THE WHO'S BUYING SERIES
BY THE NEW STRATEGIST EDITORS

Who's Buying

Transportation

5th EDITION

New Strategist Publications, Inc.
P.O. Box 242, Ithaca, New York 14851
800/848-0842; 607/273-0913
www.newstrategist.com

ISBN 1-978-935114-19-2
ISBN 1-935114-19-0

Printed in the United States of America

Contents

Household Spending on Transportation by Product Category, 2006

About the Data in Who's Buying Transportation

Introduction

The spending data in *Who's Buying Transportation* are based on the Bureau of Labor Statistics' Consumer Expenditure Survey, an ongoing, nationwide survey of household spending. The Consumer Expenditure Survey is a complete accounting of household expenditures. It includes everything from big-ticket items, such as homes and cars, to small purchases like laundry detergent and videos. The survey does not include expenditures by government, business, or institutions. The lag time between data collection and dissemination is about two years. The data in this report are from the 2006 Consumer Expenditure Survey, unless otherwise noted.

To produce this report, New Strategist Publications analyzed the Consumer Expenditure Survey's average household spending data in a variety of ways, calculating household spending indexes, aggregate (or total) household spending, and market shares. Spending data by age, household income, household type, race, Hispanic origin, region of residence, and education are shown in this report. These analyses are presented in two formats—for all product categories by demographic characteristic and for all demographic characteristics by product category.

Definition of consumer unit

The Consumer Expenditure Survey uses the consumer unit rather than the household as its sampling unit. The term "household" is used interchangeably with the term "consumer unit" in this report for convenience, although they are not exactly the same. Some households contain more than one consumer unit.

The Bureau of Labor Statistics defines consumer unit as (1) members of a household who are related by blood, marriage, adoption, or other legal arrangements; (2) a person living alone or sharing a household with others or living as a roomer in a private home or lodging house or in permanent living quarters in a hotel or motel, but who is financially independent; or (3) two or more persons living together who pool their income to make joint expenditure decisions. The bureau defines financial independence in terms of "the three major expense categories: housing, food, and other living expenses. To be considered financially independent, at least two of the three major expense categories have to be provided by the respondent."

The Census Bureau uses the household as the sampling unit in the decennial census and in the monthly Current Population Survey. The Census Bureau's household "consists of all persons who occupy a housing unit. A house, an apartment or other group of rooms, or a single room is regarded as a housing unit when it is occupied or intended for occupancy as separate living quarters; that is, when the occupants do not live and eat with any other persons in the structure and there is direct access from the outside or through a common hall."

The definition goes on to specify that "a household includes the related family members and all the unrelated persons, if any, such as lodgers, foster children, wards, or employees who share the housing unit. A person living alone in a housing unit or a group of unrelated persons sharing a housing unit as partners is also counted as a household. The count of households excludes group quarters."

Because there can be more than one consumer unit in a household, consumer units outnumber households by several million. Young adults under age 25 head most of the additional consumer units.

How to use the tables in this report

The starting point for all calculations are the unpublished, detailed average household spending data collected by the Consumer Expenditure Survey. These numbers are shown on the report's average spending tables and on each of the product-specific tables. New Strategist's editors calculated the other figures in the report based on the average figures. The indexed spending tables and the indexed spending column (Best Customers) on the product-specific tables reveal whether spending by households in a given segment is above or below the average for all households and by how much. The total (or aggregate) spending tables show the overall size of the market. The market share tables and market share column (Biggest Customers) on the product-specific tables reveal how much spending each household segment controls. These analyses are described in detail below.

• **Average Spending** The average spending figures show the average annual spending of households on transportation in 2006. The Consumer Expenditure Survey produces average spending data for all households in a segment, e.g., all households with a householder aged 25 to 34, not just for those who purchased an item. When examining spending data, it is important to remember that by including both travelers and nontravelers in the calculation, the average is less than the amount spent on the item by buyers. (See Table 1 for the percentage of households that spent on transportation in 2006 and how much the purchasers spent.)

Because average spending figures include both buyers and nonbuyers, they reveal spending patterns by demographic characteristic. By knowing who is most likely to spend on an item, marketers can target their advertising and promotions more efficiently, and businesses can determine the market potential of a product or service in a city or neighborhood. By multiplying the average amount households spend on oil changes by the number of households in an area, for example, the owners of a quick lube service can determine where to site their business.

• **Indexed Spending (Best Customers)** The indexed spending figures compare the spending of each household segment with that of the average household. To compute the indexes, New Strategist divides the average amount each household segment spends on an item by average household spending and multiplies the resulting figure by 100.

An index of 100 is the average for all households. An index of 125 means the spending of a household segment is 25 percent above average (100 plus 25). An index of 75 indicates spending that is 25 percent below the average for all households (100 minus 25). Indexed spending figures identify the best customers for a product or service. Households with an index of 178 for new cars, for example, are a strong market for this product. Those with an index below 100 are a weak or underserved market.

Spending indexes can reveal hidden markets—household segments with a high propensity to buy a particular product or service but which are overshadowed by household segments that account for a larger share of the market. Householders aged 75 or older, for example, account for 16 percent of the market for ship fares, slightly less than the 18 percent accounted for by householders aged 35 to 44. But a look at the indexed spending figures reveals that, in fact, the older householders are by far better customers. Householders aged 75 or older spend 68 percent more than the average household on ship fares, while householders aged 35 to 44 spend 13 percent less. The cruise industry can use this information to target their best customers.

Note that because of sampling errors, small differences in index values may be insignificant. But the broader patterns revealed by indexes can guide marketers to the best customers.

• **Total (Aggregate) Spending** To produce the total (aggregate) spending figures, New Strategist multiplies average spending by the number of households in a segment. The result is the dollar size of the total household market and of each market segment. All totals are shown in thousands of dollars. To convert the numbers in the total spending tables to dollars, you must append "000" to the number. For example, households headed by people aged 45 to 54 spent more than $66 billion ($66,499,166,000) on gasoline and motor oil in 2006.

When comparing the total spending figures in this report with total spending estimates from the Bureau of Economic Analysis, other government agencies, or trade associations, keep in mind that the Consumer Expenditure Survey includes only household spending, not spending by businesses or institutions. Sales data also will differ from household spending totals because sales figures for consumer products include the value of goods sold to industries, government, and foreign markets, which may be a significant proportion of sales.

• **Market Shares (Biggest Customers)** New Strategist produces market share figures by converting total (aggregate) spending data into percentages. To calculate the percentage of total spending on an item that is controlled by each demographic segment—i.e., its market share—each segment's total spending on an item is divided by aggregate household spending on the item.

Market shares reveal the biggest customers—the demographic segments that account for the largest share of spending on a particular product or service. In 2006, for example, households headed by people under age 45 accounted for 51 percent of spending on new trucks. By targeting only these householders, manufacturers could reach the majority of their customers. There is a danger here, however. By single-mindedly targeting the biggest customers, businesses cannot nurture potential growth markets. With competition for customers more heated than ever, targeting potential markets is increasingly important to business survival.

• **Product Specific Tables** The product-specific tables reveal at a glance the demographic characteristics of spending by individual product category. These tables show average spending, indexed spending (Best Customers), and market shares (Biggest Customers) by age, income, household type, race and Hispanic origin, region of residence, and education. If you want to see the spending pattern for an individual product at a glance, these are the tables for you.

History and methodology of the Consumer Expenditure Survey

The Consumer Expenditure Survey is an ongoing study of the day-to-day spending of American households. In taking the survey, government interviewers collect spending data on products and services as well as the amount and sources of household income, changes in saving and debt, and demographic and economic characteristics of household members. The Bureau of the Census collects data for the Consumer Expenditure Survey under contract with the Bureau of Labor Statistics, which is responsible for analysis and release of the survey data.

Since the late 19th century, the federal government has conducted expenditure surveys about every 10 years. Although the results have been used for a variety of purposes, their primary application is to track consumer prices. In 1980, the Consumer Expenditure Survey became continuous with annual release of data (with a lag time of about two years between data collection and release). The survey is used to update prices for the market basket of products and services used in calculating the Consumer Price Index.

The Consumer Expenditure Survey consists of two separate surveys: an interview survey and a diary survey. In the interview portion of the survey, respondents are asked each quarter for five consecutive quarters to report their expenditures for the previous three months. The purchase of big-ticket items such as houses, cars, and major appliances, or recurring expenses such as insurance premiums, utility payments, and rent are recorded by the interview survey. The interview component covers about 95 percent of all expenditures.

Expenditures on small, frequently purchased items are recorded during a two-week period by the diary survey. These detailed records include expenses for food and beverages purchased in grocery stores and at restaurants, as well as other items such as tobacco, housekeeping supplies, nonprescription drugs, and personal care products and services. The diary survey is intended to capture expenditures respondents are likely to forget or recall incorrectly over longer periods of time.

Two separate, nationally representative samples are used for the interview and diary surveys. For the interview survey, about 7,500 consumer units are interviewed on a rotating panel basis each quarter for five consecutive quarters. Another 7,500 consumer units keep weekly diaries of spending for two consecutive weeks. Data collection is carried out in 105 areas of the country.

The Bureau of Labor Statistics reviews, audits, and cleanses the data, then weights them to reflect the number and characteristics of all U.S. consumer units. Like any sample survey, the Consumer Expenditure Survey is subject to two major types of error. Nonsampling error occurs when respondents misinterpret questions or interviewers are inconsistent in the way they ask questions or record answers. Respondents may forget items, recall expenses incorrectly, or deliberately give wrong answers. A respondent may remember how much he or she spent at the grocery store but forget the items picked up at a local convenience store. Nonsampling error can also be caused by mistakes during the various stages of data processing and refinement.

Sampling error occurs when a sample does not accurately represent the population it is supposed to represent. This kind of error is present in every sample-based survey and is minimized by using a proper sampling procedure. Standard error tables documenting the extent of sampling error in the Consumer Expenditure Survey are available from the Bureau of Labor Statistics at http://www.bls.gov/cex/csxstnderror.htm.

Although the Consumer Expenditure Survey is the best source of information about the spending behavior of American households, it should be treated with caution because of the above problems.

For more information

To find out more about the Consumer Expenditure Survey, contact the specialists at the Bureau of Labor Statistics at (202) 691-6900, or visit the Consumer Expenditure Survey home page at http://www.bls .gov/cex/. The web site includes news releases, technical documentation, and current and historical summary-level data. The detailed average spending data shown in this report are available from the Bureau of Labor Statistics only by special request.

For a comprehensive look at detailed household spending data for all products and services, see the 13th edition of *Household Spending: Who Spends How Much on What*. New Strategist's books are available in hardcopy or as downloads by visiting http://www.newstrategist.com or by calling 1-800-848-0842.

Table 1. Percent reporting expenditure and amount spent, Average quarter 2006

(percent of consumer units reporting expenditure and amount spent by purchasers during the average quarter, 2006)

	average quarter	
	percent reporting expenditure	amount spent by purchasers
TRANSPORTATION	**94.0%**	**$2,252.64**
Vehicle purchases	**5.9**	**143.94**
Cars and trucks, new	1.7	26,288.30
New cars	0.9	25,083.72
New trucks	0.9	27,506.76
Cars and trucks, used	4.1	9,539.84
Used cars	2.2	8,403.35
Used trucks	1.9	10,562.31
Other vehicles	0.2	5,908.70
New motorcycles	0.1	8,750.00
Used motorcycles	0.1	3,304.17
Gasoline and motor oil	**89.7**	**620.81**
Gasoline	88.9	576.50
Diesel fuel	1.8	530.30
Gasoline on trips	21.1	150.99
Motor oil	8.4	26.10
Other vehicle expenses	**80.2**	**723.19**
Vehicle finance charges	33.0	225.96
Automobile finance charges	17.2	170.32
Truck finance charges	18.4	219.13
Motorcycle and plane finance charges	0.9	122.35
Other vehicle finance charges	1.4	276.07
Maintenance and repairs	52.4	309.72
Coolant, additives, brake, transmission fluids	5.3	17.20
Tires	7.6	339.90
Vehicle products and cleaning services	3.4	44.78
Parts, equipment, and accessories	8.6	120.47
Vechicle audio equipment	0.3	251.61
Vehicle video equipment	0.1	921.43
Body work and painting	1.2	610.12
Clutch, transmission repair	1.2	744.56
Drive shaft and rear-end repair	0.3	623.15
Brake work	5.1	303.32
Repair to steering or front-end	1.2	418.22
Repair to engine cooling system	1.9	287.37
Motor tune-up	4.7	251.75
Lube, oil change, and oil filters	34.2	48.84
Front-end alignment, wheel balance, rotation	2.6	134.67
Shock absorber replacement	0.3	398.33
Repair tires and other repair work	5.7	212.43
Exhaust system repair	0.9	285.11
Electrical system repair	2.3	274.33
Motor repair, replacement	2.7	653.68

	average quarter	
	percent reporting expenditure	amount spent by purchasers
Auto repair service policy	0.4%	$560.26
Vehicle accessories, including labor	0.5	324.54
Vehicle air conditioning repair	0.9	324.46
Vehicle insurance	49.7	445.89
Vehicle rental, leases, licenses, other charges	43.6	279.05
Leased and rented vehicles	7.3	1,005.33
Rented vehicles	3.2	290.17
Auto rental	0.6	248.83
Auto rental, on trips	2.2	290.27
Truck rental	0.3	252.78
Truck rental, on trips	0.2	301.56
Leased vehicles	4.3	1,493.43
Car lease payments	2.5	1,251.22
Truck lease payments	2.2	1,234.95
Vehicle registration, state	16.8	128.81
Vehicle registration, local	1.6	128.07
Driver's license	5.1	33.61
Vehicle inspection	5.8	40.71
Parking fees	12.2	71.48
Parking fees in home city, excluding residence	9.6	74.87
Parking fees, on trips	3.6	42.88
Tolls or electronic toll passes	8.7	54.65
Tolls on trips	7.2	13.94
Towing charges	1.1	118.29
Global positioning services	0.4	102.56
Automobile service clubs	4.7	87.39
Public transportation	**19.0**	**663.97**
Airline fares	10.9	766.73
Intercity bus fares	4.3	65.42
Intracity mass transit fares	6.8	188.66
Local transportation on trips	5.7	58.10
Taxi fares and limousine service	3.2	107.18
Intercity train fares	4.1	100.06
Ship fares	2.8	491.25
School bus	0.1	397.50

Note: Expenditures are total net outlays (vehicle purchase price less downpayment or trade-in) at the time of purchase, whether or not a vehicle is financed.
Source: Calculations by New Strategist based on the 2006 Consumer Expenditure Survey

Household Spending Trends, 2000 to 2006

Between 2000 and 2006, spending by the average household rose by 8.7 percent, after adjusting for inflation. In 2006, the average household spent $48,398, according to the Bureau of Labor Statistics' Consumer Expenditure Survey, almost $4,000 more than the inflation-adjusted $44,541 of 2000.

Spending surged on a number of items between 2000 and 2006. Perhaps not surprisingly, the biggest gainer was gasoline. The average household spent 47 percent more on gasoline in 2006 than in 2000, after adjusting for inflation, and 42 percent more on natural gas. It spent $1,465 on out-of-pocket health insurance costs, 27 percent more than in 2000. Spending on property taxes climbed 24 percent, and spending on education rose 20 percent. Households boosted their spending on a handful of discretionary categories, but by smaller margins. Spending on entertainment grew 9 percent, primarily due to a 24 percent increase in spending on audio and visual equipment and services. Behind this gain is the growing popularity of high-priced high-definition television sets. Spending on food away from home (primarily restaurant meals) climbed 8 percent.

The average household cut spending on a number of products and services between 2000 and 2006. Apparel spending fell 14 percent, after adjusting for inflation, driven in part by a 24 percent decline on footwear spending. Spending on vehicle purchases fell 15 percent partially fueled by a 24 percent spending decline on used cars and trucks. The average household's spending on reading material dropped 32 percent between 2000 and 2006. Personal taxes declined 33 percent on average, from an inflation-adjusted $3,649 in 2000 to $2,432 in 2006.

At the time the data shown in this report were collected, average household spending had recovered from the recession of 2001 and the sluggish economy that followed. But the effects of the 2008 slowdown on consumer spending had yet to be felt.

Households are spending less on some items, more on others

(percent change in spending by the average household on selected products and services, 2000 to 2006; in 2006 dollars)

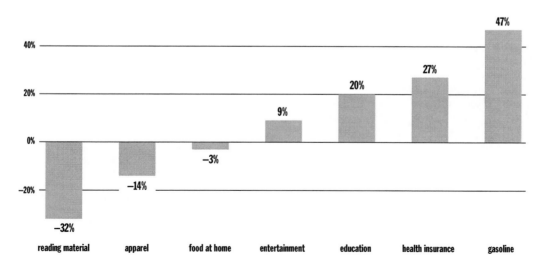

Table 2. Household spending trends, 2000 to 2006

(average annual spending of total consumer units, 2000 and 2006; percent change, 2000–06; in 2006 dollars)

	2006	2000	percent change 2000–06
Number of consumer units (in 000s)	118,843	109,367	8.7%
Average before-tax income of consumer units	$60,533	$52,272	15.8
Average annual spending of consumer units	48,398	44,541	8.7
FOOD	**6,111**	**6,039**	**1.2**
Food at home	**3,417**	**3,537**	**–3.4**
Cereals and bakery products	446	530	–15.9
Cereals and cereal products	143	183	–21.7
Bakery products	304	348	–12.6
Meats, poultry, fish, and eggs	797	931	–14.4
Beef	236	279	–15.3
Pork	157	196	–19.7
Other meats	105	118	–11.2
Poultry	141	170	–16.9
Fish and seafood	122	129	–5.3
Eggs	37	40	–7.0
Dairy products	368	380	–3.3
Fresh milk and cream	140	153	–8.7
Other dairy products	228	226	0.9
Fruits and vegetables	592	610	–2.9
Fresh fruits	195	191	2.2
Fresh vegetables	193	186	3.7
Processed fruits	109	135	–19.0
Processed vegetables	95	98	–3.4
Other food at home	1,212	1,085	11.7
Sugar and other sweets	125	137	–8.7
Fats and oils	86	97	–11.5
Miscellaneous foods	627	512	22.6
Nonalcoholic beverages	332	293	13.4
Food prepared by consumer unit on trips	43	47	–8.2
Food away from home	**2,694**	**2,502**	**7.7**
ALCOHOLIC BEVERAGES	**497**	**436**	**14.1**
HOUSING	**16,366**	**14,422**	**13.5**
Shelter	**9,673**	**8,329**	**16.1**
Owned dwellings	6,516	5,388	20.9
Mortgage interest and charges	3,753	3,090	21.5
Property taxes	1,649	1,333	23.7
Maintenance, repair, insurance, other expenses	1,115	966	15.4
Rented dwellings	2,590	2,381	8.8
Other lodging	567	560	1.3
Utilities, fuels, and public services	**3,397**	**2,914**	**16.6**
Natural gas	509	359	41.6
Electricity	1,266	1,067	18.7
Fuel oil and other fuels	138	114	21.5
Telephone services	1,087	1,027	5.9
Water and other public services	397	347	14.6
Household services	**948**	**801**	**18.4**
Personal services	393	382	3.0
Other household services	555	419	32.4
Housekeeping supplies	**640**	**564**	**13.4**
Laundry and cleaning supplies	151	153	–1.5
Other household products	330	265	24.7
Postage and stationery	159	148	7.8
Household furnishings and equipment	**1,708**	**1,813**	**–5.8**
Household textiles	154	124	24.1
Furniture	463	458	1.1

	2006	2000	percent change 2000–06
Floor coverings	$48	$52	−6.8%
Major appliances	241	221	8.9
Small appliances and miscellaneous housewares	109	102	7.0
Miscellaneous household equipment	693	856	−19.0
APPAREL AND RELATED SERVICES	**1,874**	**2,173**	**−13.8**
Men and boys	**444**	**515**	**−13.8**
Men, aged 16 or older	353	403	−12.3
Boys, aged 2 to 15	91	112	−19.0
Women and girls	**751**	**849**	**−11.5**
Women, aged 16 or older	629	711	−11.5
Girls, aged 2 to 15	122	138	−11.7
Children under age 2	**96**	**96**	**0.0**
Footwear	**304**	**402**	**−24.3**
Other apparel products and services	**280**	**311**	**−10.1**
TRANSPORTATION	**8,508**	**8,683**	**−2.0**
Vehicle purchases	**3,421**	**4,002**	**−14.5**
Cars and trucks, new	1,798	1,879	−4.3
Cars and trucks, used	1,568	2,072	−24.3
Other vehicles	54	50	7.3
Gasoline and motor oil	**2,227**	**1,511**	**47.3**
Other vehicle expenses	**2,355**	**2,670**	**−11.8**
Vehicle finance charges	298	384	−22.4
Maintenance and repairs	688	731	−5.8
Vehicle insurance	886	911	−2.7
Vehicle rentals, leases, licenses, other charges	482	645	−25.3
Public transportation	**505**	**500**	**1.0**
HEALTH CARE	**2,766**	**2,419**	**14.4**
Health insurance	1,465	1,151	27.3
Medical services	670	665	0.8
Drugs	514	487	5.5
Medical supplies	117	116	0.9
ENTERTAINMENT	**2,376**	**2,181**	**8.9**
Fees and admissions	606	603	0.5
Audio and visual equipment and services	906	728	24.4
Pets, toys, and playground equipment	412	391	5.4
Other entertainment products and services	451	460	−2.0
PERSONAL CARE PRODUCTS, SERVICES	**585**	**660**	**−11.4**
READING	**117**	**171**	**−31.5**
EDUCATION	**888**	**740**	**20.0**
TOBACCO PRODUCTS, SMOKING SUPPLIES	**327**	**373**	**−12.4**
MISCELLANEOUS	**846**	**908**	**−6.9**
CASH CONTRIBUTIONS	**1,869**	**1,396**	**33.9**
PERSONAL INSURANCE AND PENSIONS	**5,270**	**3,940**	**33.8**
Life and other personal insurance	322	467	−31.1
Pensions and Social Security	4,948	3,472	− *
PERSONAL TAXES	**2,432**	**3,649**	**−33.4**
Federal income taxes	1,711	2,820	−39.3
State and local income taxes	519	658	−21.1
Other taxes	202	171	18.2
GIFTS FOR PEOPLE IN OTHER HOUSEHOLDS	**1,154**	**1,268**	**−9.0**

Spending in 2006 on pensions and Social Security is not comparable with 2000 because of changes in methodology.
Note: Average spending is rounded to the nearest dollar, but the percent change calculation is based on unrounded figures. Spending by category will not add to total spending because gift spending is also included in the preceding product and service categories and personal taxes are not included in the total.
Source: Bureau of Labor Statistics, 2000 and 2006 Consumer Expenditure Surveys, Internet site http://www.bls.gov/cex/; calculations by New Strategist

Household Spending on Transportation, 2006

Transportation is one of the biggest expenses of American households, behind only spending on shelter. In 2006, the average household spent $8,508 on transportation, 2 percent less than in 2000 after adjusting for inflation. Consumers devote 26 percent of transportation spending to gasoline, which makes it the largest single transportation expense and one of the top six household expenses. Spending on gasoline rose 47 percent between 2000 and 2006, after adjusting for inflation.

Transportation spending patterns have changed since 2000. The share of the transportation dollar devoted to new trucks (a category that includes sport utility vehicles and minivans) climbed from 9 to 11 percent between 2000 and 2006. During those years, the average household boosted its spending on new trucks by 16 percent, after adjusting for inflation. In 2006, spending on new trucks surpassed spending on new cars, a reversal of the pattern in 2000. Average household spending on used vehicles—both cars and trucks—fell during those years as no-interest and low-interest loans lured consumers to new vehicles. Spending on leased vehicles also fell for the same reason. Vehicle maintenance expenses declined because new vehicles require fewer repairs.

Spending by age

The biggest spenders on transportation are householders aged 45 to 54. They devoted $10,111 to gasoline, trucks, cars, and other transportation items in 2006, and they spend the most on gasoline, vehicle insurance, and public transportation including air fares. The biggest spenders on new cars are householders aged 65 to 74. Spending on vehicle finance charges is above average for householders ranging in age from 25 to 54. Householders aged 35 to 44 spend the most on intracity mass transit fares.

Spending by household income

Spending on transportation rises steeply with household income as does vehicle ownership—from less than one vehicle on average for households with the lowest incomes to three vehicles for households with incomes of $100,000 or more. Households with incomes of $100,000 or more spent more than $17,000 on transportation in 2006. This income group accounts for only 16 percent of households and 33 percent of all spending, but it controls 45 percent of spending on airline fares, 44 percent of spending on new cars and trucks, and 44 percent of spending on ship fares.

Spending by household type

Transportation expenses are directly related to the number of drivers in a household and the number of vehicles owned. Married couples with adult children at home spend the most on transportation—63 percent more than the average household—because they have the most drivers and vehicles. Couples with adult children at home own 3.2 vehicles versus the average household's 1.9 vehicles. Couples with adult children at home spend 81 percent more than the average household on vehicle insurance and 65 percent more on gasoline. Couples without children at home (most of them empty-nesters) spend the most on ship fares.

Spending by race and Hispanic origin

Households headed by Asians spend 14 percent more than average on transportation, while blacks spend 28 percent less than average. Asians spend 92 percent more than the average household on new cars and more than two-and-one-half times the average on airline fares and mass transit. Blacks spend 71 percent more than average on mass transit fares, while Hispanics spend 90 percent more.

Spending by region

Spending on transportation is 19 percent above average in the West, where the average household devoted $10,156 to this category in 2006. Transportation spending is 8 percent below average in the Northeast and 12 percent below average in the Midwest. Households in the Northeast spend more than three times the average on mass transit fares, well more than twice the average on tolls, and twice the average on taxi fares.

Spending by education

Average household spending on transportation rises steadily with education, as does income. Households headed by college graduates spent an average of $10,943 on transportation in 2006 versus the $7,412 spent by householders who went no further than high school. College graduates account for 54 percent of household spending on rented vehicles. They spend 52 percent more than the average household on new cars and trucks, but their spending on used cars and trucks is average. College graduates spend twice the average on airline fares and nearly twice the average on ship fares.

Table 3. Transportation spending, 2000 to 2006

(average annual household spending on transportation, and percent distribution of spending by type, 2000 and 2006; percent change in spending, 2000–06; in 2006 dollars; ranked by amount spent)

	2006		2000		percent change 2000–06
	average household spending	percent distribution	average household spending (in 2006$)	percent distribution	
Average household spending on transportation	**$8,507.90**	**100.0%**	**$8,683.74**	**100.0%**	**–2.0%**
Gasoline and motor oil (including on trips)	2,227.46	26.2	1,511.71	17.4	47.3
Trucks, new	935.23	11.0	805.39	9.3	16.1
Vehicle insurance	886.43	10.4	910.98	10.5	–2.7
Cars, new	862.88	10.1	1,073.58	12.4	–19.6
Trucks, used	815.41	9.6	888.12	10.2	–8.2
Cars, used	752.94	8.8	1,183.90	13.6	–36.4
Vehicle maintenance and repair (incl. tires, oil changes)	688.44	8.1	730.26	8.4	–5.7
Airline fares	334.60	3.9	320.80	3.7	4.3
Vehicle finance charges	297.81	3.5	384.28	4.4	–22.5
Car lease payments	123.12	1.4	204.69	2.4	–39.9
Truck lease payments	109.17	1.3	173.80	2.0	–37.2
Tires (purchased, replaced, installed)	103.33	1.2	102.12	1.2	1.2
Oil change, lube, and oil filters	66.87	0.8	68.78	0.8	–2.8
Ship fares	55.02	0.6	42.83	0.5	28.5
Motorcycles (new and used)	54.36	0.6	41.95	0.5	29.6
Mass transit, intracity fares	51.09	0.6	55.50	0.6	–8.0
Rented vehicles (including rentals on trips)	37.49	0.4	52.62	0.6	–28.8
Parking fees, excluding residence	34.88	0.4	21.55	0.2	61.8
Taxis and local transportation on trips	20.84	0.2	34.03	0.4	–38.8
Train fares, intercity	16.29	0.2	24.73	0.3	–34.1
Automobile service clubs	16.29	0.2	9.78	0.1	66.6
Taxi fares and limousine service in home town	13.87	0.2	14.22	0.2	–2.5
Bus fares, intercity	11.33	0.1	18.85	0.2	–39.9
Towing charges	5.11	0.1	5.48	0.1	–6.7
Vehicle video equipment	2.58	0.0	–	–	–
Global positioning services	1.60	0.0	–	–	–

Note: Numbers will not add to total because spending on tires and oil changes is also included in vehicle maintenance and repairs and because some subcategories are not shown. "–" means data are unavailable.
Source: Bureau of Labor Statistics, 2000 and 2006 Consumer Expenditure Surveys; calculations by New Strategist

Table 4. Transportation: Average spending by age, 2006

(average annual spending of consumer units (CU) on transportation, by age of consumer unit reference person, 2006)

	total consumer units	under 25	25 to 34	35 to 44	45 to 54	55 to 64	65 to 74	75+
Number of consumer units (in 000s)	118,843	8,167	20,071	23,950	24,696	18,952	11,764	11,243
Number of persons per CU	2.5	2.0	2.9	3.2	2.7	2.0	1.9	1.5
Average before-tax income of CU	$60,533.00	$29,057.00	$57,208.00	$75,613.00	$77,043.00	$64,425.00	$46,064.00	$29,525.00
Average spending of CU, total	48,398.32	28,180.58	47,582.37	57,476.34	57,563.25	50,788.79	40,959.64	28,904.49
TRANSPORTATION	**8,507.90**	**5,667.15**	**9,047.11**	**9,976.76**	**10,111.13**	**8,675.59**	**7,481.39**	**3,750.59**
Vehicle purchases	3,420.83	2,395.86	3,911.62	4,056.77	3,983.39	3,165.28	3,273.04	1,284.09
Cars and trucks, new	1,798.12	943.19	1,959.80	1,999.44	2,087.09	1,866.75	2,210.47	519.62
New cars	862.88	384.64	641.28	924.06	1,150.55	851.85	1,283.05	422.57
New trucks	935.23	558.55	1,318.52	1,075.38	936.53	1,014.90	927.43	97.06
Cars and trucks, used	1,568.35	1,405.78	1,881.20	1,972.72	1,811.14	1,270.54	1,062.57	764.47
Used cars	752.94	747.58	941.18	743.71	882.38	623.40	662.20	469.41
Used trucks	815.41	658.20	940.03	1,229.00	928.75	647.14	400.37	295.06
Other vehicles	54.36	46.88	70.62	84.61	85.17	27.99	–	–
New motorcycles	38.50	–	38.38	78.97	57.21	26.45	–	–
Used motorcycles	15.86	46.88	32.24	5.65	27.96	1.54	–	–
Gasoline and motor oil	**2,227.46**	**1,637.15**	**2,346.02**	**2,635.62**	**2,692.71**	**2,288.21**	**1,765.80**	**933.80**
Other vehicle expenses	**2,354.98**	**1,413.45**	**2,341.67**	**2,725.28**	**2,819.22**	**2,638.14**	**1,971.64**	**1,178.63**
Vehicle finance charges	297.81	198.78	401.36	374.18	334.18	299.26	189.81	52.82
Automobile finance charges	116.91	93.08	161.05	122.47	141.55	114.43	85.18	26.81
Truck finance charges	161.28	98.95	221.02	235.38	168.95	154.27	76.27	25.96
Motorcycle and plane finance charges	4.16	5.71	6.80	4.70	6.43	2.06	0.06	–
Other vehicle finance charges	15.46	1.04	12.50	11.63	17.26	28.51	28.30	0.04
Maintenance and repairs	688.44	400.25	623.56	743.81	866.14	799.05	639.76	370.62
Coolant, additives, brake, transmission fluids	3.66	3.42	4.17	4.36	4.61	3.60	2.21	0.93
Tires—purchased, replaced, installed	103.33	67.49	99.33	121.48	132.73	107.13	87.94	42.97
Parts, equipment, and accessories	41.25	33.04	45.87	44.30	57.39	38.65	26.66	16.71
Vehicle products and cleaning services	5.30	2.76	4.73	5.59	8.21	5.24	4.63	2.05
Vehicle video equipment	2.58	–	3.69	0.76	4.35	0.26	8.69	–
Miscellaneous auto repair, servicing	41.15	15.48	35.50	46.42	46.37	61.62	34.71	19.56
Body work and painting	29.53	25.14	29.22	29.10	37.48	27.95	32.73	16.09
Clutch, transmission repair	36.93	10.85	28.43	56.47	40.56	36.47	41.74	17.18
Drive shaft and rear-end repair	6.73	5.83	10.17	6.51	9.35	3.97	5.14	2.25
Brake work	61.27	30.86	51.35	68.49	87.32	69.52	48.73	27.59
Repair to steering or front-end	19.74	5.70	17.10	18.76	27.58	27.12	12.13	15.08
Repair to engine cooling system	22.07	13.99	19.96	19.04	28.58	26.24	25.05	13.69
Motor tune-up	47.53	19.17	41.82	47.66	55.49	68.05	48.25	25.23
Lube, oil change, and oil filters	66.87	39.71	61.59	73.59	79.60	77.74	64.58	37.89
Front-end alignment, wheel balance, rotation	13.79	9.40	12.65	13.88	18.50	15.62	11.46	7.81
Shock absorber replacement	4.78	1.23	3.74	7.77	5.15	4.75	4.66	2.22
Tire repair and other repair work	48.52	18.11	38.46	49.42	59.01	63.07	54.96	32.32
Vehicle air conditioning repair	11.94	6.63	8.57	13.93	12.91	10.15	12.00	18.43
Exhaust system repair	10.15	3.74	8.66	14.67	8.75	12.44	10.82	6.39
Electrical system repair	24.69	8.87	22.41	23.46	29.93	29.81	26.29	21.06
Motor repair, replacement	69.29	34.49	61.43	66.61	98.25	80.52	62.21	39.18
Auto repair service policy	8.74	1.49	10.11	6.21	6.94	14.23	14.17	5.98
Vehicle insurance	886.43	548.03	822.19	976.08	1,105.17	941.06	805.89	567.68
Vehicle rental, leases, licenses, other charges	482.30	266.39	494.56	631.22	513.73	598.76	336.18	187.51
Leased and rented vehicles	294.36	153.40	305.31	429.10	293.38	374.78	175.33	81.29
Rented vehicles	37.49	18.47	29.07	41.75	52.25	42.32	42.80	11.19
Leased vehicles	256.87	134.93	276.24	387.36	241.13	332.46	132.53	70.10
Car lease payments	123.12	67.27	104.47	174.07	111.35	186.71	79.42	52.81
Truck lease payments	109.17	50.14	118.65	186.41	108.16	128.76	40.16	11.95
Vehicle registration, state	86.30	43.21	85.88	93.09	101.03	102.88	79.63	50.53
Vehicle registration, local	8.35	4.97	9.92	9.01	9.11	9.29	7.34	4.36
Driver's license	6.87	7.47	6.74	7.00	8.18	6.85	5.88	4.63
Vehicle inspection	9.51	6.19	7.95	9.99	12.03	10.57	9.60	6.23

	total consumer units	under 25	25 to 34	35 to 44	45 to 54	55 to 64	65 to 74	75+
Parking fees	$34.88	$35.90	$38.20	$40.45	$38.58	$42.39	$21.00	$10.08
Parking fees in home city, excl. residence	28.75	33.43	32.71	33.43	30.88	34.92	15.76	6.76
Parking fees on trips	6.14	2.47	5.49	7.02	7.70	7.47	5.24	3.32
Tolls	15.02	4.43	21.69	19.20	17.11	16.78	4.06	5.70
Tolls on trips	4.02	2.24	4.87	4.08	4.50	4.76	4.09	1.32
Towing charges	5.11	5.24	5.88	6.19	6.97	4.17	2.59	1.49
Global positioning services	1.60	–	0.54	1.30	2.31	1.80	3.29	1.59
Automobile service clubs	16.29	3.34	7.57	11.81	20.52	24.49	23.37	20.30
'Public transportation	504.63	220.69	447.80	559.08	615.81	583.96	470.90	354.08
Airline fares	334.60	143.75	291.43	381.28	405.79	398.09	323.16	199.45
Intercity bus fares	11.33	7.43	8.01	9.42	11.04	17.81	13.60	11.47
Intracity mass transit fares	51.09	42.69	62.36	68.41	59.16	49.42	21.61	16.09
Taxis and local transportation on trips	20.84	7.54	14.14	19.52	24.28	31.41	25.87	14.61
Taxi fares and limousine service in home town	13.87	9.79	16.33	10.90	23.30	8.60	11.58	9.72
Intercity train fares	16.29	5.77	12.18	18.75	20.62	21.94	13.04	10.39
Ship fares	55.02	3.36	43.11	47.93	68.51	56.29	59.62	92.35
School bus	1.59	0.35	0.24	2.85	3.11	0.41	2.44	–

Note: Numbers may not add to total because some categories are not shown. "–" means sample is too small to make a reliable estimate.
Source: Bureau of Labor Statistics, unpublished tables from the 2006 Consumer Expenditure Survey

Table 5. Transportation: Indexed spending by age, 2006

(indexed average annual spending of consumer units (CU) on transportation, by age of consumer unit reference person, 2006; index definition: an index of 100 is the average for all consumer units; an index of 132 means that spending by consumer units in that group is 32 percent above the average for all consumer units; an index of 68 indicates spending that is 32 percent below the average for all consumer units)

	total consumer units	under 25	25 to 34	35 to 44	45 to 54	55 to 64	65 to 74	75+
Average spending of CU, total	$48,398	$28,181	$47,582	$57,476	$57,563	$50,789	$40,960	$28,904
Average spending of CU, index	100	58	98	119	119	105	85	60
TRANSPORTATION	**100**	**67**	**106**	**117**	**119**	**102**	**88**	**44**
Vehicle purchases	**100**	**70**	**114**	**119**	**116**	**93**	**96**	**38**
Cars and trucks, new	100	52	109	111	116	104	123	29
New cars	100	45	74	107	133	99	149	49
New trucks	100	60	141	115	100	109	99	10
Cars and trucks, used	100	90	120	126	115	81	68	49
Used cars	100	99	125	99	117	83	88	62
Used trucks	100	81	115	151	114	79	49	36
Other vehicles	100	86	130	156	157	51	–	–
New motorcycles	100	–	100	205	149	69	–	–
Used motorcycles	100	296	203	36	176	10	–	–
Gasoline and motor oil	**100**	**73**	**105**	**118**	**121**	**103**	**79**	**42**
Other vehicle expenses	**100**	**60**	**99**	**116**	**120**	**112**	**84**	**50**
Vehicle finance charges	100	67	135	126	112	100	64	18
Automobile finance charges	100	80	138	105	121	98	73	23
Truck finance charges	100	61	137	146	105	96	47	16
Motorcycle and plane finance charges	100	137	163	113	155	50	1	–
Other vehicle finance charges	100	7	81	75	112	184	183	0
Maintenance and repairs	100	58	91	108	126	116	93	54
Coolant, additives, brake and transmission fluids	100	93	114	119	126	98	60	25
Tires—purchased, replaced, installed	100	65	96	118	128	104	85	42
Parts, equipment, and accessories	100	80	111	107	139	94	65	41
Vehicle products and cleaning services	100	52	89	105	155	99	87	39
Vehicle video equipment	100	–	143	29	169	10	337	–
Miscellaneous auto repair, servicing	100	38	86	113	113	150	84	48
Body work and painting	100	85	99	99	127	95	111	54
Clutch, transmission repair	100	29	77	153	110	99	113	47
Drive shaft and rear-end repair	100	87	151	97	139	59	76	33
Brake work	100	50	84	112	143	113	80	45
Repair to steering or front-end	100	29	87	95	140	137	61	76
Repair to engine cooling system	100	63	90	86	129	119	114	62
Motor tune-up	100	40	88	100	117	143	102	53
Lube, oil change, and oil filters	100	59	92	110	119	116	97	57
Front-end alignment, wheel balance, rotation	100	68	92	101	134	113	83	57
Shock absorber replacement	100	26	78	163	108	99	97	46
Tire repair and other repair work	100	37	79	102	122	130	113	67
Vehicle air conditioning repair	100	56	72	117	108	85	101	154
Exhaust system repair	100	37	85	145	86	123	107	63
Electrical system repair	100	36	91	95	121	121	106	85
Motor repair, replacement	100	50	89	96	142	116	90	57
Auto repair service policy	100	17	116	71	79	163	162	68
Vehicle insurance	100	62	93	110	125	106	91	64
Vehicle rental, leases, licenses, other charges	100	55	103	131	107	124	70	39
Leased and rented vehicles	100	52	104	146	100	127	60	28
Rented vehicles	100	49	78	111	139	113	114	30
Leased vehicles	100	53	108	151	94	129	52	27
Car lease payments	100	55	85	141	90	152	65	43
Truck lease payments	100	46	109	171	99	118	37	11
Vehicle registration, state	100	50	100	108	117	119	92	59
Vehicle registration, local	100	60	119	108	109	111	88	52
Driver's license	100	109	98	102	119	100	86	67
Vehicle inspection	100	65	84	105	126	111	101	66

	total consumer units	under 25	25 to 34	35 to 44	45 to 54	55 to 64	65 to 74	75+
Parking fees	100	103	110	116	111	122	60	29
Parking fees in home city, excl. residence	100	116	114	116	107	121	55	24
Parking fees on trips	100	40	89	114	125	122	85	54
Tolls	100	29	144	128	114	112	27	38
Tolls on trips	100	56	121	101	112	118	102	33
Towing charges	100	103	115	121	136	82	51	29
Global positioning services	100	–	34	81	144	113	206	99
Automobile service clubs	100	21	46	72	126	150	143	125
Public transportation	**100**	**44**	**89**	**111**	**122**	**116**	**93**	**70**
Airline fares	100	43	87	114	121	119	97	60
Intercity bus fares	100	66	71	83	97	157	120	101
Intracity mass transit fares	100	84	122	134	116	97	42	31
Taxis and local transportation on trips	100	36	68	94	117	151	124	70
Taxi fares and limousine service in home town	100	71	118	79	168	62	83	70
Intercity train fares	100	35	75	115	127	135	80	64
Ship fares	100	6	78	87	125	102	108	168
School bus	100	22	15	179	196	26	153	–

Note: "–" means sample is too small to make a reliable estimate.
Source: Calculations by New Strategist based on the Bureau of Labor Statistics' 2006 Consumer Expenditure Survey

Table 6. Transportation: Total spending by age, 2006

(total annual spending on transportation, by consumer unit (CU) age group, 2006; consumer units and dollars in thousands)

	total consumer units	under 25	25 to 34	35 to 44	45 to 54	55 to 64	65 to 74	75+
Number of consumer units	118,843	8,167	20,071	23,950	24,696	18,952	11,764	11,243
Total spending of all CUs	$5,751,801,544	$230,150,797	$955,025,748	$1,376,558,343	$1,421,582,022	$962,549,148	$481,849,205	$324,973,181
TRANSPORTATION	1,011,104,360	46,283,614	181,584,545	238,943,402	249,704,466	164,419,782	88,011,072	42,167,883
Vehicle purchases	406,541,700	19,566,989	78,510,125	97,159,642	98,373,799	59,988,387	38,504,043	14,437,024
Cars and trucks, new	213,693,975	7,703,033	39,335,146	47,886,588	51,542,775	35,378,646	26,003,969	5,842,088
New cars	102,547,248	3,141,355	12,871,131	22,131,237	28,413,983	16,144,261	15,093,800	4,750,955
New trucks	111,145,539	4,561,678	26,464,015	25,755,351	23,128,545	19,234,385	10,910,287	1,091,246
Cars and trucks, used	186,387,419	11,481,005	37,757,565	47,246,644	44,727,913	24,079,274	12,500,073	8,594,936
Used cars	89,481,648	6,105,486	18,890,424	17,811,855	21,791,256	11,814,677	7,790,121	5,277,577
Used trucks	96,905,771	5,375,519	18,867,342	29,434,550	22,936,410	12,264,597	4,709,953	3,317,360
Other vehicles	6,460,305	382,869	1,417,414	2,026,410	2,103,358	530,466	–	–
New motorcycles	4,575,456	–	770,325	1,891,332	1,412,858	501,280	–	–
Used motorcycles	1,884,850	382,869	647,089	135,318	690,500	29,186	–	–
Gasoline and motor oil	264,718,029	13,370,604	47,086,967	63,123,099	66,499,166	43,366,156	20,772,871	10,498,713
Other vehicle expenses	279,872,888	11,543,646	46,999,659	65,270,456	69,623,457	49,998,029	23,194,373	13,251,337
Vehicle finance charges	35,392,634	1,623,436	8,055,697	8,961,611	8,252,909	5,671,576	2,232,925	593,855
Automobile finance charges	13,893,935	760,184	3,232,435	2,933,157	3,495,719	2,168,677	1,002,058	301,425
Truck finance charges	19,166,999	808,125	4,436,092	5,637,351	4,172,389	2,923,725	897,240	291,868
Motorcycle and plane finance charges	494,387	46,634	136,483	112,565	158,795	39,041	706	–
Other vehicle finance charges	1,837,313	8,494	250,888	278,539	426,253	540,322	332,921	450
Maintenance and repairs	81,816,275	3,268,842	12,515,473	17,814,250	21,390,193	15,143,596	7,526,137	4,166,881
Coolant, additives, brake and transmission fluids	434,965	27,931	83,696	104,422	113,849	68,227	25,998	10,456
Tires—purchased, replaced, installed	12,280,047	551,191	1,993,652	2,909,446	3,277,900	2,030,328	1,034,526	483,112
Parts, equipment, and accessories	4,902,274	269,838	920,657	1,060,985	1,417,303	732,495	313,628	187,871
Vehicle products and cleaning services	629,868	22,541	94,936	133,881	202,754	99,308	54,467	23,048
Vehicle video equipment	306,615	–	74,062	18,202	107,428	4,928	102,229	–
Miscellaneous auto repair, servicing	4,890,389	126,425	712,521	1,111,759	1,145,154	1,167,822	408,328	219,913
Body work and painting	3,509,434	205,318	586,475	696,945	925,606	529,708	385,036	180,900
Clutch, transmission repair	4,388,872	88,612	570,619	1,352,457	1,001,670	691,179	491,029	193,155
Drive shaft and rear-end repair	799,813	47,614	204,122	155,915	230,908	75,239	60,467	25,297
Brake work	7,281,511	252,034	1,030,646	1,640,336	2,156,455	1,317,543	573,260	310,194
Repair to steering or front-end	2,345,961	46,552	343,214	449,302	681,116	513,978	142,697	169,544
Repair to engine cooling system	2,622,865	114,256	400,617	456,008	705,812	497,300	294,688	153,917
Motor tune-up	5,648,608	156,561	839,369	1,141,457	1,370,381	1,289,684	567,613	283,661
Lube, oil change, and oil filters	7,947,031	324,312	1,236,173	1,762,481	1,965,802	1,473,328	759,719	425,997
Front-end alignment, wheel balance, rotation	1,638,845	76,770	253,898	332,426	456,876	296,030	134,815	87,808
Shock absorber replacement	568,070	10,045	75,066	186,092	127,184	90,022	54,820	24,959
Tire repair and other repair work	5,766,262	147,904	771,931	1,183,609	1,457,311	1,195,303	646,549	363,374
Vehicle air conditioning repair	1,418,985	54,147	172,008	333,624	318,825	192,363	141,168	207,208
Exhaust system repair	1,206,256	30,545	173,815	351,347	216,090	235,763	127,286	71,843
Electrical system repair	2,934,234	72,441	449,791	561,867	739,151	564,959	309,276	236,778
Motor repair, replacement	8,234,631	281,680	1,232,962	1,595,310	2,426,382	1,526,015	731,838	440,501
Auto repair service policy	1,038,688	12,169	202,918	148,730	171,390	269,687	166,696	67,233
Vehicle insurance	105,346,000	4,475,761	16,502,175	23,377,116	27,293,278	17,834,969	9,480,490	6,382,426
Vehicle rental, leases, licenses, other charges	57,317,979	2,175,607	9,926,314	15,117,719	12,687,076	11,347,700	3,954,822	2,108,175
Leased and rented vehicles	34,982,625	1,252,818	6,127,877	10,276,945	7,245,312	7,102,831	2,062,582	913,943
Rented vehicles	4,455,424	150,844	583,464	999,913	1,290,366	802,049	503,499	125,809
Leased vehicles	30,527,201	1,101,973	5,544,413	9,277,272	5,954,946	6,300,782	1,559,083	788,134
Car lease payments	14,631,950	549,394	2,096,817	4,168,977	2,749,900	3,538,528	934,297	593,743
Truck lease payments	12,974,090	409,493	2,381,424	4,464,520	2,671,119	2,440,260	472,442	134,354
Vehicle registration, state	10,256,151	352,896	1,723,697	2,229,506	2,495,037	1,949,782	936,767	568,109
Vehicle registration, local	992,339	40,590	199,104	215,790	224,981	176,064	86,348	49,019
Driver's license	816,451	61,007	135,279	167,650	202,013	129,821	69,172	52,055
Vehicle inspection	1,130,197	50,554	159,564	239,261	297,093	200,323	112,934	70,044

	total consumer units	under 25	25 to 34	35 to 44	45 to 54	55 to 64	65 to 74	75+
Parking fees	$4,145,244	$293,195	$766,712	$968,778	$952,772	$803,375	$247,044	$113,329
Parking fees in home city, excluding residence	3,416,736	273,023	656,522	800,649	762,612	661,804	185,401	76,003
Parking fees on trips	729,696	20,172	110,190	168,129	190,159	141,571	61,643	37,327
Tolls	1,785,022	36,180	435,340	459,840	422,549	318,015	47,762	64,085
Tolls on trips	477,749	18,294	97,746	97,716	111,132	90,212	48,115	14,841
Towing charges	607,288	42,795	118,017	148,251	172,131	79,030	30,469	16,752
Global positioning services	190,149	–	10,838	31,135	57,048	34,114	38,704	17,876
Automobile service clubs	1,935,952	27,278	151,937	282,850	506,762	464,134	274,925	228,233
Public transportation	**59,971,743**	**1,802,375**	**8,987,794**	**13,389,966**	**15,208,044**	**11,067,210**	**5,539,668**	**3,980,921**
Airline fares	39,764,868	1,174,006	5,849,292	9,131,656	10,021,390	7,544,602	3,801,654	2,242,416
Intercity bus fares	1,346,491	60,681	160,769	225,609	272,644	337,535	159,990	128,957
Intracity mass transit fares	6,071,689	348,649	1,251,628	1,638,420	1,461,015	936,608	254,220	180,900
Taxis and local transportation on trips	2,476,688	61,579	283,804	467,504	599,619	595,282	304,335	164,260
Taxi fares, limousine service in home town	1,648,352	79,955	327,759	261,055	575,417	162,987	136,227	109,282
Intercity train fares	1,935,952	47,124	244,465	449,063	509,232	415,807	153,403	116,815
Ship fares	6,538,742	27,441	865,261	1,147,924	1,691,923	1,066,808	701,370	1,038,291
School bus	188,960	2,858	4,817	68,258	76,805	7,770	28,704	–

Note: Numbers may not add to total because some categories are not shown and because of rounding. "–" means sample is too small to make a reliable estimate.
Source: Calculations by New Strategist based on the Bureau of Labor Statistics' 2006 Consumer Expenditure Survey

Table 7. Transportation: Market shares by age, 2006

(percentage of total annual spending on transportation accounted for by consumer unit age groups, 2006)

	total consumer units	under 25	25 to 34	35 to 44	45 to 54	55 to 64	65 to 74	75+
Share of total consumer units	100.0%	6.9%	16.9%	20.2%	20.8%	15.9%	9.9%	9.5%
Share of total before-tax income	100.0	3.3	16.0	25.2	26.4	17.0	7.5	4.6
Share of total spending	100.0	4.0	16.6	23.9	24.7	16.7	8.4	5.6
TRANSPORTATION	100.0	4.6	18.0	23.6	24.7	16.3	8.7	4.2
Vehicle purchases	100.0	4.8	19.3	23.9	24.2	14.8	9.5	3.6
Cars and trucks, new	100.0	3.6	18.4	22.4	24.1	16.6	12.2	2.7
New cars	100.0	3.1	12.6	21.6	27.7	15.7	14.7	4.6
New trucks	100.0	4.1	23.8	23.2	20.8	17.3	9.8	1.0
Cars and trucks, used	100.0	6.2	20.3	25.3	24.0	12.9	6.7	4.6
Used cars	100.0	6.8	21.1	19.9	24.4	13.2	8.7	5.9
Used trucks	100.0	5.5	19.5	30.4	23.7	12.7	4.9	3.4
Other vehicles	100.0	5.9	21.9	31.4	32.6	8.2	–	–
New motorcycles	100.0	–	16.8	41.3	30.9	11.0	–	–
Used motorcycles	100.0	20.3	34.3	7.2	36.6	1.5	–	–
Gasoline and motor oil	100.0	5.1	17.8	23.8	25.1	16.4	7.8	4.0
Other vehicle expenses	100.0	4.1	16.8	23.3	24.9	17.9	8.3	4.7
Vehicle finance charges	100.0	4.6	22.8	25.3	23.3	16.0	6.3	1.7
Automobile finance charges	100.0	5.5	23.3	21.1	25.2	15.6	7.2	2.2
Truck finance charges	100.0	4.2	23.1	29.4	21.8	15.3	4.7	1.5
Motorcycle and plane finance charges	100.0	9.4	27.6	22.8	32.1	7.9	0.1	–
Other vehicle finance charges	100.0	0.5	13.7	15.2	23.2	29.4	18.1	0.0
Maintenance and repairs	100.0	4.0	15.3	21.8	26.1	18.5	9.2	5.1
Coolant, additives, brake, transmission fluids	100.0	6.4	19.2	24.0	26.2	15.7	6.0	2.4
Tires—purchased, replaced, installed	100.0	4.5	16.2	23.7	26.7	16.5	8.4	3.9
Parts, equipment, and accessories	100.0	5.5	18.8	21.6	28.9	14.9	6.4	3.8
Vehicle products and cleaning services	100.0	3.6	15.1	21.3	32.2	15.8	8.6	3.7
Vehicle video equipment	100.0	–	24.2	5.9	35.0	1.6	33.3	–
Miscellaneous auto repair, servicing	100.0	2.6	14.6	22.7	23.4	23.9	8.3	4.5
Body work and painting	100.0	5.9	16.7	19.9	26.4	15.1	11.0	5.2
Clutch, transmission repair	100.0	2.0	13.0	30.8	22.8	15.7	11.2	4.4
Drive shaft and rear-end repair	100.0	6.0	25.5	19.5	28.9	9.4	7.6	3.2
Brake work	100.0	3.5	14.2	22.5	29.6	18.1	7.9	4.3
Repair to steering or front-end	100.0	2.0	14.6	19.2	29.0	21.9	6.1	7.2
Repair to engine cooling system	100.0	4.4	15.3	17.4	26.9	19.0	11.2	5.9
Motor tune-up	100.0	2.8	14.9	20.2	24.3	22.8	10.0	5.0
Lube, oil change, and oil filters	100.0	4.1	15.6	22.2	24.7	18.5	9.6	5.4
Front-end alignment, wheel balance, rotation	100.0	4.7	15.5	20.3	27.9	18.1	8.2	5.4
Shock absorber replacement	100.0	1.8	13.2	32.8	22.4	15.8	9.7	4.4
Tire repair and other repair work	100.0	2.6	13.4	20.5	25.3	20.7	11.2	6.3
Vehicle air conditioning repair	100.0	3.8	12.1	23.5	22.5	13.6	9.9	14.6
Exhaust system repair	100.0	2.5	14.4	29.1	17.9	19.5	10.6	6.0
Electrical system repair	100.0	2.5	15.3	19.1	25.2	19.3	10.5	8.1
Motor repair, replacement	100.0	3.4	15.0	19.4	29.5	18.5	8.9	5.3
Auto repair service policy	100.0	1.2	19.5	14.3	16.5	26.0	16.0	6.5
Vehicle insurance	100.0	4.2	15.7	22.2	25.9	16.9	9.0	6.1
Vehicle rental, leases, licenses, other charges	100.0	3.8	17.3	26.4	22.1	19.8	6.9	3.7
Leased and rented vehicles	100.0	3.6	17.5	29.4	20.7	20.3	5.9	2.6
Rented vehicles	100.0	3.4	13.1	22.4	29.0	18.0	11.3	2.8
Leased vehicles	100.0	3.6	18.2	30.4	19.5	20.6	5.1	2.6
Car lease payments	100.0	3.8	14.3	28.5	18.8	24.2	6.4	4.1
Truck lease payments	100.0	3.2	18.4	34.4	20.6	18.8	3.6	1.0
Vehicle registration, state	100.0	3.4	16.8	21.7	24.3	19.0	9.1	5.5
Vehicle registration, local	100.0	4.1	20.1	21.7	22.7	17.7	8.7	4.9
Driver's license	100.0	7.5	16.6	20.5	24.7	15.9	8.5	6.4
Vehicle inspection	100.0	4.5	14.1	21.2	26.3	17.7	10.0	6.2

	total consumer units	under 25	25 to 34	35 to 44	45 to 54	55 to 64	65 to 74	75+
Parking fees	100.0%	7.1%	18.5%	23.4%	23.0%	19.4%	6.0%	2.7%
Parking fees in home city, excl. residence	100.0	8.0	19.2	23.4	22.3	19.4	5.4	2.2
Parking fees on trips	100.0	2.8	15.1	23.0	26.1	19.4	8.4	5.1
Tolls	100.0	2.0	24.4	25.8	23.7	17.8	2.7	3.6
Tolls on trips	100.0	3.8	20.5	20.5	23.3	18.9	10.1	3.1
Towing charges	100.0	7.0	19.4	24.4	28.3	13.0	5.0	2.8
Global positioning services	100.0	–	5.7	16.4	30.0	17.9	20.4	9.4
Automobile service clubs	100.0	1.4	7.8	14.6	26.2	24.0	14.2	11.8
Public transportation	**100.0**	**3.0**	**15.0**	**22.3**	**25.4**	**18.5**	**9.2**	**6.6**
Airline fares	100.0	3.0	14.7	23.0	25.2	19.0	9.6	5.6
Intercity bus fares	100.0	4.5	11.9	16.8	20.2	25.1	11.9	9.6
Intracity mass transit fares	100.0	5.7	20.6	27.0	24.1	15.4	4.2	3.0
Taxis and local transportation on trips	100.0	2.5	11.5	18.9	24.2	24.0	12.3	6.6
Taxi fares and limousine service in home town	100.0	4.9	19.9	15.8	34.9	9.9	8.3	6.6
Intercity train fares	100.0	2.4	12.6	23.2	26.3	21.5	7.9	6.0
Ship fares	100.0	0.4	13.2	17.6	25.9	16.3	10.7	15.9
School bus	100.0	1.5	2.5	36.1	40.6	4.1	15.2	–

Note: Numbers may not add to total because of rounding. "–" means sample is too small to make a reliable estimate.
Source: Calculations by New Strategist based on the Bureau of Labor Statistics' 2006 Consumer Expenditure Survey

Table 8. Transportation: Average spending by income, 2006

(average annual spending on transportation, by before-tax income of consumer units (CU), 2006)

	total consumer units	under $20,000	$20,000– $39,999	$40,000– $49,999	$50,000– $69,999	$70,000– $79,999	$80,000– $99,999	$100,000 or more
Number of consumer units (in 000s)	118,843	26,075	27,536	11,446	17,674	6,956	10,241	18,915
Number of persons per CU	2.5	1.7	2.2	2.5	2.8	2.8	3.0	3.2
Average before-tax income of CU	$60,533.00	$10,783.16	$29,630.20	$44,620.00	$59,253.00	$74,647.00	$88,763.00	$164,452.00
Average spending of CU, total	48,398.32	20,824.88	31,972.38	39,572.86	50,085.83	57,351.54	65,809.86	100,386.31
TRANSPORTATION	**8,507.90**	**3,077.22**	**5,889.86**	**6,843.77**	**9,422.70**	**10,920.77**	**12,206.32**	**17,058.65**
Vehicle purchases	**3,420.83**	**969.26**	**2,308.35**	**2,229.46**	**3,596.68**	**4,322.02**	**5,155.06**	**7,706.00**
Cars and trucks, new	1,798.12	409.83	837.61	927.33	1,760.63	2,265.75	2,793.51	4,961.19
New cars	862.88	321.28	353.62	553.79	771.12	894.71	1,217.41	2,419.97
New trucks	935.23	116.45	483.99	373.54	989.50	1,371.04	1,576.10	2,541.21
Cars and trucks, used	1,568.35	553.17	1,457.36	1,251.20	1,780.49	2,030.79	2,205.86	2,607.77
Used cars	752.94	336.13	689.16	564.02	742.70	1,152.84	1,006.21	1,260.02
Used trucks	815.41	217.03	768.20	687.18	1,037.79	877.95	1,199.65	1,347.75
Other vehicles	54.36	10.72	13.37	50.93	55.57	25.48	155.69	137.05
New motorcycles	38.50	3.86	6.07	20.78	35.08	9.75	104.17	130.77
Used motorcycles	15.86	8.80	10.44	30.15	20.49	15.73	51.52	6.29
Gasoline and motor oil	**2,227.46**	**1,020.62**	**1,733.41**	**2,146.62**	**2,599.07**	**2,909.33**	**3,138.28**	**3,568.09**
Other vehicle expenses	**2,354.98**	**899.17**	**1,612.77**	**2,192.71**	**2,727.57**	**3,115.40**	**3,229.42**	**4,431.61**
Vehicle finance charges	297.81	65.56	186.44	298.12	374.24	471.95	496.95	536.60
Automobile finance charges	116.91	29.11	85.89	128.18	142.39	178.52	175.35	198.17
Truck finance charges	161.28	33.75	93.69	148.92	212.68	260.35	291.86	287.79
Motorcycle and plane finance charges	4.16	0.22	1.65	2.72	6.70	11.10	7.84	7.36
Other vehicle finance charges	15.46	2.62	5.22	18.30	12.48	21.98	21.89	43.29
Maintenance and repairs	688.44	300.63	485.61	614.99	788.64	861.29	897.09	1,287.06
Coolant, additives, brake, transmission fluids	3.66	2.29	3.51	5.23	4.67	4.04	3.39	3.86
Tires—purchased, replaced, installed	103.33	40.24	64.36	89.52	124.20	133.87	161.75	193.01
Parts, equipment, and accessories	41.25	15.75	29.60	34.14	60.13	66.96	47.16	67.38
Vehicle products and cleaning services	5.30	2.23	8.39	3.68	5.63	5.47	6.36	5.14
Vehicle video equipment	2.58	0.38	0.15	0.42	1.27	–	4.10	12.37
Miscellaneous auto repair, servicing	41.15	11.79	26.49	42.77	42.90	35.09	59.88	86.38
Body work and painting	29.53	13.06	15.51	24.38	33.75	21.20	38.28	70.16
Clutch, transmission repair	36.93	7.44	23.98	35.14	45.38	65.79	48.18	72.91
Drive shaft and rear-end repair	6.73	4.46	5.48	5.90	8.13	1.05	12.64	9.77
Brake work	61.27	23.27	39.21	72.71	61.79	54.83	87.19	126.66
Repair to steering or front-end	19.74	8.22	13.14	16.14	27.92	31.93	25.98	31.91
Repair to engine cooling system	22.07	11.99	19.57	20.92	24.75	18.87	22.29	38.84
Motor tune-up	47.53	18.95	35.18	35.95	42.15	41.74	52.23	116.55
Lube, oil change, and oil filters	66.87	31.36	49.54	64.12	75.68	88.61	96.31	110.58
Front-end alignment, wheel balance, rotation	13.79	6.70	12.92	10.36	13.24	12.88	17.66	25.64
Shock absorber replacement	4.78	1.55	3.49	3.37	4.01	2.76	4.97	13.34
Tire repair and other repair work	48.52	21.01	33.74	29.55	55.19	46.72	70.07	102.19
Vehicle air conditioning repair	11.94	7.40	9.06	10.04	10.19	19.35	13.27	21.75
Exhaust system repair	10.15	7.06	8.17	8.17	11.56	11.70	9.53	16.96
Electrical system repair	24.69	14.46	21.97	17.77	27.51	29.81	34.50	37.13
Motor repair, replacement	69.29	43.48	51.42	61.44	88.06	93.04	67.44	110.36
Auto repair service policy	8.74	1.92	9.85	9.66	13.35	7.86	12.09	10.18
Vehicle insurance	886.43	374.10	694.68	911.00	1,042.81	1,159.07	1,175.85	1,453.89
Vehicle rental, leases, licenses, other charges	482.30	158.88	246.04	368.60	521.88	623.09	659.54	1,154.06
Leased and rented vehicles	294.36	83.21	119.91	208.69	325.08	381.77	414.75	765.20
Rented vehicles	37.49	9.01	20.84	24.51	33.76	41.19	51.11	103.60
Leased vehicles	256.87	74.19	99.07	184.18	291.32	340.59	363.64	661.60
Car lease payments	123.12	39.91	44.91	112.05	120.52	126.89	168.61	334.78
Truck lease payments	109.17	24.25	46.55	57.09	151.05	145.11	173.25	261.83
Vehicle registration, state	86.30	34.54	60.09	80.22	100.98	117.23	122.14	154.98
Vehicle registration, local	8.35	3.80	5.08	6.62	8.39	16.94	13.15	14.61
Driver's license	6.87	4.58	6.36	6.55	8.10	7.43	8.32	8.85
Vehicle inspection	9.51	5.07	7.65	10.89	12.62	11.96	12.28	12.16

	total consumer units	under $20,000	$20,000– $39,999	$40,000– $49,999	$50,000– $69,999	$70,000– $79,999	$80,000– $99,999	$100,000 or more
Parking fees	$34.88	$13.92	$14.65	$21.99	$29.99	$28.47	$37.34	$106.63
Parking fees in home city, excl. residence	28.75	13.01	11.89	16.80	25.59	22.82	27.85	87.82
Parking fees on trips	6.14	0.91	2.75	5.19	4.41	5.65	9.49	18.81
Tolls	15.02	2.74	12.23	6.25	10.25	25.03	18.25	38.22
Tolls on trips	4.02	1.19	2.56	3.81	3.70	4.95	5.80	9.19
Towing charges	5.11	3.48	4.58	6.03	4.61	8.85	4.47	7.01
Global positioning services	1.60	0.21	0.74	1.54	0.87	3.01	1.98	4.86
Automobile service clubs	16.29	6.24	12.19	16.00	17.28	17.45	21.04	32.36
Public transportation	**504.63**	**188.16**	**235.34**	**274.97**	**499.36**	**574.02**	**683.56**	**1,352.95**
Airline fares	334.60	101.46	138.55	169.88	324.64	424.63	470.34	943.78
Intercity bus fares	11.33	6.38	7.77	6.11	13.08	10.18	16.50	22.47
Intracity mass transit fares	51.09	43.68	43.32	41.12	45.63	41.43	33.04	97.04
Taxis and local transportation on trips	20.84	9.06	11.09	10.56	17.09	19.80	28.32	57.32
Taxi fares and limousine service in home town	13.87	7.88	10.40	14.18	8.88	18.65	12.69	29.09
Intercity train fares	16.29	5.78	10.13	9.59	10.59	17.53	19.38	47.02
Ship fares	55.02	13.74	12.35	23.28	79.18	33.81	102.77	152.61
School bus	1.59	0.39	1.73	0.24	0.28	7.99	0.52	3.61

Note: Numbers may not add to total because some categories are not shown. "–" means sample is too small to make a reliable estimate.
Source: Bureau of Labor Statistics, unpublished tables from the 2006 Consumer Expenditure Survey

Table 9. Transportation: Indexed spending by income, 2006

(indexed average annual spending of consumer units (CU) on transportation, by before-tax income of consumer unit, 2006; index definition: an index of 100 is the average for all consumer units; an index of 132 means that spending by consumer units in that group is 32 percent above the average for all consumer units; an index of 68 indicates spending that is 32 percent below the average for all consumer units)

	total consumer units	under $20,000	$20,000– $39,999	$40,000– $49,999	$50,000– $69,999	$70,000– $79,999	$80,000– $99,999	$100,000 or more
Average spending of CU, total	$48,398	$20,825	$31,972	$39,573	$50,086	$57,352	$65,810	$100,386
Average spending of CU, index	100	43	66	82	103	118	136	207
TRANSPORTATION	100	36	69	80	111	128	143	201
Vehicle purchases	100	28	67	65	105	126	151	225
Cars and trucks, new	100	23	47	52	98	126	155	276
New cars	100	37	41	64	89	104	141	280
New trucks	100	12	52	40	106	147	169	272
Cars and trucks, used	100	35	93	80	114	129	141	166
Used cars	100	45	92	75	99	153	134	167
Used trucks	100	27	94	84	127	108	147	165
Other vehicles	100	20	25	94	102	47	286	252
New motorcycles	100	10	16	54	91	25	271	340
Used motorcycles	100	55	66	190	129	99	325	40
Gasoline and motor oil	100	46	78	96	117	131	141	160
Other vehicle expenses	100	38	68	93	116	132	137	188
Vehicle finance charges	100	22	63	100	126	158	167	180
Automobile finance charges	100	25	73	110	122	153	150	170
Truck finance charges	100	21	58	92	132	161	181	178
Motorcycle and plane finance charges	100	5	40	65	161	267	188	177
Other vehicle finance charges	100	17	34	118	81	142	142	280
Maintenance and repairs	100	44	71	89	115	125	130	187
Coolant, additives, brake, transmission fluids	100	63	96	143	128	110	93	105
Tires—purchased, replaced, installed	100	39	62	87	120	130	157	187
Parts, equipment, and accessories	100	38	72	83	146	162	114	163
Vehicle products and cleaning services	100	42	158	69	106	103	120	97
Vehicle video equipment	100	15	6	16	49	–	159	479
Miscellaneous auto repair, servicing	100	29	64	104	104	85	146	210
Body work and painting	100	44	53	83	114	72	130	238
Clutch, transmission repair	100	20	65	95	123	178	130	197
Drive shaft and rear-end repair	100	66	81	88	121	16	188	145
Brake work	100	38	64	119	101	89	142	207
Repair to steering or front-end	100	42	67	82	141	162	132	162
Repair to engine cooling system	100	54	89	95	112	86	101	176
Motor tune-up	100	40	74	76	89	88	110	245
Lube, oil change, and oil filters	100	47	74	96	113	133	144	165
Front-end alignment, wheel balance, rotation	100	49	94	75	96	93	128	186
Shock absorber replacement	100	32	73	71	84	58	104	279
Tire repair and other repair work	100	43	70	61	114	96	144	211
Vehicle air conditioning repair	100	62	76	84	85	162	111	182
Exhaust system repair	100	70	80	80	114	115	94	167
Electrical system repair	100	59	89	72	111	121	140	150
Motor repair, replacement	100	63	74	89	127	134	97	159
Auto repair service policy	100	22	113	111	153	90	138	116
Vehicle insurance	100	42	78	103	118	131	133	164
Vehicle rental, leases, licenses, other charges	100	33	51	76	108	129	137	239
Leased and rented vehicles	100	28	41	71	110	130	141	260
Rented vehicles	100	24	56	65	90	110	136	276
Leased vehicles	100	29	39	72	113	133	142	258
Car lease payments	100	32	36	91	98	103	137	272
Truck lease payments	100	22	43	52	138	133	159	240
Vehicle registration, state	100	40	70	93	117	136	142	180
Vehicle registration, local	100	46	61	79	100	203	157	175
Driver's license	100	67	93	95	118	108	121	129
Vehicle inspection	100	53	80	115	133	126	129	128

	total consumer units	under $20,000	$20,000–$39,999	$40,000–$49,999	$50,000–$69,999	$70,000–$79,999	$80,000–$99,999	$100,000 or more
Parking fees	100	40	42	63	86	82	107	306
Parking fees in home city, excluding residence	100	45	41	58	89	79	97	305
Parking fees on trips	100	15	45	85	72	92	155	306
Tolls	100	18	81	42	68	167	122	254
Tolls on trips	100	30	64	95	92	123	144	229
Towing charges	100	68	90	118	90	173	87	137
Global positioning services	100	13	46	96	54	188	124	304
Automobile service clubs	100	38	75	98	106	107	129	199
Public transportation	**100**	**37**	**47**	**54**	**99**	**114**	**135**	**268**
Airline fares	100	30	41	51	97	127	141	282
Intercity bus fares	100	56	69	54	115	90	146	198
Intracity mass transit fares	100	85	85	80	89	81	65	190
Taxis and local transportation on trips	100	43	53	51	82	95	136	275
Taxi fares and limousine service in home town	100	57	75	102	64	134	91	210
Intercity train fares	100	35	62	59	65	108	119	289
Ship fares	100	25	22	42	144	61	187	277
School bus	100	24	109	15	18	503	33	227

Note: "–" means sample is too small to make a reliable estimate.
Source: Calculations by New Strategist based on the Bureau of Labor Statistics' 2006 Consumer Expenditure Survey

Table 10. Transportation: Total spending by income, 2006

(total annual spending on transportation, by before-tax income group of consumer units (CU), 2006; consumer units and dollars in thousands)

	total consumer units	under $20,000	$20,000–$39,999	$40,000–$49,999	$50,000–$69,999	$70,000–$79,999	$80,000–$99,999	$100,000 or more
Number of consumer units	118,843	26,075	27,536	11,446	17,674	6,956	10,241	18,915
Total spending of all CUs	$5,751,801,544	$543,008,700	$880,391,370	$452,950,956	$885,216,959	$398,937,312	$673,958,776	$1,898,807,054
TRANSPORTATION	1,011,104,360	80,238,399	162,183,202	78,333,791	166,536,800	75,964,876	125,004,923	322,664,365
Vehicle purchases	406,541,700	25,273,521	63,562,703	25,518,399	63,567,722	30,063,971	52,792,969	145,758,990
Cars and trucks, new	213,693,975	10,686,257	23,064,492	10,614,219	31,117,375	15,760,557	28,608,336	93,840,909
New cars	102,547,248	8,377,317	9,737,238	6,338,680	13,628,775	6,223,603	12,467,496	45,773,733
New trucks	111,145,539	3,036,393	13,327,121	4,275,539	17,488,423	9,536,954	16,140,840	48,066,987
Cars and trucks, used	186,387,419	14,423,780	40,129,932	14,321,235	31,468,380	14,126,175	22,590,212	49,325,970
Used cars	89,481,648	8,764,640	18,976,750	6,455,773	13,126,480	8,019,155	10,304,597	23,833,278
Used trucks	96,905,771	5,659,139	21,153,173	7,865,462	18,341,900	6,107,020	12,285,616	25,492,691
Other vehicles	6,460,305	279,421	368,279	582,945	982,144	177,239	1,594,421	2,592,301
New motorcycles	4,575,456	100,650	167,144	237,848	620,004	67,821	1,066,805	2,473,515
Used motorcycles	1,884,850	229,380	287,524	345,097	362,140	109,418	527,616	118,975
Gasoline and motor oil	264,718,029	26,612,676	47,731,188	24,570,213	45,935,963	20,237,299	32,139,125	67,490,422
Other vehicle expenses	279,872,888	23,445,757	44,409,164	25,097,759	48,207,072	21,670,722	33,072,490	83,823,903
Vehicle finance charges	35,392,634	1,709,601	5,133,753	3,412,282	6,614,318	3,282,884	5,089,265	10,149,789
Automobile finance charges	13,893,935	758,976	2,365,101	1,467,148	2,516,601	1,241,785	1,795,759	3,748,386
Truck finance charges	19,166,999	879,990	2,579,718	1,704,538	3,758,906	1,810,995	2,988,938	5,443,548
Motorcycle and plane finance charges	494,387	5,784	45,394	31,133	118,416	77,212	80,289	139,214
Other vehicle finance charges	1,837,313	68,205	143,682	209,462	220,572	152,893	224,175	818,830
Maintenance and repairs	81,816,275	7,838,865	13,371,657	7,039,176	13,938,423	5,991,133	9,187,099	24,344,740
Coolant, additives, brake and transmission fluids	434,965	59,734	96,574	59,863	82,538	28,102	34,717	73,012
Tires—purchased, replaced, installed	12,280,047	1,049,351	1,772,308	1,024,646	2,195,111	931,200	1,656,482	3,650,784
Parts, equipment, and accessories	4,902,274	410,766	815,041	390,766	1,062,738	465,774	482,966	1,274,493
Vehicle products and cleaning services	629,868	58,018	231,149	42,121	99,505	38,049	65,133	97,223
Vehicle video equipment	306,615	9,909	4,130	4,807	22,446	–	41,988	233,979
Miscellaneous auto repair, servicing	4,890,389	307,483	729,460	489,545	758,215	244,086	613,231	1,633,878
Body work and painting	3,509,434	340,624	427,127	279,053	596,498	147,467	392,025	1,327,076
Clutch, transmission repair	4,388,872	193,964	660,414	402,212	802,046	457,635	493,411	1,379,093
Drive shaft and rear-end repair	799,813	116,235	150,897	67,531	143,690	7,304	129,446	184,800
Brake work	7,281,511	606,885	1,079,651	832,239	1,092,076	381,397	892,913	2,395,774
Repair to steering or front-end	2,345,961	214,249	361,906	184,738	493,458	222,105	266,061	603,578
Repair to engine cooling system	2,622,865	312,550	538,967	239,450	437,432	131,260	228,272	734,659
Motor tune-up	5,648,608	494,067	968,708	411,484	744,959	290,343	534,887	2,204,543
Lube, oil change, and oil filters	7,947,031	817,658	1,364,137	733,918	1,337,568	616,371	986,311	2,091,621
Front-end alignment, wheel balance, rotation	1,638,845	174,818	355,858	118,581	234,004	89,593	180,856	484,981
Shock absorber replacement	568,070	40,480	96,138	38,573	70,873	19,199	50,898	252,326
Tire repair and other repair work	5,766,262	547,882	929,162	338,229	975,428	324,984	717,587	1,932,924
Vehicle air conditioning repair	1,418,985	192,987	249,498	114,918	180,098	134,599	135,898	411,401
Exhaust system repair	1,206,256	184,147	224,873	93,514	204,311	81,385	97,597	320,798
Electrical system repair	2,934,234	377,012	604,914	203,395	486,212	207,358	353,315	702,314
Motor repair, replacement	8,234,631	1,133,859	1,415,834	703,242	1,556,372	647,186	690,653	2,087,459
Auto repair service policy	1,038,688	50,069	271,125	110,568	235,948	54,674	123,814	192,555
Vehicle insurance	105,346,000	9,754,558	19,128,679	10,427,306	18,430,624	8,062,491	12,041,880	27,500,329
Vehicle rental, leases, licenses, other charges	57,317,979	4,142,871	6,774,933	4,218,996	9,223,707	4,334,214	6,754,349	21,829,045
Leased and rented vehicles	34,982,625	2,169,583	3,301,879	2,388,666	5,745,464	2,655,592	4,247,455	14,473,758
Rented vehicles	4,455,424	234,888	573,975	280,541	596,674	286,518	523,418	1,959,594
Leased vehicles	30,527,201	1,934,619	2,727,904	2,108,124	5,148,790	2,369,144	3,724,037	12,514,164
Car lease payments	14,631,950	1,040,737	1,236,769	1,282,524	2,130,070	882,647	1,726,735	6,332,364
Truck lease payments	12,974,090	632,394	1,281,781	653,452	2,669,658	1,009,385	1,774,253	4,952,514
Vehicle registration, state	10,256,151	900,572	1,654,763	918,198	1,784,721	815,452	1,250,836	2,931,447
Vehicle registration, local	992,339	99,101	139,765	75,773	148,285	117,835	134,669	276,348
Driver's license	816,451	119,453	175,021	74,971	143,159	51,683	85,205	167,398
Vehicle inspection	1,130,197	132,302	210,669	124,647	223,046	83,194	125,759	230,006

	total consumer units	under $20,000	$20,000– $39,999	$40,000– $49,999	$50,000– $69,999	$70,000– $79,999	$80,000– $99,999	$100,000 or more
Parking fees	$4,145,244	$362,881	$403,378	$251,698	$530,043	$198,037	$382,399	$2,016,906
Parking fees in home city, excluding residence	3,416,736	339,148	327,462	192,293	452,278	158,736	285,212	1,661,115
Parking fees on trips	729,696	23,734	75,774	59,405	77,942	39,301	97,187	355,791
Tolls	1,785,022	71,481	336,774	71,538	181,159	174,109	186,898	722,931
Tolls on trips	477,749	31,030	70,415	43,609	65,394	34,432	59,398	173,829
Towing charges	607,288	90,693	126,223	69,019	81,477	61,561	45,777	132,594
Global positioning services	190,149	5,370	20,401	17,627	15,376	20,938	20,277	91,927
Automobile service clubs	1,935,952	162,692	335,655	183,136	305,407	121,382	215,471	612,089
Public transportation	**59,971,743**	**4,906,400**	**6,480,423**	**3,147,307**	**8,825,689**	**3,992,883**	**7,000,338**	**25,591,049**
Airline fares	39,764,868	2,645,622	3,815,045	1,944,446	5,737,687	2,953,726	4,816,752	17,851,599
Intercity bus fares	1,346,491	166,384	214,045	69,935	231,176	70,812	168,977	425,020
Intracity mass transit fares	6,071,689	1,138,983	1,192,887	470,660	806,465	288,187	338,363	1,835,512
Taxis and local transportation on trips	2,476,688	236,192	305,384	120,870	302,049	137,729	290,025	1,084,208
Taxi fares and limousine service in home town	1,648,352	205,508	286,309	162,304	156,945	129,729	129,958	550,237
Intercity train fares	1,935,952	150,620	279,074	109,767	187,168	121,939	198,471	889,383
Ship fares	6,538,742	358,392	340,131	266,463	1,399,427	235,182	1,052,468	2,886,618
School bus	188,960	10,109	47,557	2,747	4,949	55,578	5,325	68,283

Note: Numbers may not add to total because some categories are not shown and because of rounding. "–" means sample is too small to make a reliable estimate.
Source: Calculations by New Strategist based on the Bureau of Labor Statistics' 2006 Consumer Expenditure Survey

Table 11. Transportation: Market shares by income, 2006

(percentage of total annual spending on transportation accounted for by before-tax income group of consumer units, 2006)

	total consumer units	under $20,000	$20,000–$39,999	$40,000–$49,999	$50,000–$69,999	$70,000–$79,999	$80,000–$99,999	$100,000 or more
Share of total consumer units	100.0%	21.9%	23.2%	9.6%	14.9%	5.9%	8.6%	15.9%
Share of total before-tax income	100.0	3.9	11.3	7.1	14.6	7.2	12.6	43.2
Share of total spending	100.0	9.4	15.3	7.9	15.4	6.9	11.7	33.0
TRANSPORTATION	**100.0**	**7.9**	**16.0**	**7.7**	**16.5**	**7.5**	**12.4**	**31.9**
Vehicle purchases	**100.0**	**6.2**	**15.6**	**6.3**	**15.6**	**7.4**	**13.0**	**35.9**
Cars and trucks, new	100.0	5.0	10.8	5.0	14.6	7.4	13.4	43.9
New cars	100.0	8.2	9.5	6.2	13.3	6.1	12.2	44.6
New trucks	100.0	2.7	12.0	3.8	15.7	8.6	14.5	43.2
Cars and trucks, used	100.0	7.7	21.5	7.7	16.9	7.6	12.1	26.5
Used cars	100.0	9.8	21.2	7.2	14.7	9.0	11.5	26.6
Used trucks	100.0	5.8	21.8	8.1	18.9	6.3	12.7	26.3
Other vehicles	100.0	4.3	5.7	9.0	15.2	2.7	24.7	40.1
New motorcycles	100.0	2.2	3.7	5.2	13.6	1.5	23.3	54.1
Used motorcycles	100.0	12.2	15.3	18.3	19.2	5.8	28.0	6.3
Gasoline and motor oil	**100.0**	**10.1**	**18.0**	**9.3**	**17.4**	**7.6**	**12.1**	**25.5**
Other vehicle expenses	**100.0**	**8.4**	**15.9**	**9.0**	**17.2**	**7.7**	**11.8**	**30.0**
Vehicle finance charges	100.0	4.8	14.5	9.6	18.7	9.3	14.4	28.7
Automobile finance charges	100.0	5.5	17.0	10.6	18.1	8.9	12.9	27.0
Truck finance charges	100.0	4.6	13.5	8.9	19.6	9.4	15.6	28.4
Motorcycle and plane finance charges	100.0	1.2	9.2	6.3	24.0	15.6	16.2	28.2
Other vehicle finance charges	100.0	3.7	7.8	11.4	12.0	8.3	12.2	44.6
Maintenance and repairs	100.0	9.6	16.3	8.6	17.0	7.3	11.2	29.8
Coolant, additives, brake and transmission fluids	100.0	13.7	22.2	13.8	19.0	6.5	8.0	16.8
Tires—purchased, replaced, installed	100.0	8.5	14.4	8.3	17.9	7.6	13.5	29.7
Parts, equipment, and accessories	100.0	8.4	16.6	8.0	21.7	9.5	9.9	26.0
Vehicle products and cleaning services	100.0	9.2	36.7	6.7	15.8	6.0	10.3	15.4
Vehicle video equipment	100.0	3.2	1.3	1.6	7.3	–	13.7	76.3
Miscellaneous auto repair, servicing	100.0	6.3	14.9	10.0	15.5	5.0	12.5	33.4
Body work and painting	100.0	9.7	12.2	8.0	17.0	4.2	11.2	37.8
Clutch, transmission repair	100.0	4.4	15.0	9.2	18.3	10.4	11.2	31.4
Drive shaft and rear-end repair	100.0	14.5	18.9	8.4	18.0	0.9	16.2	23.1
Brake work	100.0	8.3	14.8	11.4	15.0	5.2	12.3	32.9
Repair to steering or front-end	100.0	9.1	15.4	7.9	21.0	9.5	11.3	25.7
Repair to engine cooling system	100.0	11.9	20.5	9.1	16.7	5.0	8.7	28.0
Motor tune-up	100.0	8.7	17.1	7.3	13.2	5.1	9.5	39.0
Lube, oil change, and oil filters	100.0	10.3	17.2	9.2	16.8	7.8	12.4	26.3
Front-end alignment, wheel balance, rotation	100.0	10.7	21.7	7.2	14.3	5.5	11.0	29.6
Shock absorber replacement	100.0	7.1	16.9	6.8	12.5	3.4	9.0	44.4
Tire repair and other repair work	100.0	9.5	16.1	5.9	16.9	5.6	12.4	33.5
Vehicle air conditioning repair	100.0	13.6	17.6	8.1	12.7	9.5	9.6	29.0
Exhaust system repair	100.0	15.3	18.6	7.8	16.9	6.7	8.1	26.6
Electrical system repair	100.0	12.8	20.6	6.9	16.6	7.1	12.0	23.9
Motor repair, replacement	100.0	13.8	17.2	8.5	18.9	7.9	8.4	25.3
Auto repair service policy	100.0	4.8	26.1	10.6	22.7	5.3	11.9	18.5
Vehicle insurance	100.0	9.3	18.2	9.9	17.5	7.7	11.4	26.1
Vehicle rental, leases, licenses, other charges	100.0	7.2	11.8	7.4	16.1	7.6	11.8	38.1
Leased and rented vehicles	100.0	6.2	9.4	6.8	16.4	7.6	12.1	41.4
Rented vehicles	100.0	5.3	12.9	6.3	13.4	6.4	11.7	44.0
Leased vehicles	100.0	6.3	8.9	6.9	16.9	7.8	12.2	41.0
Car lease payments	100.0	7.1	8.5	8.8	14.6	6.0	11.8	43.3
Truck lease payments	100.0	4.9	9.9	5.0	20.6	7.8	13.7	38.2
Vehicle registration, state	100.0	8.8	16.1	9.0	17.4	8.0	12.2	28.6
Vehicle registration, local	100.0	10.0	14.1	7.6	14.9	11.9	13.6	27.8
Driver's license	100.0	14.6	21.4	9.2	17.5	6.3	10.4	20.5
Vehicle inspection	100.0	11.7	18.6	11.0	19.7	7.4	11.1	20.4

	total consumer units	under $20,000	$20,000– $39,999	$40,000– $49,999	$50,000– $69,999	$70,000– $79,999	$80,000– $99,999	$100,000 or more
Parking fees	100.0%	8.8%	9.7%	6.1%	12.8%	4.8%	9.2%	48.7%
Parking fees in home city, excl. residence	100.0	9.9	9.6	5.6	13.2	4.6	8.3	48.6
Parking fees on trips	100.0	3.3	10.4	8.1	10.7	5.4	13.3	48.8
Tolls	100.0	4.0	18.9	4.0	10.1	9.8	10.5	40.5
Tolls on trips	100.0	6.5	14.7	9.1	13.7	7.2	12.4	36.4
Towing charges	100.0	14.9	20.8	11.4	13.4	10.1	7.5	21.8
Global positioning services	100.0	2.8	10.7	9.3	8.1	11.0	10.7	48.3
Automobile service clubs	100.0	8.4	17.3	9.5	15.8	6.3	11.1	31.6
Public transportation	**100.0**	**8.2**	**10.8**	**5.2**	**14.7**	**6.7**	**11.7**	**42.7**
Airline fares	100.0	6.7	9.6	4.9	14.4	7.4	12.1	44.9
Intercity bus fares	100.0	12.4	15.9	5.2	17.2	5.3	12.5	31.6
Intracity mass transit fares	100.0	18.8	19.6	7.8	13.3	4.7	5.6	30.2
Taxis and local transportation on trips	100.0	9.5	12.3	4.9	12.2	5.6	11.7	43.8
Taxi fares and limousine service in home town	100.0	12.5	17.4	9.8	9.5	7.9	7.9	33.4
Intercity train fares	100.0	7.8	14.4	5.7	9.7	6.3	10.3	45.9
Ship fares	100.0	5.5	5.2	4.1	21.4	3.6	16.1	44.1
School bus	100.0	5.3	25.2	1.5	2.6	29.4	2.8	36.1

Note: Numbers may not add to total because of rounding. "–" means sample is too small to make a reliable estimate.
Source: Calculations by New Strategist based on the Bureau of Labor Statistics' 2006 Consumer Expenditure Survey

Table 12. Transportation: Average spending by high-income consumer units, 2006

(average annual spending on transportation, by before-tax income of consumer units with high incomes, 2006)

	total consumer units	$100,000 or more	$100,000– $119,999	$120,000– $149,999	$150,000 or more
Number of consumer units (in 000s)	118,843	18,915	6,300	5,357	7,258
Number of persons per consumer unit	2.5	3.2	3.2	3.1	3.2
Average before-tax income of consumer units	$60,533.00	$164,452.00	$108,417.00	$132,682.00	$236,545.00
Average spending of consumer units, total	48,398.32	100,386.31	78,128.93	88,646.65	128,681.21
TRANSPORTATION	**8,507.90**	**17,058.65**	**13,600.60**	**15,661.40**	**21,096.89**
Vehicle purchases	**3,420.83**	**7,706.00**	**5,502.16**	**6,805.21**	**10,283.99**
Cars and trucks, new	1,798.12	4,961.19	3,091.96	4,005.75	7,289.02
New cars	862.88	2,419.97	1,559.85	1,411.68	3,910.82
New trucks	935.23	2,541.21	1,532.11	2,594.07	3,378.20
Cars and trucks, used	1,568.35	2,607.77	2,276.45	2,662.63	2,854.88
Used cars	752.94	1,260.02	1,032.37	1,400.19	1,354.18
Used trucks	815.41	1,347.75	1,244.08	1,262.44	1,500.71
Other vehicles	54.36	137.05	133.75	136.83	140.08
New motorcycles	38.50	130.77	118.01	133.15	140.08
Used motorcycles	15.86	6.29	15.74	3.69	–
Gasoline and motor oil	**2,227.46**	**3,568.09**	**3,317.88**	**3,598.03**	**3,763.19**
Other vehicle expenses	**2,354.98**	**4,431.61**	**3,731.73**	**4,205.89**	**5,208.90**
Vehicle finance charges	297.81	536.60	526.20	531.21	549.61
Automobile finance charges	116.91	198.17	188.51	196.07	208.10
Truck finance charges	161.28	287.79	306.81	291.35	268.64
Motorcycle and plane finance charges	4.16	7.36	4.94	10.84	6.88
Other vehicle finance charges	15.46	43.29	25.94	32.95	65.99
Maintenance and repairs	688.44	1,287.06	1,050.58	1,285.14	1,495.45
Coolant, additives, brake and transmission fluids	3.66	3.86	3.95	4.76	3.13
Tires—purchased, replaced, installed	103.33	193.01	161.47	180.15	229.88
Parts, equipment, and accessories	41.25	67.38	73.92	76.26	55.16
Vehicle products and cleaning services	5.30	5.14	4.25	4.58	6.44
Vehicle video equipment	2.58	12.37	0.32	6.63	27.06
Miscellaneous auto repair, servicing	41.15	86.38	81.47	72.12	102.20
Body work and painting	29.53	70.16	36.90	83.85	88.94
Clutch, transmission repair	36.93	72.91	67.10	71.05	79.34
Drive shaft and rear-end repair	6.73	9.77	8.63	11.29	9.62
Brake work	61.27	126.66	94.20	138.91	145.80
Repair to steering or front-end	19.74	31.91	20.69	31.97	41.61
Repair to engine cooling system	22.07	38.84	28.11	43.34	44.84
Motor tune-up	47.53	116.55	85.51	110.75	147.78
Lube, oil change, and oil filters	66.87	110.58	97.03	107.70	124.46
Front-end alignment, wheel balance, rotation	13.79	25.64	19.31	34.76	24.41
Shock absorber replacement	4.78	13.34	6.67	13.23	19.20
Tire repair and other repair work	48.52	102.19	97.40	92.94	113.17
Vehicle air conditioning repair	11.94	21.75	17.15	34.01	16.68
Exhaust system repair	10.15	16.96	11.20	12.79	25.05
Electrical system repair	24.69	37.13	38.15	27.81	43.12
Motor repair, replacement	69.29	110.36	85.10	113.88	129.70
Auto repair service policy	8.74	10.18	12.06	10.02	8.67
Vehicle insurance	886.43	1,453.89	1,307.19	1,481.64	1,560.75
Vehicle rental, leases, licenses, other charges	482.30	1,154.06	847.76	907.90	1,603.08
Leased and rented vehicles	294.36	765.20	552.21	572.67	1,092.18
Rented vehicles	37.49	103.60	71.58	75.41	152.20
Leased vehicles	256.87	661.60	480.63	497.26	939.98
Car lease payments	123.12	334.78	227.36	237.48	499.86
Truck lease payments	109.17	261.83	211.68	193.73	355.62
Vehicle registration, state	86.30	154.98	133.19	144.35	181.73
Vehicle registration, local	8.35	14.61	16.36	12.47	14.68
Driver's license	6.87	8.85	8.77	8.08	9.48
Vehicle inspection	9.51	12.16	12.17	11.99	12.29

	total consumer units	$100,000 or more	$100,000–$119,999	$120,000–$149,999	$150,000 or more
Parking fees	$34.88	$106.63	$59.54	$69.99	$174.56
Parking fees in home city, excluding residence	28.75	87.82	48.55	53.56	147.20
Parking fees on trips	6.14	18.81	10.99	16.43	27.36
Tolls	15.02	38.22	26.86	37.48	50.06
Tolls on trips	4.02	9.19	6.71	9.95	10.78
Towing charges	5.11	7.01	5.91	7.36	7.70
Global positioning services	1.60	4.86	4.11	3.65	6.39
Automobile service clubs	16.29	32.36	21.92	29.90	43.24
Public transportation	**504.63**	**1,352.95**	**1,048.83**	**1,052.27**	**1,840.81**
Airline fares	334.60	943.78	736.03	736.08	1,277.42
Intercity bus fares	11.33	22.47	19.16	14.62	31.14
Intracity mass transit fares	51.09	97.04	73.08	79.63	130.69
Taxis and local transportation on trips	20.84	57.32	39.43	34.32	89.82
Taxi fares and limousine service in home town	13.87	29.09	12.26	34.17	41.89
Intercity train fares	16.29	47.02	42.86	35.16	59.40
Ship fares	55.02	152.61	121.90	116.39	206.02
School bus	1.59	3.61	4.11	1.91	4.43

Note: Numbers may not add to total because some categories are not shown.
Source: Bureau of Labor Statistics, unpublished tables from the 2006 Consumer Expenditure Survey

Table 13. Transportation: Indexed spending by high-income consumer units, 2006

(indexed average annual spending of consumer units with high incomes on transportation, by before-tax income of consumer unit, 2006; index definition: an index of 100 is the average for all consumer units; an index of 132 means that spending by consumer units in that group is 32 percent above the average for all consumer units; an index of 68 indicates spending that is 32 percent below the average for all consumer units)

	total consumer units	$100,000 or more	$100,000– $119,999	$120,000– $149,999	$150,000 or more
Average spending of consumer units, total	$48,398	$100,386	$78,129	$88,647	$128,681
Average spending of consumer units, index	100	207	161	183	266
TRANSPORTATION	100	201	160	184	248
Vehicle purchases	100	225	161	199	301
Cars and trucks, new	100	276	172	223	405
New cars	100	280	181	164	453
New trucks	100	272	164	277	361
Cars and trucks, used	100	166	145	170	182
Used cars	100	167	137	186	180
Used trucks	100	165	153	155	184
Other vehicles	100	252	246	252	258
New motorcycles	100	340	307	346	364
Used motorcycles	100	40	99	23	–
Gasoline and motor oil	100	160	149	162	169
Other vehicle expenses	100	188	158	179	221
Vehicle finance charges	100	180	177	178	185
Automobile finance charges	100	170	161	168	178
Truck finance charges	100	178	190	181	167
Motorcycle and plane finance charges	100	177	119	261	165
Other vehicle finance charges	100	280	168	213	427
Maintenance and repairs	100	187	153	187	217
Coolant, additives, brake and transmission fluids	100	105	108	130	86
Tires—purchased, replaced, installed	100	187	156	174	222
Parts, equipment, and accessories	100	163	179	185	134
Vehicle products and cleaning services	100	97	80	86	122
Vehicle video equipment	100	479	12	257	1049
Miscellaneous auto repair, servicing	100	210	198	175	248
Body work and painting	100	238	125	284	301
Clutch, transmission repair	100	197	182	192	215
Drive shaft and rear-end repair	100	145	128	168	143
Brake work	100	207	154	227	238
Repair to steering or front-end	100	162	105	162	211
Repair to engine cooling system	100	176	127	196	203
Motor tune-up	100	245	180	233	311
Lube, oil change, and oil filters	100	165	145	161	186
Front-end alignment, wheel balance, rotation	100	186	140	252	177
Shock absorber replacement	100	279	140	277	402
Tire repair and other repair work	100	211	201	192	233
Vehicle air conditioning repair	100	182	144	285	140
Exhaust system repair	100	167	110	126	247
Electrical system repair	100	150	155	113	175
Motor repair, replacement	100	159	123	164	187
Auto repair service policy	100	116	138	115	99
Vehicle insurance	100	164	147	167	176
Vehicle rental, leases, licenses, other charges	100	239	176	188	332
Leased and rented vehicles	100	260	188	195	371
Rented vehicles	100	276	191	201	406
Leased vehicles	100	258	187	194	366
Car lease payments	100	272	185	193	406
Truck lease payments	100	240	194	177	326
Vehicle registration, state	100	180	154	167	211
Vehicle registration, local	100	175	196	149	176
Driver's license	100	129	128	118	138
Vehicle inspection	100	128	128	126	129

	total consumer units	$100,000 or more	$100,000–$119,999	$120,000–$149,999	$150,000 or more
Parking fees	100	306	171	201	500
Parking fees in home city, excluding residence	100	305	169	186	512
Parking fees on trips	100	306	179	268	446
Tolls	100	254	179	250	333
Tolls on trips	100	229	167	248	268
Towing charges	100	137	116	144	151
Global positioning services	100	304	257	228	399
Automobile service clubs	100	199	135	184	265
Public transportation	**100**	**268**	**208**	**209**	**365**
Airline fares	100	282	220	220	382
Intercity bus fares	100	198	169	129	275
Intracity mass transit fares	100	190	143	156	256
Taxis and local transportation on trips	100	275	189	165	431
Taxi fares and limousine service in home town	100	210	88	246	302
Intercity train fares	100	289	263	216	365
Ship fares	100	277	222	212	374
School bus	100	227	258	120	279

Source: Calculations by New Strategist based on the Bureau of Labor Statistics' 2006 Consumer Expenditure Survey

Table 14. Transportation: Total spending by high-income consumer units, 2006

(total annual spending on transportation, by before-tax income group of consumer units with high incomes, 2006; consumer units and dollars in thousands)

	total consumer units	$100,000 or more	$100,000– $119,999	$120,000– $149,999	$150,000 or more
Number of consumer units	118,843	18,915	6,300	5,357	7,258
Total spending of all consumer units	$5,751,801,544	$1,898,807,054	$492,212,259	$474,880,104	$933,968,222
TRANSPORTATION	**1,011,104,360**	**322,664,365**	**85,683,780**	**83,898,120**	**153,121,228**
Vehicle purchases	406,541,700	145,758,990	34,663,608	36,455,510	74,641,199
Cars and trucks, new	213,693,975	93,840,909	19,479,348	21,458,803	52,903,707
New cars	102,547,248	45,773,733	9,827,055	7,562,370	28,384,732
New trucks	111,145,539	48,066,987	9,652,293	13,896,433	24,518,976
Cars and trucks, used	186,387,419	49,325,970	14,341,635	14,263,709	20,720,719
Used cars	89,481,648	23,833,278	6,503,931	7,500,818	9,828,638
Used trucks	96,905,771	25,492,691	7,837,704	6,762,891	10,892,153
Other vehicles	6,460,305	2,592,301	842,625	732,998	1,016,701
New motorcycles	4,575,456	2,473,515	743,463	713,285	1,016,701
Used motorcycles	1,884,850	118,975	99,162	19,767	–
Gasoline and motor oil	**264,718,029**	**67,490,422**	**20,902,644**	**19,274,647**	**27,313,233**
Other vehicle expenses	**279,872,888**	**83,823,903**	**23,509,899**	**22,530,953**	**37,806,196**
Vehicle finance charges	35,392,634	10,149,789	3,315,060	2,845,692	3,989,069
Automobile finance charges	13,893,935	3,748,386	1,187,613	1,050,347	1,510,390
Truck finance charges	19,166,999	5,443,548	1,932,903	1,560,762	1,949,789
Motorcycle and plane finance charges	494,387	139,214	31,122	58,070	49,935
Other vehicle finance charges	1,837,313	818,830	163,422	176,513	478,955
Maintenance and repairs	81,816,275	24,344,740	6,618,654	6,884,495	10,853,976
Coolant, additives, brake and transmission fluids	434,965	73,012	24,885	25,499	22,718
Tires—purchased, replaced, installed	12,280,047	3,650,784	1,017,261	965,064	1,668,469
Parts, equipment, and accessories	4,902,274	1,274,493	465,696	408,525	400,351
Vehicle products and cleaning services	629,868	97,223	26,775	24,535	46,742
Vehicle video equipment	306,615	233,979	2,016	35,517	196,401
Miscellaneous auto repair, servicing	4,890,389	1,633,878	513,261	386,347	741,768
Body work and painting	3,509,434	1,327,076	232,470	449,184	645,527
Clutch, transmission repair	4,388,872	1,379,093	422,730	380,615	575,850
Drive shaft and rear-end repair	799,813	184,800	54,369	60,481	69,822
Brake work	7,281,511	2,395,774	593,460	744,141	1,058,216
Repair to steering or front-end	2,345,961	603,578	130,347	171,263	302,005
Repair to engine cooling system	2,622,865	734,659	177,093	232,172	325,449
Motor tune-up	5,648,608	2,204,543	538,713	593,288	1,072,587
Lube, oil change, and oil filters	7,947,031	2,091,621	611,289	576,949	903,331
Front-end alignment, wheel balance, rotation	1,638,845	484,981	121,653	186,209	177,168
Shock absorber replacement	568,070	252,326	42,021	70,873	139,354
Tire repair and other repair work	5,766,262	1,932,924	613,620	497,880	821,388
Vehicle air conditioning repair	1,418,985	411,401	108,045	182,192	121,063
Exhaust system repair	1,206,256	320,798	70,560	68,516	181,813
Electrical system repair	2,934,234	702,314	240,345	148,978	312,965
Motor repair, replacement	8,234,631	2,087,459	536,130	610,055	941,363
Auto repair service policy	1,038,688	192,555	75,978	53,677	62,927
Vehicle insurance	105,346,000	27,500,329	8,235,297	7,937,145	11,327,924
Vehicle rental, leases, licenses, other charges	57,317,979	21,829,045	5,340,888	4,863,620	11,635,155
Leased and rented vehicles	34,982,625	14,473,758	3,478,923	3,067,793	7,927,042
Rented vehicles	4,455,424	1,959,594	450,954	403,971	1,104,668
Leased vehicles	30,527,201	12,514,164	3,027,969	2,663,822	6,822,375
Car lease payments	14,631,950	6,332,364	1,432,368	1,272,180	3,627,984
Truck lease payments	12,974,090	4,952,514	1,333,584	1,037,812	2,581,090
Vehicle registration, state	10,256,151	2,931,447	839,097	773,283	1,318,996
Vehicle registration, local	992,339	276,348	103,068	66,802	106,547
Driver's license	816,451	167,398	55,251	43,285	68,806
Vehicle inspection	1,130,197	230,006	76,671	64,230	89,201

	total consumer units	$100,000 or more	$100,000–$119,999	$120,000–$149,999	$150,000 or more
Parking fees	$4,145,244	$2,016,906	$375,102	$374,936	$1,266,956
Parking fees in home city, excluding residence	3,416,736	1,661,115	305,865	286,921	1,068,378
Parking fees on trips	729,696	355,791	69,237	88,016	198,579
Tolls	1,785,022	722,931	169,218	200,780	363,335
Tolls on trips	477,749	173,829	42,273	53,302	78,241
Towing charges	607,288	132,594	37,233	39,428	55,887
Global positioning services	190,149	91,927	25,893	19,553	46,379
Automobile service clubs	1,935,952	612,089	138,096	160,174	313,836
Public transportation	**59,971,743**	**25,591,049**	**6,607,629**	**5,637,010**	**13,360,599**
Airline fares	39,764,868	17,851,599	4,636,989	3,943,181	9,271,514
Intercity bus fares	1,346,491	425,020	120,708	78,319	226,014
Intracity mass transit fares	6,071,689	1,835,512	460,404	426,578	948,548
Taxis and local transportation on trips	2,476,688	1,084,208	248,409	183,852	651,914
Taxi fares and limousine service in home town	1,648,352	550,237	77,238	183,049	304,038
Intercity train fares	1,935,952	889,383	270,018	188,352	431,125
Ship fares	6,538,742	2,886,618	767,970	623,501	1,495,293
School bus	188,960	68,283	25,893	10,232	32,153

Note: Numbers may not add to total because some categories are not shown and because of rounding.
Source: Calculations by New Strategist based on the Bureau of Labor Statistics' 2006 Consumer Expenditure Survey

Table 15. Transportation: Market shares by high-income consumer units, 2006

(percentage of total annual spending on transportation accounted for by before-tax income group of consumer units with high incomes, 2006)

	total consumer units	$100,000 or more	$100,000– $119,999	$120,000– $149,999	$150,000 or more
Share of total consumer units	100.0%	15.9%	5.3%	4.5%	6.1%
Share of total before-tax income	100.0	43.2	9.5	9.9	23.9
Share of total spending	100.0	33.0	8.6	8.3	16.2
TRANSPORTATION	100.0	31.9	8.5	8.3	15.1
Vehicle purchases	100.0	35.9	8.5	9.0	18.4
Cars and trucks, new	100.0	43.9	9.1	10.0	24.8
New cars	100.0	44.6	9.6	7.4	27.7
New trucks	100.0	43.2	8.7	12.5	22.1
Cars and trucks, used	100.0	26.5	7.7	7.7	11.1
Used cars	100.0	26.6	7.3	8.4	11.0
Used trucks	100.0	26.3	8.1	7.0	11.2
Other vehicles	100.0	40.1	13.0	11.3	15.7
New motorcycles	100.0	54.1	16.2	15.6	22.2
Used motorcycles	100.0	6.3	5.3	1.0	–
Gasoline and motor oil	100.0	25.5	7.9	7.3	10.3
Other vehicle expenses	100.0	30.0	8.4	8.1	13.5
Vehicle finance charges	100.0	28.7	9.4	8.0	11.3
Automobile finance charges	100.0	27.0	8.5	7.6	10.9
Truck finance charges	100.0	28.4	10.1	8.1	10.2
Motorcycle and plane finance charges	100.0	28.2	6.3	11.7	10.1
Other vehicle finance charges	100.0	44.6	8.9	9.6	26.1
Maintenance and repairs	100.0	29.8	8.1	8.4	13.3
Coolant, additives, brake and transmission fluids	100.0	16.8	5.7	5.9	5.2
Tires—purchased, replaced, installed	100.0	29.7	8.3	7.9	13.6
Parts, equipment, and accessories	100.0	26.0	9.5	8.3	8.2
Vehicle products and cleaning services	100.0	15.4	4.3	3.9	7.4
Vehicle video equipment	100.0	76.3	0.7	11.6	64.1
Miscellaneous auto repair, servicing	100.0	33.4	10.5	7.9	15.2
Body work and painting	100.0	37.8	6.6	12.8	18.4
Clutch, transmission repair	100.0	31.4	9.6	8.7	13.1
Drive shaft and rear-end repair	100.0	23.1	6.8	7.6	8.7
Brake work	100.0	32.9	8.2	10.2	14.5
Repair to steering or front-end	100.0	25.7	5.6	7.3	12.9
Repair to engine cooling system	100.0	28.0	6.8	8.9	12.4
Motor tune-up	100.0	39.0	9.5	10.5	19.0
Lube, oil change, and oil filters	100.0	26.3	7.7	7.3	11.4
Front-end alignment, wheel balance, rotation	100.0	29.6	7.4	11.4	10.8
Shock absorber replacement	100.0	44.4	7.4	12.5	24.5
Tire repair and other repair work	100.0	33.5	10.6	8.6	14.2
Vehicle air conditioning repair	100.0	29.0	7.6	12.8	8.5
Exhaust system repair	100.0	26.6	5.8	5.7	15.1
Electrical system repair	100.0	23.9	8.2	5.1	10.7
Motor repair, replacement	100.0	25.3	6.5	7.4	11.4
Auto repair service policy	100.0	18.5	7.3	5.2	6.1
Vehicle insurance	100.0	26.1	7.8	7.5	10.8
Vehicle rental, leases, licenses, other charges	100.0	38.1	9.3	8.5	20.3
Leased and rented vehicles	100.0	41.4	9.9	8.8	22.7
Rented vehicles	100.0	44.0	10.1	9.1	24.8
Leased vehicles	100.0	41.0	9.9	8.7	22.3
Car lease payments	100.0	43.3	9.8	8.7	24.8
Truck lease payments	100.0	38.2	10.3	8.0	19.9
Vehicle registration, state	100.0	28.6	8.2	7.5	12.9
Vehicle registration, local	100.0	27.8	10.4	6.7	10.7
Driver's license	100.0	20.5	6.8	5.3	8.4
Vehicle inspection	100.0	20.4	6.8	5.7	7.9

	total consumer units	$100,000 or more	$100,000– $119,999	$120,000– $149,999	$150,000 or more
Parking fees	100.0%	48.7%	9.0%	9.0%	30.6%
Parking fees in home city, excluding residence	100.0	48.6	9.0	8.4	31.3
Parking fees on trips	100.0	48.8	9.5	12.1	27.2
Tolls	100.0	40.5	9.5	11.2	20.4
Tolls on trips	100.0	36.4	8.8	11.2	16.4
Towing charges	100.0	21.8	6.1	6.5	9.2
Global positioning services	100.0	48.3	13.6	10.3	24.4
Automobile service clubs	100.0	31.6	7.1	8.3	16.2
Public transportation	**100.0**	**42.7**	**11.0**	**9.4**	**22.3**
Airline fares	100.0	44.9	11.7	9.9	23.3
Intercity bus fares	100.0	31.6	9.0	5.8	16.8
Intracity mass transit fares	100.0	30.2	7.6	7.0	15.6
Taxis and local transportation on trips	100.0	43.8	10.0	7.4	26.3
Taxi fares and limousine service in home town	100.0	33.4	4.7	11.1	18.4
Intercity train fares	100.0	45.9	13.9	9.7	22.3
Ship fares	100.0	44.1	11.7	9.5	22.9
School bus	100.0	36.1	13.7	5.4	17.0

Note: Numbers may not add to total because of rounding. "–" means sample is too small to make a reliable estimate.
Source: Calculations by New Strategist based on the Bureau of Labor Statistics' 2006 Consumer Expenditure Survey

Table 16. Transportation: Average spending by household type, 2006

(average annual spending of consumer units (CU) on transportation, by type of consumer unit, 2006)

	total consumer units	total married couples	married couples, no children	married couples with children total	married couples with children oldest child under 6	married couples with children oldest child 6 to 17	married couples with children oldest child 18 or older	single parent, at least one child <18	single person
Number of consumer units (in 000s)	118,843	59,428	25,306	29,381	5,763	15,166	8,452	7,225	35,221
Number of persons per CU	2.5	3.2	2.0	3.9	3.5	4.1	3.9	2.9	1.0
Average before-tax income of CU	$60,533.00	$82,195.00	$73,032.00	$89,351.00	$81,372.00	$89,792.00	$93,999.00	$34,852.00	$31,557.00
Average spending of CU, total	48,398.32	62,503.18	55,631.38	68,354.25	63,415.54	69,157.47	70,233.96	35,490.95	29,374.35
TRANSPORTATION	**8,507.90**	**11,387.79**	**9,673.87**	**12,786.99**	**11,188.25**	**12,768.81**	**13,909.28**	**5,503.65**	**4,433.23**
Vehicle purchases	**3,420.83**	**4,744.72**	**3,803.18**	**5,552.65**	**5,211.13**	**5,586.58**	**5,724.64**	**1,917.01**	**1,558.29**
Cars and trucks, new	1,798.12	2,664.55	2,392.38	2,977.63	3,064.64	3,078.24	2,737.77	552.79	825.83
New cars	862.88	1,201.16	1,139.58	1,328.45	1,241.67	1,229.76	1,564.70	152.08	612.23
New trucks	935.23	1,463.39	1,252.80	1,649.18	1,822.97	1,848.48	1,173.07	400.71	213.60
Cars and trucks, used	1,568.35	2,001.32	1,343.82	2,491.60	2,130.72	2,414.41	2,876.17	1,352.59	726.10
Used cars	752.94	882.60	694.32	1,015.26	778.48	845.44	1,481.41	832.73	417.51
Used trucks	815.41	1,118.72	649.50	1,476.34	1,352.23	1,568.97	1,394.76	519.86	308.58
Other vehicles	54.36	78.86	66.97	83.42	15.77	93.93	110.70	11.63	6.37
New motorcycles	38.50	62.88	45.94	72.21	–	83.74	100.76	9.06	4.49
Used motorcycles	15.86	15.98	21.03	11.21	15.77	10.19	9.94	2.57	1.88
Gasoline and motor oil	**2,227.46**	**2,900.65**	**2,419.28**	**3,245.75**	**2,608.88**	**3,245.96**	**3,679.66**	**1,697.30**	**1,187.61**
Other vehicle expenses	**2,354.98**	**3,086.99**	**2,733.15**	**3,381.01**	**2,909.14**	**3,326.25**	**3,799.83**	**1,628.17**	**1,324.40**
Vehicle finance charges	297.81	418.78	323.31	496.97	518.91	494.49	486.44	192.60	116.64
Automobile finance charges	116.91	147.42	121.40	162.22	172.03	142.67	190.62	106.33	57.26
Truck finance charges	161.28	240.23	167.55	304.67	331.54	320.72	257.55	82.00	52.44
Motorcycle and plane finance charges	4.16	5.37	2.39	7.54	2.38	11.25	4.40	0.39	1.66
Other vehicle finance charges	15.46	25.75	31.96	22.53	12.96	19.85	33.88	3.87	5.28
Maintenance and repairs	688.44	882.02	789.86	957.79	645.87	995.06	1,102.10	467.44	418.96
Coolant, additives, brake, transmission fluids	3.66	4.34	2.81	5.18	3.08	5.22	6.54	3.05	2.00
Tires—purchased, replaced, installed	103.33	137.03	122.41	154.03	98.26	178.39	148.34	78.01	54.48
Parts, equipment, and accessories	41.25	51.47	33.41	68.02	35.82	58.62	106.84	33.30	26.42
Vehicle products and cleaning services	5.30	5.82	5.72	6.27	6.43	5.63	7.46	3.63	4.87
Vehicle video equipment	2.58	4.57	6.00	3.81	12.41	2.29	0.68	–	0.96
Miscellaneous auto repair, servicing	41.15	53.30	56.62	52.62	33.63	65.18	40.04	21.75	21.39
Body work and painting	29.53	38.40	33.67	39.52	28.69	39.31	47.28	10.39	16.32
Clutch, transmission repair	36.93	53.51	43.52	59.20	36.38	66.26	62.08	38.02	15.79
Drive shaft and rear-end repair	6.73	8.43	6.27	9.56	3.21	9.04	14.80	0.84	6.70
Brake work	61.27	76.18	69.47	81.99	44.51	82.51	106.60	58.54	34.28
Repair to steering or front-end	19.74	25.75	19.32	30.89	24.42	31.08	34.97	20.12	10.94
Repair to engine cooling system	22.07	24.93	24.89	26.13	25.25	24.77	29.18	16.37	16.58
Motor tune-up	47.53	62.45	59.74	66.29	56.95	62.14	80.09	28.96	28.99
Lube, oil change, and oil filters	66.87	83.66	81.03	87.38	77.18	88.30	92.71	51.60	45.64
Front-end alignment, wheel balance, rotation	13.79	18.43	15.48	20.35	9.51	22.98	23.03	8.02	8.21
Shock absorber replacement	4.78	6.42	5.34	7.07	4.38	5.23	12.20	2.55	3.53
Tire repair and other repair work	48.52	58.87	60.69	57.48	36.12	53.85	78.57	23.30	36.99
Vehicle air conditioning repair	11.94	14.91	15.63	14.88	16.08	15.98	12.10	7.42	7.91
Exhaust system repair	10.15	10.69	9.42	12.09	6.89	13.85	12.47	5.01	8.18
Electrical system repair	24.69	29.85	26.04	32.09	22.80	30.25	41.73	13.50	18.02
Motor repair, replacement	69.29	93.39	73.05	100.73	58.16	117.69	99.34	37.37	40.40
Auto repair service policy	8.74	11.44	13.79	10.37	5.70	11.21	12.04	5.69	7.09
Vehicle insurance	886.43	1,131.80	993.80	1,234.92	947.36	1,137.36	1,606.06	665.61	507.90
Vehicle rental, leases, licenses, other charges	482.30	654.38	626.18	691.33	797.01	699.35	605.24	302.52	280.90
Leased and rented vehicles	294.36	411.98	394.37	442.56	550.85	463.14	331.78	179.57	161.66
Rented vehicles	37.49	49.96	52.93	49.06	36.71	52.41	51.46	27.86	24.12
Leased vehicles	256.87	362.02	341.44	393.50	514.14	410.73	280.33	151.72	137.54
Car lease payments	123.12	149.33	180.51	130.82	119.03	124.32	150.54	78.63	91.23
Truck lease payments	109.17	180.93	139.67	220.52	307.51	242.78	121.26	67.88	29.20
Vehicle registration, state	86.30	115.26	108.60	119.96	112.60	114.15	135.41	55.69	48.43
Vehicle registration, local	8.35	11.68	11.20	11.62	10.49	12.42	10.97	3.68	3.92
Driver's license	6.87	8.24	8.09	8.51	6.76	9.17	8.54	7.23	4.43
Vehicle inspection	9.51	11.78	10.86	12.47	8.45	12.35	15.43	7.67	6.40

	total consumer units	total married couples	married couples, no children	married couples with children				single parent, at least one child <18	single person
				total	oldest child under 6	oldest child 6 to 17	oldest child 18 or older		
Parking fees	$34.88	$40.59	$39.77	$43.86	$59.37	$39.57	$40.96	$21.97	$29.97
Parking fees in home city, excl. residence	28.75	32.38	30.89	35.83	52.34	31.67	32.03	19.49	25.92
Parking fees on trips	6.14	8.21	8.89	8.03	7.03	7.90	8.94	2.47	4.06
Tolls	15.02	20.55	15.21	21.79	26.18	20.48	21.48	10.44	7.74
Tolls on trips	4.02	5.69	5.21	6.26	7.28	6.05	5.93	1.84	2.57
Towing charges	5.11	5.56	2.92	6.42	4.44	5.86	8.77	8.33	3.15
Global positioning services	1.60	2.51	3.52	1.63	0.87	2.22	1.09	0.64	0.61
Automobile service clubs	16.29	20.56	26.43	16.25	9.72	13.94	24.87	5.45	12.02
Public transportation	**504.63**	**655.43**	**718.25**	**607.58**	**459.09**	**610.02**	**705.14**	**261.17**	**362.93**
Airline fares	334.60	458.34	494.19	431.62	374.60	440.13	455.23	156.61	222.57
Intercity bus fares	11.33	14.57	23.40	7.70	3.58	7.71	10.49	4.13	8.91
Intracity mass transit fares	51.09	46.39	32.99	53.53	38.74	48.37	72.87	52.49	47.43
Taxis and local transportation on trips	20.84	26.79	36.16	20.60	9.13	22.19	25.59	5.16	18.79
Taxi fares and limousine service in home town	13.87	11.54	9.32	12.44	4.78	9.03	24.44	10.47	17.43
Intercity train fares	16.29	20.26	24.27	17.81	9.95	16.32	25.82	6.09	13.91
Ship fares	55.02	74.69	97.77	59.12	16.76	58.32	89.43	26.46	33.55
School bus	1.59	2.84	0.15	4.76	1.54	7.93	1.27	0.29	0.33

Note: Numbers may not add to total because some categories are not shown. "–" means sample is too small to make a reliable estimate.
Source: Bureau of Labor Statistics, unpublished tables from the 2006 Consumer Expenditure Survey

Table 17. Transportation: Indexed spending by household type, 2006

(indexed average annual spending of consumer units (CU) on transportation, by type of consumer unit, 2006; index definition: an index of 100 is the average for all consumer units; an index of 132 means that spending by consumer units in that group is 32 percent above the average for all consumer units; an index of 68 indicates spending that is 32 percent below the average for all consumer units)

	total consumer units	total married couples	married couples, no children	married couples with children total	oldest child under 6	oldest child 6 to 17	oldest child 18 or older	single parent, at least one child <18	single person
Average spending of CU, total	$48,398	$62,503	$55,631	$68,354	$63,416	$69,157	$70,234	$35,491	$29,374
Average spending of CU, index	100	129	115	141	131	143	145	73	61
TRANSPORTATION	100	134	114	150	132	150	163	65	52
Vehicle purchases	100	139	111	162	152	163	167	56	46
Cars and trucks, new	100	148	133	166	170	171	152	31	46
New cars	100	139	132	154	144	143	181	18	71
New trucks	100	156	134	176	195	198	125	43	23
Cars and trucks, used	100	128	86	159	136	154	183	86	46
Used cars	100	117	92	135	103	112	197	111	55
Used trucks	100	137	80	181	166	192	171	64	38
Other vehicles	100	145	123	153	29	173	204	21	12
New motorcycles	100	163	119	188	–	218	262	24	12
Used motorcycles	100	101	133	71	99	64	63	16	12
Gasoline and motor oil	100	130	109	146	117	146	165	76	53
Other vehicle expenses	100	131	116	144	124	141	161	69	56
Vehicle finance charges	100	141	109	167	174	166	163	65	39
Automobile finance charges	100	126	104	139	147	122	163	91	49
Truck finance charges	100	149	104	189	206	199	160	51	33
Motorcycle and plane finance charges	100	129	57	181	57	270	106	9	40
Other vehicle finance charges	100	167	207	146	84	128	219	25	34
Maintenance and repairs	100	128	115	139	94	145	160	68	61
Coolant, additives, brake and transmission fluids	100	119	77	142	84	143	179	83	55
Tires—purchased, replaced, installed	100	133	118	149	95	173	144	75	53
Parts, equipment, and accessories	100	125	81	165	87	142	259	81	64
Vehicle products and cleaning services	100	110	108	118	121	106	141	68	92
Vehicle video equipment	100	177	233	148	481	89	26	–	37
Miscellaneous auto repair, servicing	100	130	138	128	82	158	97	53	52
Body work and painting	100	130	114	134	97	133	160	35	55
Clutch, transmission repair	100	145	118	160	99	179	168	103	43
Drive shaft and rear-end repair	100	125	93	142	48	134	220	12	100
Brake work	100	124	113	134	73	135	174	96	56
Repair to steering or front-end	100	130	98	156	124	157	177	102	55
Repair to engine cooling system	100	113	113	118	114	112	132	74	75
Motor tune-up	100	131	126	139	120	131	169	61	61
Lube, oil change, and oil filters	100	125	121	131	115	132	139	77	68
Front-end alignment, wheel balance, rotation	100	134	112	148	69	167	167	58	60
Shock absorber replacement	100	134	112	148	92	109	255	53	74
Tire repair and other repair work	100	121	125	118	74	111	162	48	76
Vehicle air conditioning repair	100	125	131	125	135	134	101	62	66
Exhaust system repair	100	105	93	119	68	136	123	49	81
Electrical system repair	100	121	105	130	92	123	169	55	73
Motor repair, replacement	100	135	105	145	84	170	143	54	58
Auto repair service policy	100	131	158	119	65	128	138	65	81
Vehicle insurance	100	128	112	139	107	128	181	75	57
Vehicle rental, leases, licenses, other charges	100	136	130	143	165	145	125	63	58
Leased and rented vehicles	100	140	134	150	187	157	113	61	55
Rented vehicles	100	133	141	131	98	140	137	74	64
Leased vehicles	100	141	133	153	200	160	109	59	54
Car lease payments	100	121	147	106	97	101	122	64	74
Truck lease payments	100	166	128	202	282	222	111	62	27
Vehicle registration, state	100	134	126	139	130	132	157	65	56
Vehicle registration, local	100	140	134	139	126	149	131	44	47
Driver's license	100	120	118	124	98	133	124	105	64
Vehicle inspection	100	124	114	131	89	130	162	81	67

	total consumer units	total married couples	married couples, no children	married couples with children				single parent, at least one child <18	single person
				total	oldest child under 6	oldest child 6 to 17	oldest child 18 or older		
Parking fees	100	116	114	126	170	113	117	63	86
Parking fees in home city, excl. residence	100	113	107	125	182	110	111	68	90
Parking fees on trips	100	134	145	131	114	129	146	40	66
Tolls	100	137	101	145	174	136	143	70	52
Tolls on trips	100	142	130	156	181	150	148	46	64
Towing charges	100	109	57	126	87	115	172	163	62
Global positioning services	100	157	220	102	54	139	68	40	38
Automobile service clubs	100	126	162	100	60	86	153	33	74
Public transportation	**100**	**130**	**142**	**120**	**91**	**121**	**140**	**52**	**72**
Airline fares	100	137	148	129	112	132	136	47	67
Intercity bus fares	100	129	207	68	32	68	93	36	79
Intracity mass transit fares	100	91	65	105	76	95	143	103	93
Taxis and local transportation on trips	100	129	174	99	44	106	123	25	90
Taxi fares and limousine service in home town	100	83	67	90	34	65	176	75	126
Intercity train fares	100	124	149	109	61	100	159	37	85
Ship fares	100	136	178	107	30	106	163	48	61
School bus	100	179	9	299	97	499	80	18	21

Note: "–" means sample is too small to make a reliable estimate.
Source: Calculations by New Strategist based on the Bureau of Labor Statistics' 2006 Consumer Expenditure Survey

Table 18. Transportation: Total spending by household type, 2006

(total annual spending on transportation, by consumer unit (CU) type, 2002; consumer units and dollars in thousands)

	total consumer units	total married couples	married couples, no children	married couples with children total	oldest child under 6	oldest child 6 to 17	oldest child 18 or older	single parent, at least one child <18	single person
Number of consumer units	118,843	59,428	25,306	29,381	5,763	15,166	8,452	7,225	35,221
Total spending of all CUs	$5,751,801,544	$3,714,438,981	$1,407,807,702	$2,008,316,219	$365,463,757	$1,048,842,190	$593,617,430	$256,422,114	$1,034,593,981
TRANSPORTATION	**1,011,104,360**	**676,753,584**	**244,806,954**	**375,694,553**	**64,477,885**	**193,651,772**	**117,561,235**	**39,763,871**	**156,142,794**
Vehicle purchases	**406,541,700**	**281,969,220**	**96,243,273**	**163,142,410**	**30,031,742**	**84,726,072**	**48,384,657**	**13,850,397**	**54,884,532**
Cars and trucks, new	213,693,975	158,348,877	60,541,568	87,485,747	17,661,520	46,684,588	23,139,632	3,993,908	29,086,558
New cars	102,547,248	71,382,536	28,838,211	39,031,189	7,155,744	18,650,540	13,224,844	1,098,778	21,563,353
New trucks	111,145,539	86,966,341	31,703,357	48,454,558	10,505,776	28,034,048	9,914,788	2,895,130	7,523,206
Cars and trucks, used	186,387,419	118,934,445	34,006,709	73,205,700	12,279,339	36,616,942	24,309,389	9,772,463	25,573,968
Used cars	89,481,648	52,451,153	17,570,462	29,829,354	4,486,380	12,821,943	12,520,877	6,016,474	14,705,120
Used trucks	96,905,771	66,483,292	16,436,247	43,376,346	7,792,901	23,794,999	11,788,512	3,755,989	10,868,496
Other vehicles	6,460,305	4,686,492	1,694,743	2,450,963	90,883	1,424,542	935,636	84,027	224,358
New motorcycles	4,575,456	3,736,833	1,162,558	2,121,602	–	1,270,001	851,624	65,459	158,142
Used motorcycles	1,884,850	949,659	532,185	329,361	90,883	154,542	84,013	18,568	66,215
Gasoline and motor oil	**264,718,029**	**172,379,828**	**61,222,300**	**95,363,381**	**15,034,975**	**49,228,229**	**31,100,486**	**12,262,993**	**41,828,812**
Other vehicle expenses	**279,872,888**	**183,453,642**	**69,165,094**	**99,337,455**	**16,765,374**	**50,445,908**	**32,116,163**	**11,763,528**	**46,646,692**
Vehicle finance charges	35,392,634	24,887,258	8,181,683	14,601,476	2,990,478	7,499,435	4,111,391	1,391,535	4,108,177
Automobile finance charges	13,893,935	8,760,876	3,072,148	4,766,186	991,409	2,163,733	1,611,120	768,234	2,016,754
Truck finance charges	19,166,999	14,276,388	4,240,020	8,951,509	1,910,665	4,864,040	2,176,813	592,450	1,846,989
Motorcycle and plane finance charges	494,387	319,128	60,481	221,533	13,716	170,618	37,189	2,818	58,467
Other vehicle finance charges	1,837,313	1,530,271	808,780	661,954	74,688	301,045	286,354	27,961	185,967
Maintenance and repairs	81,816,275	52,416,685	19,988,197	28,140,828	3,722,149	15,091,080	9,314,949	3,377,254	14,756,190
Coolant, additives, brake and transmission fluids	434,965	257,918	71,110	152,194	17,750	79,167	55,276	22,036	70,442
Tires—purchased, replaced, installed	12,280,047	8,143,419	3,097,707	4,525,555	566,272	2,705,463	1,253,770	563,622	1,918,840
Parts, equipment, and accessories	4,902,274	3,058,759	845,473	1,998,496	206,431	889,031	903,012	240,593	930,539
Vehicle products and cleaning services	629,868	345,871	144,750	184,219	37,056	85,385	63,052	26,227	171,526
Vehicle video equipment	306,615	271,586	151,836	111,942	71,519	34,730	5,747	–	33,812
Miscellaneous auto repair, servicing	4,890,389	3,167,512	1,432,826	1,546,028	193,810	988,520	338,418	157,144	753,377
Body work and painting	3,509,434	2,282,035	852,053	1,161,137	165,340	596,175	399,611	75,068	574,807
Clutch, transmission repair	4,388,872	3,179,992	1,101,317	1,739,355	209,658	1,004,899	524,700	274,695	556,140
Drive shaft and rear-end repair	799,813	500,978	158,669	280,882	18,499	137,101	125,090	6,069	235,981
Brake work	7,281,511	4,527,225	1,758,008	2,408,948	256,511	1,251,347	900,983	422,952	1,207,376
Repair to steering or front-end	2,345,961	1,530,271	488,912	907,579	140,732	471,359	295,566	145,367	385,318
Repair to engine cooling system	2,622,865	1,481,540	629,866	767,726	145,516	375,662	246,629	118,273	583,964
Motor tune-up	5,648,608	3,711,279	1,511,780	1,947,666	328,203	942,415	676,921	209,236	1,021,057
Lube, oil change, and oil filters	7,947,031	4,971,746	2,050,545	2,567,312	444,788	1,339,158	783,585	372,810	1,607,486
Front-end alignment, wheel balance, rotation	1,638,845	1,095,258	391,737	597,903	54,806	348,515	194,650	57,945	289,164
Shock absorber replacement	568,070	381,528	135,134	207,724	25,242	79,318	103,114	18,424	124,330
Tire repair and other repair work	5,766,262	3,498,526	1,535,821	1,688,820	208,160	816,689	664,074	168,343	1,302,825
Vehicle air conditioning repair	1,418,985	886,071	395,533	437,189	92,669	242,353	102,269	53,610	278,598
Exhaust system repair	1,206,256	635,285	238,383	355,216	39,707	210,049	105,396	36,197	288,108
Electrical system repair	2,934,234	1,773,926	658,968	942,836	131,396	458,772	352,702	97,538	634,682
Motor repair, replacement	8,234,631	5,549,981	1,848,603	2,959,548	335,176	1,784,887	839,622	269,998	1,422,928
Auto repair service policy	1,038,688	679,856	348,970	304,681	32,849	170,011	101,762	41,110	249,717
Vehicle insurance	105,346,000	67,260,610	25,149,103	36,283,185	5,459,636	17,249,202	13,574,419	4,809,032	17,888,746
Vehicle rental, leases, licenses, other charges	57,317,979	38,888,495	15,846,111	20,311,967	4,593,169	10,606,342	5,115,488	2,185,707	9,893,579
Leased and rented vehicles	34,982,625	24,483,147	9,979,927	13,002,855	3,174,549	7,023,981	2,804,205	1,297,393	5,693,827
Rented vehicles	4,455,424	2,969,023	1,339,447	1,441,432	211,560	794,850	434,940	201,289	849,531
Leased vehicles	30,527,201	21,514,125	8,640,481	11,561,424	2,962,989	6,229,131	2,369,349	1,096,177	4,844,296
Car lease payments	14,631,950	8,874,383	4,567,986	3,843,622	685,970	1,885,437	1,272,364	568,102	3,213,212
Truck lease payments	12,974,090	10,752,308	ˉ3,534,489	6,479,098	1,772,180	3,682,001	1,024,890	490,433	1,028,453
Vehicle registration, state	10,256,151	6,849,671	2,748,232	3,524,545	648,914	1,731,199	1,144,485	402,360	1,705,753
Vehicle registration, local	992,339	694,119	283,427	341,407	60,454	188,362	92,718	26,588	138,066
Driver's license	816,451	489,687	204,726	250,032	38,958	139,072	72,180	52,237	156,029
Vehicle inspection	1,130,197	700,062	274,823	366,381	48,697	187,300	130,414	55,416	225,414

	total consumer units	total married couples	married couples, no children	married couples with children				single parent, at least one child <18	single person
				total	oldest child under 6	oldest child 6 to 17	oldest child 18 or older		
Parking fees	$4,145,244	$2,412,183	$1,006,420	$1,288,651	$342,149	$600,119	$346,194	$158,733	$1,055,573
Parking fees in home city, excluding residence	3,416,736	1,924,279	781,702	1,052,721	301,635	480,307	270,718	140,815	912,928
Parking fees on trips	729,696	487,904	224,970	235,929	40,514	119,811	75,561	17,846	142,997
Tolls	1,785,022	1,221,245	384,904	640,212	150,875	310,600	181,549	75,429	272,611
Tolls on trips	477,749	338,145	131,844	183,925	41,955	91,754	50,120	13,294	90,518
Towing charges	607,288	330,420	73,894	188,626	25,588	88,873	74,124	60,184	110,946
Global positioning services	190,149	149,164	89,077	47,891	5,014	33,669	9,213	4,624	21,485
Automobile service clubs	1,935,952	1,221,840	668,838	477,441	56,016	211,414	210,201	39,376	423,356
Public transportation	**59,971,743**	**38,950,894**	**18,176,035**	**17,851,308**	**2,645,736**	**9,251,563**	**5,959,843**	**1,886,953**	**12,782,758**
Airline fares	39,764,868	27,238,230	12,505,972	12,681,427	2,158,820	6,675,012	3,847,604	1,127,678	7,839,138
Intercity bus fares	1,346,491	865,866	592,160	226,234	20,632	116,930	88,661	29,839	313,819
Intracity mass transit fares	6,071,689	2,756,865	834,845	1,572,765	223,259	733,579	615,897	379,240	1,670,532
Taxis and local transportation on trips	2,476,688	1,592,076	915,065	605,249	52,616	336,534	216,287	37,281	661,803
Taxi fares, limousine service in home town	1,648,352	685,799	235,852	365,500	27,547	136,949	206,567	75,646	613,902
Intercity train fares	1,935,952	1,204,011	614,177	523,276	57,342	247,509	218,231	44,000	489,924
Ship fares	6,538,742	4,438,677	2,474,168	1,737,005	96,588	884,481	755,862	191,174	1,181,665
School bus	188,960	168,776	3,796	139,854	8,875	120,266	10,734	2,095	11,623

Note: Numbers will not add to total because not all types of consumer units are shown and because of rounding. "–" means sample is too small to make a reliable estimate.
Source: Calculations by New Strategist based on the Bureau of Labor Statistics' 2006 Consumer Expenditure Survey

Table 19. Transportation: Market shares by household type, 2006

(percentage of total annual spending on transportation accounted for by types of consumer units, 2006)

	total consumer units	total married couples	married couples, no children	married couples with children				single parent, at least one child <18	single person
				total	oldest child under 6	oldest child 6 to 17	oldest child 18 or older		
Share of total consumer units	100.0%	50.0%	21.3%	24.7%	4.8%	12.8%	7.1%	6.1%	29.6%
Share of total before-tax income	100.0	67.9	25.7	36.5	6.5	18.9	11.0	3.5	15.5
Share of total spending	100.0	64.6	24.5	34.9	6.4	18.2	10.3	4.5	18.0
TRANSPORTATION	100.0	66.9	24.2	37.2	6.4	19.2	11.6	3.9	15.4
Vehicle purchases	100.0	69.4	23.7	40.1	7.4	20.8	11.9	3.4	13.5
Cars and trucks, new	100.0	74.1	28.3	40.9	8.3	21.8	10.8	1.9	13.6
New cars	100.0	69.6	28.1	38.1	7.0	18.2	12.9	1.1	21.0
New trucks	100.0	78.2	28.5	43.6	9.5	25.2	8.9	2.6	6.8
Cars and trucks, used	100.0	63.8	18.2	39.3	6.6	19.6	13.0	5.2	13.7
Used cars	100.0	58.6	19.6	33.3	5.0	14.3	14.0	6.7	16.4
Used trucks	100.0	68.6	17.0	44.8	8.0	24.6	12.2	3.9	11.2
Other vehicles	100.0	72.5	26.2	37.9	1.4	22.1	14.5	1.3	3.5
New motorcycles	100.0	81.7	25.4	46.4	–	27.8	18.6	1.4	3.5
Used motorcycles	100.0	50.4	28.2	17.5	4.8	8.2	4.5	1.0	3.5
Gasoline and motor oil	100.0	65.1	23.1	36.0	5.7	18.6	11.7	4.6	15.8
Other vehicle expenses	100.0	65.5	24.7	35.5	6.0	18.0	11.5	4.2	16.7
Vehicle finance charges	100.0	70.3	23.1	41.3	8.4	21.2	11.6	3.9	11.6
Automobile finance charges	100.0	63.1	22.1	34.3	7.1	15.6	11.6	5.5	14.5
Truck finance charges	100.0	74.5	22.1	46.7	10.0	25.4	11.4	3.1	9.6
Motorcycle and plane finance charges	100.0	64.6	12.2	44.8	2.8	34.5	7.5	0.6	11.8
Other vehicle finance charges	100.0	83.3	44.0	36.0	4.1	16.4	15.6	1.5	10.1
Maintenance and repairs	100.0	64.1	24.4	34.4	4.5	18.4	11.4	4.1	18.0
Coolant, additives, brake, transmission fluids	100.0	59.3	16.3	35.0	4.1	18.2	12.7	5.1	16.2
Tires—purchased, replaced, installed	100.0	66.3	25.2	36.9	4.6	22.0	10.2	4.6	15.6
Parts, equipment, and accessories	100.0	62.4	17.2	40.8	4.2	18.1	18.4	4.9	19.0
Vehicle products and cleaning services	100.0	54.9	23.0	29.2	5.9	13.6	10.0	4.2	27.2
Vehicle video equipment	100.0	88.6	49.5	36.5	23.3	11.3	1.9	–	11.0
Miscellaneous auto repair, servicing	100.0	64.8	29.3	31.6	4.0	20.2	6.9	3.2	15.4
Body work and painting	100.0	65.0	24.3	33.1	4.7	17.0	11.4	2.1	16.4
Clutch, transmission repair	100.0	72.5	25.1	39.6	4.8	22.9	12.0	6.3	12.7
Drive shaft and rear-end repair	100.0	62.6	19.8	35.1	2.3	17.1	15.6	0.8	29.5
Brake work	100.0	62.2	24.1	33.1	3.5	17.2	12.4	5.8	16.6
Repair to steering or front-end	100.0	65.2	20.8	38.7	6.0	20.1	12.6	6.2	16.4
Repair to engine cooling system	100.0	56.5	24.0	29.3	5.5	14.3	9.4	4.5	22.3
Motor tune-up	100.0	65.7	26.8	34.5	5.8	16.7	12.0	3.7	18.1
Lube, oil change, and oil filters	100.0	62.6	25.8	32.3	5.6	16.9	9.9	4.7	20.2
Front-end alignment, wheel balance, rotation	100.0	66.8	23.9	36.5	3.3	21.3	11.9	3.5	17.6
Shock absorber replacement	100.0	67.2	23.8	36.6	4.4	14.0	18.2	3.2	21.9
Tire repair and other repair work	100.0	60.7	26.6	29.3	3.6	14.2	11.5	2.9	22.6
Vehicle air conditioning repair	100.0	62.4	27.9	30.8	6.5	17.1	7.2	3.8	19.6
Exhaust system repair	100.0	52.7	19.8	29.4	3.3	17.4	8.7	3.0	23.9
Electrical system repair	100.0	60.5	22.5	32.1	4.5	15.6	12.0	3.3	21.6
Motor repair, replacement	100.0	67.4	22.4	35.9	4.1	21.7	10.2	3.3	17.3
Auto repair service policy	100.0	65.5	33.6	29.3	3.2	16.4	9.8	4.0	24.0
Vehicle insurance	100.0	63.8	23.9	34.4	5.2	16.4	12.9	4.6	17.0
Vehicle rental, leases, licenses, other charges	100.0	67.8	27.6	35.4	8.0	18.5	8.9	3.8	17.3
Leased and rented vehicles	100.0	70.0	28.5	37.2	9.1	20.1	8.0	3.7	16.3
Rented vehicles	100.0	66.6	30.1	32.4	4.7	17.8	9.8	4.5	19.1
Leased vehicles	100.0	70.5	28.3	37.9	9.7	20.4	7.8	3.6	15.9
Car lease payments	100.0	60.7	31.2	26.3	4.7	12.9	8.7	3.9	22.0
Truck lease payments	100.0	82.9	27.2	49.9	13.7	28.4	7.9	3.8	7.9
Vehicle registration, state	100.0	66.8	26.8	34.4	6.3	16.9	11.2	3.9	16.6
Vehicle registration, local	100.0	69.9	28.6	34.4	6.1	19.0	9.3	2.7	13.9
Driver's license	100.0	60.0	25.1	30.6	4.8	17.0	8.8	6.4	19.1
Vehicle inspection	100.0	61.9	24.3	32.4	4.3	16.6	11.5	4.9	19.9

	total consumer units	total married couples	married couples, no children	married couples with children				single parent, at least one child <18	single person
				total	oldest child under 6	oldest child 6 to 17	oldest child 18 or older		
Parking fees	100.0%	58.2%	24.3%	31.1%	8.3%	14.5%	8.4%	3.8%	25.5%
Parking fees in home city, excl. residence	100.0	56.3	22.9	30.8	8.8	14.1	7.9	4.1	26.7
Parking fees on trips	100.0	66.9	30.8	32.3	5.6	16.4	10.4	2.4	19.6
Tolls	100.0	68.4	21.6	35.9	8.5	17.4	10.2	4.2	15.3
Tolls on trips	100.0	70.8	27.6	38.5	8.8	19.2	10.5	2.8	18.9
Towing charges	100.0	54.4	12.2	31.1	4.2	14.6	12.2	9.9	18.3
Global positioning services	100.0	78.4	46.8	25.2	2.6	17.7	4.8	2.4	11.3
Automobile service clubs	100.0	63.1	34.5	24.7	2.9	10.9	10.9	2.0	21.9
Public transportation	**100.0**	**64.9**	**30.3**	**29.8**	**4.4**	**15.4**	**9.9**	**3.1**	**21.3**
Airline fares	100.0	68.5	31.4	31.9	5.4	16.8	9.7	2.8	19.7
Intercity bus fares	100.0	64.3	44.0	16.8	1.5	8.7	6.6	2.2	23.3
Intracity mass transit fares	100.0	45.4	13.7	25.9	3.7	12.1	10.1	6.2	27.5
Taxis and local transportation on trips	100.0	64.3	36.9	24.4	2.1	13.6	8.7	1.5	26.7
Taxi fares and limousine service in home town	100.0	41.6	14.3	22.2	1.7	8.3	12.5	4.6	37.2
Intercity train fares	100.0	62.2	31.7	27.0	3.0	12.8	11.3	2.3	25.3
Ship fares	100.0	67.9	37.8	26.6	1.5	13.5	11.6	2.9	18.1
School bus	100.0	89.3	2.0	74.0	4.7	63.6	5.7	1.1	6.2

Note: Market shares by type of consumer unit will not add to total because not all types of consumer units are shown. "−" means sample is too small to make a reliable estimate.
Source: Calculations by New Strategist based on the Bureau of Labor Statistics' 2006 Consumer Expenditure Survey

Table 20. Transportation: Average spending by race and Hispanic origin, 2006

(average annual spending of consumer units on transportation, by race and Hispanic origin of consumer unit reference person, 2006)

	total consumer units	Asian	black	Hispanic	non-Hispanic white and other
Number of consumer units (in 000s)	118,843	4,098	14,265	13,664	91,049
Number of persons per consumer unit	2.5	2.7	2.6	3.2	2.3
Average before-tax income of consumer units	$60,533.00	$75,865.00	$41,142.00	$48,108.00	$65,417.00
Average spending of consumer units, total	48,398.32	57,544.40	34,583.43	43,053.47	51,350.56
TRANSPORTATION	**8,507.90**	**9,721.77**	**6,129.52**	**8,285.67**	**8,913.37**
Vehicle purchases	**3,420.83**	**3,822.96**	**2,361.71**	**3,400.29**	**3,590.18**
Cars and trucks, new	1,798.12	2,672.02	1,045.87	1,661.04	1,933.86
New cars	862.88	1,656.16	390.78	598.38	975.26
New trucks	935.23	1,015.86	655.09	1,062.66	958.61
Cars and trucks, used	1,568.35	1,150.94	1,279.80	1,689.57	1,598.46
Used cars	752.94	962.61	698.43	628.74	778.99
Used trucks	815.41	188.33	581.36	1,060.83	819.47
Other vehicles	54.36	–	36.05	49.69	57.85
New motorcycles	38.50	–	25.26	39.61	40.35
Used motorcycles	15.86	–	10.78	10.07	17.50
Gasoline and motor oil	**2,227.46**	**2,191.17**	**1,740.01**	**2,318.83**	**2,289.47**
Other vehicle expenses	**2,354.98**	**2,518.53**	**1,742.17**	**2,152.26**	**2,480.74**
Vehicle finance charges	297.81	219.86	245.75	326.48	301.56
Automobile finance charges	116.91	141.93	119.55	111.14	117.30
Truck finance charges	161.28	77.93	125.98	206.18	160.06
Motorcycle and plane finance charges	4.16	–	0.22	2.76	4.98
Other vehicle finance charges	15.46	–	–	6.40	19.22
Maintenance and repairs	688.44	677.61	456.41	609.71	736.28
Coolant, additives, brake and transmission fluids	3.66	1.92	3.22	5.19	3.49
Tires—purchased, replaced, installed	103.33	71.73	71.30	86.03	111.06
Parts, equipment, and accessories	41.25	33.68	17.40	35.27	45.83
Vehicle products and cleaning services	5.30	3.69	10.65	4.09	4.62
Vehicle video equipment	2.58	–	–	2.27	3.03
Miscellaneous auto repair, servicing	41.15	39.39	26.25	29.96	45.15
Body work and painting	29.53	26.37	16.93	29.66	31.61
Clutch, transmission repair	36.93	29.39	24.96	44.41	37.63
Drive shaft and rear-end repair	6.73	6.59	2.67	1.33	8.17
Brake work	61.27	60.18	41.55	46.34	66.50
Repair to steering or front-end	19.74	30.14	11.78	15.61	21.58
Repair to engine cooling system	22.07	7.27	14.61	15.61	24.17
Motor tune-up	47.53	75.49	28.22	48.76	50.38
Lube, oil change, and oil filters	66.87	65.40	45.68	54.53	71.98
Front-end alignment, wheel balance, rotation	13.79	10.62	6.37	8.44	15.73
Shock absorber replacement	4.78	4.75	3.92	4.55	4.95
Tire repair and other repair work	48.52	41.27	34.98	39.20	52.07
Vehicle air conditioning repair	11.94	14.43	5.31	16.99	12.21
Exhaust system repair	10.15	11.18	6.28	8.50	10.99
Electrical system repair	24.69	19.42	13.74	21.06	26.92
Motor repair, replacement	69.29	114.66	51.73	74.16	71.25
Auto repair service policy	8.74	10.03	6.90	4.57	9.64
Vehicle insurance	886.43	1,037.37	709.87	814.24	925.06
Vehicle rental, leases, licenses, other charges	482.30	583.69	330.14	401.83	517.85
Leased and rented vehicles	294.36	373.03	230.18	246.54	311.41
Rented vehicles	37.49	51.79	27.19	20.61	41.60
Leased vehicles	256.87	321.24	202.99	225.93	269.81
Car lease payments	123.12	142.34	110.22	112.75	126.51
Truck lease payments	109.17	162.56	81.48	91.17	116.28
Vehicle registration, state	86.30	97.55	42.91	74.29	94.82
Vehicle registration, local	8.35	12.22	5.83	4.40	9.32
Driver's license	6.87	6.36	4.48	5.56	7.44
Vehicle inspection	9.51	9.50	5.75	9.01	10.15

	total consumer units	Asian	black	Hispanic	non-Hispanic white and other
Parking fees	$34.88	$50.16	$15.16	$19.94	$40.19
Parking fees in home city, excluding residence	28.75	45.48	13.80	16.17	32.95
Parking fees on trips	6.14	4.68	1.35	3.77	7.24
Tolls	15.02	13.22	11.43	21.82	14.54
Tolls on trips	4.02	2.54	1.86	3.76	4.40
Towing charges	5.11	3.18	5.63	7.51	4.66
Global positioning services	1.60	1.55	0.33	0.37	1.98
Automobile service clubs	16.29	14.37	6.58	8.62	18.95
Public transportation	**504.63**	**1,189.11**	**285.63**	**414.29**	**552.99**
Airline fares	334.60	877.54	137.61	238.53	380.37
Intercity bus fares	11.33	22.31	5.94	8.05	12.67
Intracity mass transit fares	51.09	132.91	87.56	96.84	38.52
Taxis and local transportation on trips	20.84	43.11	6.30	11.32	24.52
Taxi fares and limousine service in home town	13.87	14.17	10.21	18.24	13.76
Intercity train fares	16.29	27.20	9.35	8.56	18.52
Ship fares	55.02	70.57	28.24	28.08	63.32
School bus	1.59	1.30	0.41	4.67	1.31

Note: "Asian" and "black" include Hispanics and non-Hispanics who identify themselves as being of the respective race alone. "Hispanic" includes people of any race who identify themselves as Hispanic. "Other" includes people who identify themselves as non-Hispanic and as Alaska Native, American Indian, Asian (who are also included in the Asian column), Native Hawaiian or other Pacific Islander, as well as non-Hispanics reporting more than one race. Numbers will not add to total because not all categories are shown. "–" means sample is too small to make a reliable estimate.
Source: Bureau of Labor Statistics, unpublished tables from the 2006 Consumer Expenditure Survey

Table 21. Transportation: Indexed spending by race and Hispanic origin, 2006

(indexed average annual spending of consumer units on transportation, by race and Hispanic origin of consumer unit reference person, 2006; index definition: an index of 100 is the average for all consumer units; an index of 132 means that spending by consumer units in that group is 32 percent above the average for all consumer units; an index of 68 indicates spending that is 32 percent below the average for all consumer units)

	total consumer units	Asian	black	Hispanic	non-Hispanic white and other
Average spending of consumer units, total	$48,398	$57,544	$34,583	$43,053	$51,351
Average spending of consumer units, index	100	119	71	89	106
TRANSPORTATION	100	114	72	97	105
Vehicle purchases	100	112	69	99	105
Cars and trucks, new	100	149	58	92	108
New cars	100	192	45	69	113
New trucks	100	109	70	114	102
Cars and trucks, used	100	73	82	108	102
Used cars	100	128	93	84	103
Used trucks	100	23	71	130	100
Other vehicles	100	–	66	91	106
New motorcycles	100	–	66	103	105
Used motorcycles	100	–	68	63	110
Gasoline and motor oil	100	98	78	104	103
Other vehicle expenses	100	107	74	91	105
Vehicle finance charges	100	74	83	110	101
Automobile finance charges	100	121	102	95	100
Truck finance charges	100	48	78	128	99
Motorcycle and plane finance charges	100	–	5	66	120
Other vehicle finance charges	100	–	–	41	124
Maintenance and repairs	100	98	66	89	107
Coolant, additives, brake and transmission fluids	100	52	88	142	95
Tires—purchased, replaced, installed	100	69	69	83	107
Parts, equipment, and accessories	100	82	42	86	111
Vehicle products and cleaning services	100	70	201	77	87
Vehicle video equipment	100	–	–	88	117
Miscellaneous auto repair, servicing	100	96	64	73	110
Body work and painting	100	89	57	100	107
Clutch, transmission repair	100	80	68	120	102
Drive shaft and rear-end repair	100	98	40	20	121
Brake work	100	98	68	76	109
Repair to steering or front-end	100	153	60	79	109
Repair to engine cooling system	100	33	66	71	110
Motor tune-up	100	159	59	103	106
Lube, oil change, and oil filters	100	98	68	82	108
Front-end alignment, wheel balance, rotation	100	77	46	61	114
Shock absorber replacement	100	99	82	95	104
Tire repair and other repair work	100	85	72	81	107
Vehicle air conditioning repair	100	121	44	142	102
Exhaust system repair	100	110	62	84	108
Electrical system repair	100	79	56	85	109
Motor repair, replacement	100	165	75	107	103
Auto repair service policy	100	115	79	52	110
Vehicle insurance	100	117	80	92	104
Vehicle rental, leases, licenses, other charges	100	121	68	83	107
Leased and rented vehicles	100	127	78	84	106
Rented vehicles	100	138	73	55	111
Leased vehicles	100	125	79	88	105
Car lease payments	100	116	90	92	103
Truck lease payments	100	149	75	84	107
Vehicle registration, state	100	113	50	86	110
Vehicle registration, local	100	146	70	53	112
Driver's license	100	93	65	81	108
Vehicle inspection	100	100	60	95	107

	total consumer units	Asian	black	Hispanic	non-Hispanic white and other
Parking fees	100	144	43	57	115
Parking fees in home city, excluding residence	100	158	48	56	115
Parking fees on trips	100	76	22	61	118
Tolls	100	88	76	145	97
Tolls on trips	100	63	46	94	109
Towing charges	100	62	110	147	91
Global positioning services	100	97	21	23	124
Automobile service clubs	100	88	40	53	116
Public transportation	**100**	**236**	**57**	**82**	**110**
Airline fares	100	262	41	71	114
Intercity bus fares	100	197	52	71	112
Intracity mass transit fares	100	260	171	190	75
Taxis and local transportation on trips	100	207	30	54	118
Taxi fares and limousine service in home town	100	102	74	132	99
Intercity train fares	100	167	57	53	114
Ship fares	100	128	51	51	115
School bus	100	82	26	294	82

Note: "Asian" and "black" include Hispanics and non-Hispanics who identify themselves as being of the respective race alone. "Hispanic" includes people of any race who identify themselves as Hispanic. "Other" includes people who identify themselves as non-Hispanic and as Alaska Native, American Indian, Asian (who are also included in the Asian column), Native Hawaiian or other Pacific Islander, as well as non-Hispanics reporting more than one race. "–" means sample is too small to make a reliable estimate.

Source: Calculations by New Strategist based on the Bureau of Labor Statistics' 2006 Consumer Expenditure Survey

Table 22. Transportation: Total spending by race and Hispanic origin, 2006

(total annual spending on transportation, by consumer unit race and Hispanic origin groups, 2006; consumer units and dollars in thousands)

	total consumer units	Asian	black	Hispanic	non-Hispanic white and other
Number of consumer units	118,843	4,098	14,265	13,664	91,049
Total spending of all consumer units	$5,751,801,544	$235,816,951	$493,332,629	$588,282,614	$4,675,417,137
TRANSPORTATION	**1,011,104,360**	**39,839,813**	**87,437,603**	**113,215,395**	**811,553,425**
Vehicle purchases	**406,541,700**	**15,666,490**	**33,689,793**	**46,461,563**	**326,882,299**
Cars and trucks, new	213,693,975	10,949,938	14,919,336	22,696,451	176,076,019
New cars	102,547,248	6,786,944	5,574,477	8,176,264	88,796,448
New trucks	111,145,539	4,162,994	9,344,859	14,520,186	87,280,482
Cars and trucks, used	186,387,419	4,716,552	18,256,347	23,086,284	145,538,185
Used cars	89,481,648	3,944,776	9,963,104	8,591,103	70,926,261
Used trucks	96,905,771	771,776	8,293,100	14,495,181	74,611,924
Other vehicles	6,460,305	–	514,253	678,964	5,267,185
New motorcycles	4,575,456	–	360,334	541,231	3,673,827
Used motorcycles	1,884,850	–	153,777	137,596	1,593,358
Gasoline and motor oil	**264,718,029**	**8,979,415**	**24,821,243**	**31,684,493**	**208,453,954**
Other vehicle expenses	**279,872,888**	**10,320,936**	**24,852,055**	**29,408,481**	**225,868,896**
Vehicle finance charges	35,392,634	900,986	3,505,624	4,461,023	27,456,736
Automobile finance charges	13,893,935	581,629	1,705,381	1,518,617	10,680,048
Truck finance charges	19,166,999	319,357	1,797,105	2,817,244	14,573,303
Motorcycle and plane finance charges	494,387	–	3,138	37,713	453,424
Other vehicle finance charges	1,837,313	–	–	87,450	1,749,962
Maintenance and repairs	81,816,275	2,776,846	6,510,689	8,331,077	67,037,558
Coolant, additives, brake and transmission fluids	434,965	7,868	45,933	70,916	317,761
Tires—purchased, replaced, installed	12,280,047	293,950	1,017,095	1,175,514	10,111,902
Parts, equipment, and accessories	4,902,274	138,021	248,211	481,929	4,172,776
Vehicle products and cleaning services	629,868	15,122	151,922	55,886	420,646
Vehicle video equipment	306,615	–	–	31,017	275,878
Miscellaneous auto repair, servicing	4,890,389	161,420	374,456	409,373	4,110,862
Body work and painting	3,509,434	108,064	241,506	405,274	2,878,059
Clutch, transmission repair	4,388,872	120,440	356,054	606,818	3,426,174
Drive shaft and rear-end repair	799,813	27,006	38,088	18,173	743,870
Brake work	7,281,511	246,618	592,711	633,190	6,054,759
Repair to steering or front-end	2,345,961	123,514	168,042	213,295	1,964,837
Repair to engine cooling system	2,622,865	29,792	208,412	213,295	2,200,654
Motor tune-up	5,648,608	309,358	402,558	666,257	4,587,049
Lube, oil change, and oil filters	7,947,031	268,009	651,625	745,098	6,553,707
Front-end alignment, wheel balance, rotation	1,638,845	43,521	90,868	115,324	1,432,201
Shock absorber replacement	568,070	19,466	55,919	62,171	450,693
Tire repair and other repair work	5,766,262	169,124	498,990	535,629	4,740,921
Vehicle air conditioning repair	1,418,985	59,134	75,747	232,151	1,111,708
Exhaust system repair	1,206,256	45,816	89,584	116,144	1,000,629
Electrical system repair	2,934,234	79,583	196,001	287,764	2,451,039
Motor repair, replacement	8,234,631	469,877	737,928	1,013,322	6,487,241
Auto repair service policy	1,038,688	41,103	98,429	62,444	877,712
Vehicle insurance	105,346,000	4,251,142	10,126,296	11,125,775	84,225,788
Vehicle rental, leases, licenses, other charges	57,317,979	2,391,962	4,709,447	5,490,605	47,149,725
Leased and rented vehicles	34,982,625	1,528,677	3,283,518	3,368,723	28,353,569
Rented vehicles	4,455,424	212,235	387,865	281,615	3,787,638
Leased vehicles	30,527,201	1,316,442	2,895,652	3,087,108	24,565,931
Car lease payments	14,631,950	583,309	1,572,288	1,540,616	11,518,609
Truck lease payments	12,974,090	666,171	1,162,312	1,245,747	10,587,178
Vehicle registration, state	10,256,151	399,760	612,111	1,015,099	8,633,266
Vehicle registration, local	992,339	50,078	83,165	60,122	848,577
Driver's license	816,451	26,063	63,907	75,972	677,405
Vehicle inspection	1,130,197	38,931	82,024	123,113	924,147

	total consumer units	Asian	black	Hispanic	non-Hispanic white and other
Parking fees	$4,145,244	$205,556	$216,257	$272,460	$3,659,259
Parking fees in home city, excluding residence	3,416,736	186,377	196,857	220,947	3,000,065
Parking fees on trips	729,696	19,179	19,258	51,513	659,195
Tolls	1,785,022	54,176	163,049	298,148	1,323,852
Tolls on trips	477,749	10,409	26,533	51,377	400,616
Towing charges	607,288	13,032	80,312	102,617	424,288
Global positioning services	190,149	6,352	4,707	5,056	180,277
Automobile service clubs	1,935,952	58,888	93,864	117,784	1,725,379
Public transportation	**59,971,743**	**4,872,973**	**4,074,512**	**5,660,859**	**50,349,187**
Airline fares	39,764,868	3,596,159	1,963,007	3,259,274	34,632,308
Intercity bus fares	1,346,491	91,426	84,734	109,995	1,153,591
Intracity mass transit fares	6,071,689	544,665	1,249,043	1,323,222	3,507,207
Taxis and local transportation on trips	2,476,688	176,665	89,870	154,676	2,232,521
Taxi fares and limousine service in home town	1,648,352	58,069	145,646	249,231	1,252,834
Intercity train fares	1,935,952	111,466	133,378	116,964	1,686,227
Ship fares	6,538,742	289,196	402,844	383,685	5,765,223
School bus	188,960	5,327	5,849	63,811	119,274

Note: "Asian" and "black" include Hispanics and non-Hispanics who identify themselves as being of the respective race alone. "Hispanic" includes people of any race who identify themselves as Hispanic. "Other" includes people who identify themselves as non-Hispanic and as Alaska Native, American Indian, Asian (who are also included in the Asian column), Native Hawaiian or other Pacific Islander, as well as non-Hispanics reporting more than one race. Numbers may not add to total because of rounding and missing subcategories. "–" means sample is too small to make a reliable estimate.
Source: Calculations by New Strategist based on the Bureau of Labor Statistics' 2006 Consumer Expenditure Survey

Table 23. Transportation: Market shares by race and Hispanic origin, 2006

(percentage of total annual spending on transportation accounted for by consumer unit race and Hispanic origin groups, 2006)

	total consumer units	Asian	black	Hispanic	non-Hispanic white and other
Share of total consumer units	100.0%	3.4%	12.0%	11.5%	76.6%
Share of total before-tax income	100.0	4.3	8.2	9.1	82.8
Share of total spending	100.0	4.1	8.6	10.2	81.3
TRANSPORTATION	100.0	3.9	8.6	11.2	80.3
Vehicle purchases	100.0	3.9	8.3	11.4	80.4
Cars and trucks, new	100.0	5.1	7.0	10.6	82.4
New cars	100.0	6.6	5.4	8.0	86.6
New trucks	100.0	3.7	8.4	13.1	78.5
Cars and trucks, used	100.0	2.5	9.8	12.4	78.1
Used cars	100.0	4.4	11.1	9.6	79.3
Used trucks	100.0	0.8	8.6	15.0	77.0
Other vehicles	100.0	–	8.0	10.5	81.5
New motorcycles	100.0	–	7.9	11.8	80.3
Used motorcycles	100.0	–	8.2	7.3	84.5
Gasoline and motor oil	100.0	3.4	9.4	12.0	78.7
Other vehicle expenses	100.0	3.7	8.9	10.5	80.7
Vehicle finance charges	100.0	2.5	9.9	12.6	77.6
Automobile finance charges	100.0	4.2	12.3	10.9	76.9
Truck finance charges	100.0	1.7	9.4	14.7	76.0
Motorcycle and plane finance charges	100.0	–	0.6	7.6	91.7
Other vehicle finance charges	100.0	–	–	4.8	95.2
Maintenance and repairs	100.0	3.4	8.0	10.2	81.9
Coolant, additives, brake and transmission fluids	100.0	1.8	10.6	16.3	73.1
Tires—purchased, replaced, installed	100.0	2.4	8.3	9.6	82.3
Parts, equipment, and accessories	100.0	2.8	5.1	9.8	85.1
Vehicle products and cleaning services	100.0	2.4	24.1	8.9	66.8
Vehicle video equipment	100.0	–	–	10.1	90.0
Miscellaneous auto repair, servicing	100.0	3.3	7.7	8.4	84.1
Body work and painting	100.0	3.1	6.9	11.5	82.0
Clutch, transmission repair	100.0	2.7	8.1	13.8	78.1
Drive shaft and rear-end repair	100.0	3.4	4.8	2.3	93.0
Brake work	100.0	3.4	8.1	8.7	83.2
Repair to steering or front-end	100.0	5.3	7.2	9.1	83.8
Repair to engine cooling system	100.0	1.1	7.9	8.1	83.9
Motor tune-up	100.0	5.5	7.1	11.8	81.2
Lube, oil change, and oil filters	100.0	3.4	8.2	9.4	82.5
Front-end alignment, wheel balance, rotation	100.0	2.7	5.5	7.0	87.4
Shock absorber replacement	100.0	3.4	9.8	10.9	79.3
Tire repair and other repair work	100.0	2.9	8.7	9.3	82.2
Vehicle air conditioning repair	100.0	4.2	5.3	16.4	78.3
Exhaust system repair	100.0	3.8	7.4	9.6	83.0
Electrical system repair	100.0	2.7	6.7	9.8	83.5
Motor repair, replacement	100.0	5.7	9.0	12.3	78.8
Auto repair service policy	100.0	4.0	9.5	6.0	84.5
Vehicle insurance	100.0	4.0	9.6	10.6	80.0
Vehicle rental, leases, licenses, other charges	100.0	4.2	8.2	9.6	82.3
Leased and rented vehicles	100.0	4.4	9.4	9.6	81.1
Rented vehicles	100.0	4.8	8.7	6.3	85.0
Leased vehicles	100.0	4.3	9.5	10.1	80.5
Car lease payments	100.0	4.0	10.7	10.5	78.7
Truck lease payments	100.0	5.1	9.0	9.6	81.6
Vehicle registration, state	100.0	3.9	6.0	9.9	84.2
Vehicle registration, local	100.0	5.0	8.4	6.1	85.5
Driver's license	100.0	3.2	7.8	9.3	83.0
Vehicle inspection	100.0	3.4	7.3	10.9	81.8

	total consumer units	Asian	black	Hispanic	non-Hispanic white and other
Parking fees	100.0%	5.0%	5.2%	6.6%	88.3%
Parking fees in home city, excluding residence	100.0	5.5	5.8	6.5	87.8
Parking fees on trips	100.0	2.6	2.6	7.1	90.3
Tolls	100.0	3.0	9.1	16.7	74.2
Tolls on trips	100.0	2.2	5.6	10.8	83.9
Towing charges	100.0	2.1	13.2	16.9	69.9
Global positioning services	100.0	3.3	2.5	2.7	94.8
Automobile service clubs	100.0	3.0	4.8	6.1	89.1
Public transportation	**100.0**	**8.1**	**6.8**	**9.4**	**84.0**
Airline fares	100.0	9.0	4.9	8.2	87.1
Intercity bus fares	100.0	6.8	6.3	8.2	85.7
Intracity mass transit fares	100.0	9.0	20.6	21.8	57.8
Taxis and local transportation on trips	100.0	7.1	3.6	6.2	90.1
Taxi fares and limousine service in home town	100.0	3.5	8.8	15.1	76.0
Intercity train fares	100.0	5.8	6.9	6.0	87.1
Ship fares	100.0	4.4	6.2	5.9	88.2
School bus	100.0	2.8	3.1	33.8	63.1

Note: "Asian" and "black" include Hispanics and non-Hispanics who identify themselves as being of the respective race alone. "Hispanic" includes people of any race who identify themselves as Hispanic. "Other" includes people who identify themselves as non-Hispanic and as Alaska Native, American Indian, Asian (who are also included in the Asian column), Native Hawaiian or other Pacific Islander, as well as non-Hispanics reporting more than one race. "–" means sample is too small to make a reliable estimate.
Source: Calculations by New Strategist based on the 2002 Consumer Expenditure Survey

Table 24. Transportation: Average spending by region, 2006

(average annual spending of consumer units on transportation, by region in which consumer unit lives, 2006)

	total consumer units	Northeast	Midwest	South	West
Number of consumer units (in 000s)	118,843	22,757	27,206	42,457	26,423
Number of persons per consumer unit	2.5	2.4	2.4	2.5	2.6
Average before-tax income of consumer units	$60,533.00	$64,232.00	$57,980.00	$56,190.00	$66,955.00
Average spending of consumer units, total	48,398.32	49,164.09	45,084.61	44,501.24	57,485.71
TRANSPORTATION	**8,507.90**	**7,819.03**	**7,501.97**	**8,496.63**	**10,156.30**
Vehicle purchases	3,420.83	2,894.22	2,729.66	3,642.51	4,229.81
Cars and trucks, new	1,798.12	1,617.34	1,316.87	1,889.21	2,302.94
New cars	862.88	922.15	580.64	861.39	1,104.82
New trucks	935.23	695.20	736.22	1,027.82	1,198.12
Cars and trucks, used	1,568.35	1,238.79	1,369.21	1,715.54	1,820.71
Used cars	752.94	708.54	640.39	820.76	798.09
Used trucks	815.41	530.26	728.83	894.78	1,022.62
Other vehicles	54.36	38.09	43.59	37.76	106.17
New motorcycles	38.50	29.89	25.30	28.21	76.07
Used motorcycles	15.86	8.19	18.29	9.55	30.10
Gasoline and motor oil	**2,227.46**	**1,910.35**	**2,142.22**	**2,355.80**	**2,382.14**
Other vehicle expenses	**2,354.98**	**2,385.95**	**2,224.72**	**2,182.37**	**2,740.63**
Vehicle finance charges	297.81	236.68	249.98	337.94	335.21
Automobile finance charges	116.91	108.08	102.41	126.51	124.01
Truck finance charges	161.28	119.27	127.20	194.93	178.46
Motorcycle and plane finance charges	4.16	2.15	5.79	3.81	4.76
Other vehicle finance charges	15.46	7.19	14.57	12.68	27.98
Maintenance and repairs	688.44	651.45	625.35	650.33	847.06
Coolant, additives, brake and transmission fluids	3.66	2.35	3.06	4.13	4.63
Tires—purchased, replaced, installed	103.33	88.33	93.75	105.35	122.86
Parts, equipment, and accessories	41.25	33.66	33.77	35.97	63.99
Vehicle products and cleaning services	5.30	3.42	3.80	5.61	8.05
Vehicle video equipment	2.58	1.02	0.32	2.62	6.19
Miscellaneous auto repair, servicing	41.15	34.79	37.29	44.34	45.60
Body work and painting	29.53	31.15	27.04	28.46	32.43
Clutch, transmission repair	36.93	27.35	30.88	35.74	53.31
Drive shaft and rear-end repair	6.73	7.17	3.24	8.44	7.20
Brake work	61.27	87.92	62.80	47.39	59.02
Repair to steering or front-end	19.74	20.58	25.39	11.50	26.45
Repair to engine cooling system	22.07	17.60	20.31	19.51	31.84
Motor tune-up	47.53	49.67	31.18	43.20	69.49
Lube, oil change, and oil filters	66.87	56.41	72.67	66.21	70.99
Front-end alignment, wheel balance, rotation	13.79	13.65	13.92	13.50	14.23
Shock absorber replacement	4.78	3.81	5.29	4.82	5.05
Tire repair and other repair work	48.52	57.26	44.37	42.40	55.09
Vehicle air conditioning repair	11.94	8.08	13.76	10.93	15.03
Exhaust system repair	10.15	14.04	12.88	6.62	9.67
Electrical system repair	24.69	22.97	26.16	21.59	29.64
Motor repair, replacement	69.29	53.60	54.94	75.10	88.25
Auto repair service policy	8.74	7.28	5.28	9.98	11.56
Vehicle insurance	886.43	859.79	823.68	874.24	993.60
Vehicle rental, leases, licenses, other charges	482.30	638.03	525.73	319.86	564.76
Leased and rented vehicles	294.36	423.90	330.35	186.41	319.18
Rented vehicles	37.49	44.76	30.87	24.45	59.00
Leased vehicles	256.87	379.14	299.48	161.96	260.18
Car lease payments	123.12	208.62	111.23	71.68	144.38
Truck lease payments	109.17	142.72	165.25	71.70	82.73
Vehicle registration, state	86.30	47.71	110.84	56.56	142.05
Vehicle registration, local	8.35	4.34	5.58	12.97	7.22
Driver's license	6.87	7.96	7.33	6.41	6.22
Vehicle inspection	9.51	23.59	1.42	7.64	8.69

	total consumer units	Northeast	Midwest	South	West
Parking fees	$34.88	$54.88	$38.87	$18.32	$40.17
Parking fees in home city, excluding residence	28.75	48.24	32.80	13.86	31.70
Parking fees on trips	6.14	6.64	6.07	4.46	8.47
Tolls	15.02	35.40	6.52	12.64	10.31
Tolls on trips	4.02	8.10	3.14	2.90	3.22
Towing charges	5.11	4.72	5.69	3.97	6.69
Global positioning services	1.60	1.67	2.26	1.66	0.75
Automobile service clubs	16.29	25.75	13.73	10.38	20.27
Public transportation	**504.63**	**628.51**	**405.37**	**315.95**	**803.71**
Airline fares	334.60	335.47	279.39	223.27	569.58
Intercity bus fares	11.33	12.68	10.68	6.85	18.03
Intracity mass transit fares	51.09	154.65	25.64	16.33	43.93
Taxis and local transportation on trips	20.84	30.11	18.97	11.14	30.36
Taxi fares and limousine service in home town	13.87	32.02	10.47	5.87	15.01
Intercity train fares	16.29	16.92	15.48	10.40	26.06
Ship fares	55.02	46.12	44.48	39.29	98.81
School bus	1.59	0.54	0.24	2.81	1.93

Note: Numbers may not add to total because some categories are not shown.
Source: Bureau of Labor Statistics, unpublished tables from the 2006 Consumer Expenditure Survey

Table 25. Transportation: Indexed spending by region, 2006

(indexed average annual spending of consumer units on transportation, by region in which consumer unit lives, 2006; index definition: an index of 100 is the average for all consumer units; an index of 132 means that spending by consumer units in that group is 32 percent above the average for all consumer units; an index of 68 indicates spending that is 32 percent below the average for all consumer units)

	total consumer units	Northeast	Midwest	South	West
Average spending of consumer units, total	$48,398	$49,164	$45,085	$44,501	$57,486
Average spending of consumer units, index	100	102	93	92	119
TRANSPORTATION	100	92	88	100	119
Vehicle purchases	100	85	80	106	124
Cars and trucks, new	100	90	73	105	128
New cars	100	107	67	100	128
New trucks	100	74	79	110	128
Cars and trucks, used	100	79	87	109	116
Used cars	100	94	85	109	106
Used trucks	100	65	89	110	125
Other vehicles	100	70	80	69	195
New motorcycles	100	78	66	73	198
Used motorcycles	100	52	115	60	190
Gasoline and motor oil	100	86	96	106	107
Other vehicle expenses	100	101	94	93	116
Vehicle finance charges	100	79	84	113	113
Automobile finance charges	100	92	88	108	106
Truck finance charges	100	74	79	121	111
Motorcycle and plane finance charges	100	52	139	92	114
Other vehicle finance charges	100	47	94	82	181
Maintenance and repairs	100	95	91	94	123
Coolant, additives, brake and transmission fluids	100	64	84	113	127
Tires—purchased, replaced, installed	100	85	91	102	119
Parts, equipment, and accessories	100	82	82	87	155
Vehicle products and cleaning services	100	65	72	106	152
Vehicle video equipment	100	40	12	102	240
Miscellaneous auto repair, servicing	100	85	91	108	111
Body work and painting	100	105	92	96	110
Clutch, transmission repair	100	74	84	97	144
Drive shaft and rear-end repair	100	107	48	125	107
Brake work	100	143	102	77	96
Repair to steering or front-end	100	104	129	58	134
Repair to engine cooling system	100	80	92	88	144
Motor tune-up	100	105	66	91	146
Lube, oil change, and oil filters	100	84	109	99	106
Front-end alignment, wheel balance, rotation	100	99	101	98	103
Shock absorber replacement	100	80	111	101	106
Tire repair and other repair work	100	118	91	87	114
Vehicle air conditioning repair	100	68	115	92	126
Exhaust system repair	100	138	127	65	95
Electrical system repair	100	93	106	87	120
Motor repair, replacement	100	77	79	108	127
Auto repair service policy	100	83	60	114	132
Vehicle insurance	100	97	93	99	112
Vehicle rental, leases, licenses, other charges	100	132	109	66	117
Leased and rented vehicles	100	144	112	63	108
Rented vehicles	100	119	82	65	157
Leased vehicles	100	148	117	63	101
Car lease payments	100	169	90	58	117
Truck lease payments	100	131	151	66	76
Vehicle registration, state	100	55	128	66	165
Vehicle registration, local	100	52	67	155	86
Driver's license	100	116	107	93	91
Vehicle inspection	100	248	15	80	91

	total consumer units	Northeast	Midwest	South	West
Parking fees	100	157	111	53	115
Parking fees in home city, excluding residence	100	168	114	48	110
Parking fees on trips	100	108	99	73	138
Tolls	100	236	43	84	69
Tolls on trips	100	201	78	72	80
Towing charges	100	92	111	78	131
Global positioning services	100	104	141	104	47
Automobile service clubs	100	158	84	64	124
Public transportation	**100**	**125**	**80**	**63**	**159**
Airline fares	100	100	83	67	170
Intercity bus fares	100	112	94	60	159
Intracity mass transit fares	100	303	50	32	86
Taxis and local transportation on trips	100	144	91	53	146
Taxi fares and limousine service in home town	100	231	75	42	108
Intercity train fares	100	104	95	64	160
Ship fares	100	84	81	71	180
School bus	100	34	15	177	121

Source: Calculations by New Strategist based on the Bureau of Labor Statistics' 2006 Consumer Expenditure Survey

Table 26. Transportation: Total spending by region, 2006

(total annual spending on transportation, by region in which consumer unit lives, 2006; consumer units and dollars in thousands)

	total consumer units	Northeast	Midwest	South	West
Number of consumer units	118,843	22,757	27,206	42,457	26,423
Total spending of all consumer units	$5,751,801,544	$1,118,827,196	$1,226,571,900	$1,889,389,147	$1,518,944,915
TRANSPORTATION	**1,011,104,360**	**177,937,666**	**204,098,596**	**360,741,420**	**268,359,915**
Vehicle purchases	**406,541,700**	**65,863,765**	**74,263,130**	**154,650,047**	**111,764,270**
Cars and trucks, new	213,693,975	36,805,806	35,826,765	80,210,189	60,850,584
New cars	102,547,248	20,985,368	15,796,892	36,572,035	29,192,659
New trucks	111,145,539	15,820,666	20,029,601	43,638,154	31,657,925
Cars and trucks, used	186,387,419	28,191,144	37,250,727	72,836,682	48,108,620
Used cars	89,481,648	16,124,245	17,422,450	34,847,007	21,087,932
Used trucks	96,905,771	12,067,127	19,828,549	37,989,674	27,020,688
Other vehicles	6,460,305	866,814	1,185,910	1,603,176	2,805,330
New motorcycles	4,575,456	680,207	688,312	1,197,712	2,009,998
Used motorcycles	1,884,850	186,380	497,598	405,464	795,332
Gasoline and motor oil	**264,718,029**	**43,473,835**	**58,281,237**	**100,020,201**	**62,943,285**
Other vehicle expenses	**279,872,888**	**54,297,064**	**60,525,732**	**92,656,883**	**72,415,666**
Vehicle finance charges	35,392,634	5,386,127	6,800,956	14,347,919	8,857,254
Automobile finance charges	13,893,935	2,459,577	2,786,166	5,371,235	3,276,716
Truck finance charges	19,166,999	2,714,227	3,460,603	8,276,143	4,715,449
Motorcycle and plane finance charges	494,387	48,928	157,523	161,761	125,773
Other vehicle finance charges	1,837,313	163,623	396,391	538,355	739,316
Maintenance and repairs	81,816,275	14,825,048	17,013,272	27,611,061	22,381,866
Coolant, additives, brake and transmission fluids	434,965	53,479	83,250	175,347	122,338
Tires—purchased, replaced, installed	12,280,047	2,010,126	2,550,563	4,472,845	3,246,330
Parts, equipment, and accessories	4,902,274	766,001	918,747	1,527,178	1,690,808
Vehicle products and cleaning services	629,868	77,829	103,383	238,184	212,705
Vehicle video equipment	306,615	23,212	8,706	111,237	163,558
Miscellaneous auto repair, servicing	4,890,389	791,716	1,014,512	1,882,543	1,204,889
Body work and painting	3,509,434	708,881	735,650	1,208,326	856,898
Clutch, transmission repair	4,388,872	622,404	840,121	1,517,413	1,408,610
Drive shaft and rear-end repair	799,813	163,168	88,147	358,337	190,246
Brake work	7,281,511	2,000,795	1,708,537	2,012,037	1,559,485
Repair to steering or front-end	2,345,961	468,339	690,760	488,256	698,888
Repair to engine cooling system	2,622,865	400,523	552,554	828,336	841,308
Motor tune-up	5,648,608	1,130,340	848,283	1,834,142	1,836,134
Lube, oil change, and oil filters	7,947,031	1,283,722	1,977,060	2,811,078	1,875,769
Front-end alignment, wheel balance, rotation	1,638,845	310,633	378,708	573,170	375,999
Shock absorber replacement	568,070	86,704	143,920	204,643	133,436
Tire repair and other repair work	5,766,262	1,303,066	1,207,130	1,800,177	1,455,643
Vehicle air conditioning repair	1,418,985	183,877	374,355	464,055	397,138
Exhaust system repair	1,206,256	319,508	350,413	281,065	255,510
Electrical system repair	2,934,234	522,728	711,709	916,647	783,178
Motor repair, replacement	8,234,631	1,219,775	1,494,698	3,188,521	2,331,830
Auto repair service policy	1,038,688	165,671	143,648	423,721	305,450
Vehicle insurance	105,346,000	19,566,241	22,409,038	37,117,608	26,253,893
Vehicle rental, leases, licenses, other charges	57,317,979	14,519,649	14,303,010	13,580,296	14,922,653
Leased and rented vehicles	34,982,625	9,646,692	8,987,502	7,914,409	8,433,693
Rented vehicles	4,455,424	1,018,603	839,849	1,038,074	1,558,957
Leased vehicles	30,527,201	8,628,089	8,147,653	6,876,336	6,874,736
Car lease payments	14,631,950	4,747,565	3,026,123	3,043,318	3,814,953
Truck lease payments	12,974,090	3,247,879	4,495,792	3,044,167	2,185,975
Vehicle registration, state	10,256,151	1,085,736	3,015,513	2,401,368	3,753,387
Vehicle registration, local	992,339	98,765	151,809	550,667	190,774
Driver's license	816,451	181,146	199,420	272,149	164,351
Vehicle inspection	1,130,197	536,838	38,633	324,371	229,616

	total consumer units	Northeast	Midwest	South	West
Parking fees	$4,145,244	$1,248,904	$1,057,497	$777,812	$1,061,412
Parking fees in home city, excluding residence	3,416,736	1,097,798	892,357	588,454	837,609
Parking fees on trips	729,696	151,106	165,140	189,358	223,803
Tolls	1,785,022	805,598	177,383	536,656	272,421
Tolls on trips	477,749	184,332	85,427	123,125	85,082
Towing charges	607,288	107,413	154,802	168,554	176,770
Global positioning services	190,149	38,004	61,486	70,479	19,817
Automobile service clubs	1,935,952	585,993	373,538	440,704	535,594
Public transportation	**59,971,743**	**14,303,002**	**11,028,496**	**13,414,289**	**21,236,429**
Airline fares	39,764,868	7,634,291	7,601,084	9,479,374	15,050,012
Intercity bus fares	1,346,491	288,559	290,560	290,830	476,407
Intracity mass transit fares	6,071,689	3,519,370	697,562	693,323	1,160,762
Taxis and local transportation on trips	2,476,688	685,213	516,098	472,971	802,202
Taxi fares and limousine service in home town	1,648,352	728,679	284,847	249,223	396,609
Intercity train fares	1,935,952	385,048	421,149	441,553	688,583
Ship fares	6,538,742	1,049,553	1,210,123	1,668,136	2,610,857
School bus	188,960	12,289	6,529	119,304	50,996

Note: Numbers may not add to total because some categories are not shown and because of rounding.
Source: Calculations by New Strategist based on the Bureau of Labor Statistics' 2006 Consumer Expenditure Survey

Table 27. Transportation: Market shares by region, 2006

(percentage of total annual spending on transportation accounted for by consumer units by region of residence, 2006)

	total consumer units	Northeast	Midwest	South	West
Share of total consumer units	100.0%	19.1%	22.9%	35.7%	22.2%
Share of total before-tax income	100.0	20.3	21.9	33.2	24.6
Share of total spending	100.0	19.5	21.3	32.8	26.4
TRANSPORTATION	100.0	17.6	20.2	35.7	26.5
Vehicle purchases	100.0	16.2	18.3	38.0	27.5
Cars and trucks, new	100.0	17.2	16.8	37.5	28.5
New cars	100.0	20.5	15.4	35.7	28.5
New trucks	100.0	14.2	18.0	39.3	28.5
Cars and trucks, used	100.0	15.1	20.0	39.1	25.8
Used cars	100.0	18.0	19.5	38.9	23.6
Used trucks	100.0	12.5	20.5	39.2	27.9
Other vehicles	100.0	13.4	18.4	24.8	43.4
New motorcycles	100.0	14.9	15.0	26.2	43.9
Used motorcycles	100.0	9.9	26.4	21.5	42.2
Gasoline and motor oil	100.0	16.4	22.0	37.8	23.8
Other vehicle expenses	100.0	19.4	21.6	33.1	25.9
Vehicle finance charges	100.0	15.2	19.2	40.5	25.0
Automobile finance charges	100.0	17.7	20.1	38.7	23.6
Truck finance charges	100.0	14.2	18.1	43.2	24.6
Motorcycle and plane finance charges	100.0	9.9	31.9	32.7	25.4
Other vehicle finance charges	100.0	8.9	21.6	29.3	40.2
Maintenance and repairs	100.0	18.1	20.8	33.7	27.4
Coolant, additives, brake and transmission fluids	100.0	12.3	19.1	40.3	28.1
Tires—purchased, replaced, installed	100.0	16.4	20.8	36.4	26.4
Parts, equipment, and accessories	100.0	15.6	18.7	31.2	34.5
Vehicle products and cleaning services	100.0	12.4	16.4	37.8	33.8
Vehicle video equipment	100.0	7.6	2.8	36.3	53.3
Miscellaneous auto repair, servicing	100.0	16.2	20.7	38.5	24.6
Body work and painting	100.0	20.2	21.0	34.4	24.4
Clutch, transmission repair	100.0	14.2	19.1	34.6	32.1
Drive shaft and rear-end repair	100.0	20.4	11.0	44.8	23.8
Brake work	100.0	27.5	23.5	27.6	21.4
Repair to steering or front-end	100.0	20.0	29.4	20.8	29.8
Repair to engine cooling system	100.0	15.3	21.1	31.6	32.1
Motor tune-up	100.0	20.0	15.0	32.5	32.5
Lube, oil change, and oil filters	100.0	16.2	24.9	35.4	23.6
Front-end alignment, wheel balance, rotation	100.0	19.0	23.1	35.0	22.9
Shock absorber replacement	100.0	15.3	25.3	36.0	23.5
Tire repair and other repair work	100.0	22.6	20.9	31.2	25.2
Vehicle air conditioning repair	100.0	13.0	26.4	32.7	28.0
Exhaust system repair	100.0	26.5	29.0	23.3	21.2
Electrical system repair	100.0	17.8	24.3	31.2	26.7
Motor repair, replacement	100.0	14.8	18.2	38.7	28.3
Auto repair service policy	100.0	16.0	13.8	40.8	29.4
Vehicle insurance	100.0	18.6	21.3	35.2	24.9
Vehicle rental, leases, licenses, other charges	100.0	25.3	25.0	23.7	26.0
Leased and rented vehicles	100.0	27.6	25.7	22.6	24.1
Rented vehicles	100.0	22.9	18.9	23.3	35.0
Leased vehicles	100.0	28.3	26.7	22.5	22.5
Car lease payments	100.0	32.4	20.7	20.8	26.1
Truck lease payments	100.0	25.0	34.7	23.5	16.8
Vehicle registration, state	100.0	10.6	29.4	23.4	36.6
Vehicle registration, local	100.0	10.0	15.3	55.5	19.2
Driver's license	100.0	22.2	24.4	33.3	20.1
Vehicle inspection	100.0	47.5	3.4	28.7	20.3

	total consumer units	Northeast	Midwest	South	West
Parking fees	100.0%	30.1%	25.5%	18.8%	25.6%
Parking fees in home city, excluding residence	100.0	32.1	26.1	17.2	24.5
Parking fees on trips	100.0	20.7	22.6	26.0	30.7
Tolls	100.0	45.1	9.9	30.1	15.3
Tolls on trips	100.0	38.6	17.9	25.8	17.8
Towing charges	100.0	17.7	25.5	27.8	29.1
Global positioning services	100.0	20.0	32.3	37.1	10.4
Automobile service clubs	100.0	30.3	19.3	22.8	27.7
Public transportation	**100.0**	**23.8**	**18.4**	**22.4**	**35.4**
Airline fares	100.0	19.2	19.1	23.8	37.8
Intercity bus fares	100.0	21.4	21.6	21.6	35.4
Intracity mass transit fares	100.0	58.0	11.5	11.4	19.1
Taxis and local transportation on trips	100.0	27.7	20.8	19.1	32.4
Taxi fares and limousine service in home town	100.0	44.2	17.3	15.1	24.1
Intercity train fares	100.0	19.9	21.8	22.8	35.6
Ship fares	100.0	16.1	18.5	25.5	39.9
School bus	100.0	6.5	3.5	63.1	27.0

Note: Numbers may not add to total because of rounding.
Source: Calculations by New Strategist based on the Bureau of Labor Statistics' 2006 Consumer Expenditure Survey

Table 28. Transportation: Average spending by education, 2006

(average annual spending of consumer units (CU) on transportation, by education of consumer unit reference person, 2006)

	total consumer units	less than high school graduate	high school graduate	some college	associate's degree	college graduate total	college graduate bachelor's degree	college graduate master's, professional, doctorate
Number of consumer units (in 000s)	118,843	17,747	31,134	25,135	11,582	33,244	21,277	11,967
Number of persons per CU	2.5	2.6	2.5	2.4	2.5	2.4	2.4	2.4
Average before-tax income of CU	$60,533.00	$31,775.00	$45,962.00	$53,809.00	$67,353.00	$92,241.00	$82,860.00	$108,918.00
Average spending of CU, total	48,398.32	28,760.01	39,304.72	45,891.39	52,272.22	67,835.51	63,863.98	74,905.99
TRANSPORTATION	8,507.90	5,043.13	7,411.81	8,634.28	9,494.90	10,942.92	10,648.26	11,466.90
Vehicle purchases	3,420.83	1,955.68	2,979.19	3,626.82	3,720.35	4,356.50	4,193.02	4,647.15
Cars and trucks, new	1,798.12	741.46	1,398.99	1,781.29	1,864.52	2,725.59	2,612.47	2,926.70
New cars	862.88	371.81	585.01	708.47	891.91	1,491.90	1,358.06	1,729.86
New trucks	935.23	369.65	813.99	1,072.82	972.60	1,233.68	1,254.41	1,196.84
Cars and trucks, used	1,568.35	1,198.63	1,510.54	1,770.07	1,790.24	1,590.03	1,541.47	1,676.37
Used cars	752.94	513.77	614.25	947.83	929.42	801.66	727.32	933.84
Used trucks	815.41	684.86	896.29	822.24	860.82	788.37	814.15	742.53
Other vehicles	54.36	15.59	69.65	75.46	65.59	40.89	39.08	44.09
New motorcycles	38.50	12.45	40.53	62.95	48.59	28.52	27.18	30.90
Used motorcycles	15.86	3.14	29.13	12.51	17.01	12.36	11.90	13.19
Gasoline and motor oil	2,227.46	1,575.32	2,130.57	2,288.09	2,552.92	2,507.12	2,510.12	2,501.79
Other vehicle expenses	2,354.98	1,326.16	2,028.38	2,323.91	2,703.04	3,110.82	3,073.49	3,177.23
Vehicle finance charges	297.81	161.52	289.72	339.13	357.59	326.07	330.27	318.59
Automobile finance charges	116.91	67.63	109.88	126.38	134.04	136.67	141.86	127.44
Truck finance charges	161.28	90.11	157.87	190.87	208.74	163.55	165.89	159.39
Motorcycle and plane finance charges	4.16	0.82	4.80	7.29	4.04	3.01	3.77	1.65
Other vehicle finance charges	15.46	2.97	17.17	14.59	10.77	22.84	18.75	30.11
Maintenance and repairs	688.44	395.94	547.57	673.27	799.93	948.01	939.73	962.72
Coolant, additives, brake, transmission fluids	3.66	3.82	4.41	4.23	3.56	2.47	2.85	1.80
Tires—purchased, replaced, installed	103.33	61.47	83.15	99.55	132.47	137.28	144.79	123.94
Parts, equipment, and accessories	41.25	31.19	35.94	45.40	57.79	42.71	40.04	47.45
Vehicle products and cleaning services	5.30	3.31	4.86	8.20	3.99	5.12	5.91	3.69
Vehicle video equipment	2.58	0.33	0.16	2.47	0.29	6.94	8.94	3.39
Miscellaneous auto repair, servicing	41.15	19.18	34.41	37.02	37.27	62.80	61.12	65.84
Body work and painting	29.53	18.38	19.71	23.85	41.53	44.81	48.76	37.77
Clutch, transmission repair	36.93	22.93	28.60	40.83	52.64	43.78	45.66	40.43
Drive shaft and rear-end repair	6.73	2.04	5.14	8.50	7.18	9.23	10.75	6.54
Brake work	61.27	26.29	51.50	60.42	68.51	87.20	78.60	102.49
Repair to steering or front-end	19.74	8.71	17.47	21.23	23.02	25.49	27.41	22.08
Repair to engine cooling system	22.07	12.20	18.33	26.05	24.79	26.87	29.54	22.14
Motor tune-up	47.53	22.25	31.76	39.61	50.98	80.59	69.89	99.61
Lube, oil change, and oil filters	66.87	33.94	55.39	66.47	76.10	92.30	89.56	97.16
Front-end alignment, wheel balance, rotation	13.79	7.44	12.90	11.45	17.19	18.60	19.13	17.64
Shock absorber replacement	4.78	3.53	4.86	4.31	2.39	6.57	6.37	6.94
Tire repair and other repair work	48.52	26.71	36.46	42.68	63.72	70.57	67.64	75.79
Vehicle air conditioning repair	11.94	5.77	8.40	15.32	10.30	16.57	18.05	13.94
Exhaust system repair	10.15	3.19	8.41	8.61	13.23	15.60	16.26	14.43
Electrical system repair	24.69	16.24	17.48	28.36	28.25	31.94	29.30	36.63
Motor repair, replacement	69.29	52.59	55.60	66.75	70.12	92.66	91.33	95.03
Auto repair service policy	8.74	7.98	3.60	9.63	9.40	13.06	11.57	15.73
Vehicle insurance	886.43	583.03	847.97	883.86	1,018.71	1,040.30	1,049.91	1,023.20
Vehicle rental, leases, licenses, other charges	482.30	185.67	343.12	427.66	526.81	796.44	753.58	872.72
Leased and rented vehicles	294.36	92.72	196.24	244.45	325.50	520.78	499.78	558.11
Rented vehicles	37.49	13.36	18.61	27.44	47.33	72.23	66.20	82.96
Leased vehicles	256.87	79.36	177.63	217.01	278.16	448.55	433.58	475.15
Car lease payments	123.12	46.44	61.97	115.20	148.67	218.41	200.55	250.16
Truck lease payments	109.17	29.16	88.19	87.88	89.15	194.59	193.55	196.44
Vehicle registration, state	86.30	52.44	77.06	89.41	100.08	105.87	105.35	106.79
Vehicle registration, local	8.35	5.83	8.20	7.19	11.53	9.60	9.28	10.15
Driver's license	6.87	5.32	6.90	7.45	7.43	7.06	7.00	7.15
Vehicle inspection	9.51	6.47	9.21	9.41	9.76	11.39	11.43	11.32

	total consumer units	less than high school graduate	high school graduate	some college	associate's degree	college graduate		
						total	bachelor's degree	master's, professional, doctorate
Parking fees	$34.88	$5.07	$13.37	$29.07	$31.35	$76.57	$63.72	$99.41
Parking fees in home city, excl. residence	28.75	3.86	10.42	24.73	24.62	63.66	52.16	84.11
Parking fees on trips	6.14	1.21	2.95	4.33	6.72	12.90	11.56	15.30
Tolls	15.02	5.18	11.00	13.99	10.44	26.02	23.12	31.26
Tolls on trips	4.02	1.40	2.82	3.42	4.58	6.81	5.94	8.35
Towing charges	5.11	4.95	3.70	6.52	5.80	5.22	4.78	6.00
Global positioning services	1.60	0.12	1.40	1.45	3.08	2.17	1.86	2.72
Automobile service clubs	16.29	6.15	13.23	15.30	17.28	24.97	21.32	31.46
Public transportation	**504.63**	**185.97**	**273.67**	**395.47**	**518.58**	**968.48**	**871.63**	**1,140.73**
Airline fares	334.60	92.80	170.62	251.07	372.40	667.25	588.35	807.52
Intercity bus fares	11.33	5.24	7.08	9.99	14.64	18.41	16.28	22.19
Intracity mass transit fares	51.09	54.52	34.13	31.73	38.39	84.18	83.00	86.28
Taxis and local transportation on trips	20.84	4.48	9.36	17.05	19.82	43.54	40.09	49.67
Taxi fares and limousine service in home town	13.87	10.25	7.39	13.98	12.32	22.11	20.16	25.62
Intercity train fares	16.29	4.39	9.03	14.98	16.26	30.45	26.75	37.02
Ship fares	55.02	13.22	33.72	56.17	44.76	99.99	94.83	109.17
School bus	1.59	1.07	2.33	0.50	–	2.56	2.17	3.25

Note: Numbers may not add to total because some categories are not shown. "–" means sample is too small to make a reliable estimate.
Source: Bureau of Labor Statistics, unpublished tables from the 2006 Consumer Expenditure Survey

Table 29. Transportation: Indexed spending by education, 2006

(indexed average annual spending of consumer units (CU) on transportation, by education of consumer unit reference person, 2006; index definition: an index of 100 is the average for all consumer units; an index of 132 means that spending by consumer units in that group is 32 percent above the average for all consumer units; an index of 68 indicates spending that is 32 percent below the average for all consumer units)

	total consumer units	less than high school graduate	high school graduate	some college	associate's degree	college graduate total	bachelor's degree	master's, professional, doctorate
Average spending of CU, total	$48,398	$28,760	$39,305	$45,891	$52,272	$67,836	$63,864	$74,906
Average spending of CU, index	100	59	81	95	108	140	132	155
TRANSPORTATION	100	59	87	101	112	129	125	135
Vehicle purchases	100	57	87	106	109	127	123	136
Cars and trucks, new	100	41	78	99	104	152	145	163
New cars	100	43	68	82	103	173	157	200
New trucks	100	40	87	115	104	132	134	128
Cars and trucks, used	100	76	96	113	114	101	98	107
Used cars	100	68	82	126	123	106	97	124
Used trucks	100	84	110	101	106	97	100	91
Other vehicles	100	29	128	139	121	75	72	81
New motorcycles	100	32	105	164	126	74	71	80
Used motorcycles	100	20	184	79	107	78	75	83
Gasoline and motor oil	100	71	96	103	115	113	113	112
Other vehicle expenses	100	56	86	99	115	132	131	135
Vehicle finance charges	100	54	97	114	120	109	111	107
Automobile finance charges	100	58	94	108	115	117	121	109
Truck finance charges	100	56	98	118	129	101	103	99
Motorcycle and plane finance charges	100	20	115	175	97	72	91	40
Other vehicle finance charges	100	19	111	94	70	148	121	195
Maintenance and repairs	100	58	80	98	116	138	137	140
Coolant, additives, brake and transmission fluids	100	104	120	116	97	67	78	49
Tires—purchased, replaced, installed	100	59	80	96	128	133	140	120
Parts, equipment, and accessories	100	76	87	110	140	104	97	115
Vehicle products and cleaning services	100	62	92	155	75	97	112	70
Vehicle video equipment	100	13	6	96	11	269	347	131
Miscellaneous auto repair, servicing	100	47	84	90	91	153	149	160
Body work and painting	100	62	67	81	141	152	165	128
Clutch, transmission repair	100	62	77	111	143	119	124	109
Drive shaft and rear-end repair	100	30	76	126	107	137	160	97
Brake work	100	43	84	99	112	142	128	167
Repair to steering or front-end	100	44	89	108	117	129	139	112
Repair to engine cooling system	100	55	83	118	112	122	134	100
Motor tune-up	100	47	67	83	107	170	147	210
Lube, oil change, and oil filters	100	51	83	99	114	138	134	145
Front-end alignment, wheel balance, rotation	100	54	94	83	125	135	139	128
Shock absorber replacement	100	74	102	90	50	137	133	145
Tire repair and other repair work	100	55	75	88	131	145	139	156
Vehicle air conditioning repair	100	48	70	128	86	139	151	117
Exhaust system repair	100	31	83	85	130	154	160	142
Electrical system repair	100	66	71	115	114	129	119	148
Motor repair, replacement	100	76	80	96	101	134	132	137
Auto repair service policy	100	91	41	110	108	149	132	180
Vehicle insurance	100	66	96	100	115	117	118	115
Vehicle rental, leases, licenses, other charges	100	38	71	89	109	165	156	181
Leased and rented vehicles	100	31	67	83	111	177	170	190
Rented vehicles	100	36	50	73	126	193	177	221
Leased vehicles	100	31	69	84	108	175	169	185
Car lease payments	100	38	50	94	121	177	163	203
Truck lease payments	100	27	81	80	82	178	177	180
Vehicle registration, state	100	61	89	104	116	123	122	124
Vehicle registration, local	100	70	98	86	138	115	111	122
Driver's license	100	77	100	108	108	103	102	104
Vehicle inspection	100	68	97	99	103	120	120	119

	total consumer units	less than high school graduate	high school graduate	some college	associate's degree	college graduate		
						total	bachelor's degree	master's, professional, doctorate
Parking fees	100	15	38	83	90	220	183	285
Parking fees in home city, excl. residence	100	13	36	86	86	221	181	293
Parking fees on trips	100	20	48	71	109	210	188	249
Tolls	100	34	73	93	70	173	154	208
Tolls on trips	100	35	70	85	114	169	148	208
Towing charges	100	97	72	128	114	102	94	117
Global positioning services	100	8	88	91	193	136	116	170
Automobile service clubs	100	38	81	94	106	153	131	193
Public transportation	**100**	**37**	**54**	**78**	**103**	**192**	**173**	**226**
Airline fares	100	28	51	75	111	199	176	241
Intercity bus fares	100	46	62	88	129	162	144	196
Intracity mass transit fares	100	107	67	62	75	165	162	169
Taxis and local transportation on trips	100	21	45	82	95	209	192	238
Taxi fares and limousine service in home town	100	74	53	101	89	159	145	185
Intercity train fares	100	27	55	92	100	187	164	227
Ship fares	100	24	61	102	81	182	172	198
School bus	100	67	147	31	–	161	136	204

Note: "–" means sample is too small to make a reliable estimate.
Source: Calculations by New Strategist based on the Bureau of Labor Statistics' 2006 Consumer Expenditure Survey

Table 30. Transportation: Total spending by education, 2006

(total annual spending on transportation, by education of consumer unit (CU) reference person, 2006; consumer units and dollars in thousands)

	total consumer units	less than high school graduate	high school graduate	some college	associate's degree	college graduate total	college graduate bachelor's degree	master's, professional, doctorate
Number of consumer units	118,843	17,747	31,134	25,135	11,582	33,244	21,277	11,967
Total spending of all CUs	$5,751,801,544	$510,403,897	$1,223,713,152	$1,153,480,088	$605,416,852	$2,255,123,694	$1,358,833,902	$896,399,982
TRANSPORTATION	1,011,104,360	89,500,428	230,759,293	217,022,628	109,969,932	363,786,432	226,563,028	137,224,392
Vehicle purchases	406,541,700	34,707,453	92,754,101	91,160,121	43,089,094	144,827,486	89,214,887	55,612,444
Cars and trucks, new	213,693,975	13,158,691	43,556,155	44,772,724	21,594,871	90,609,514	55,585,524	35,023,819
New cars	102,547,248	6,598,512	18,213,701	17,807,393	10,330,102	49,596,724	28,895,443	20,701,235
New trucks	111,145,539	6,560,179	25,342,765	26,965,331	11,264,653	41,012,458	26,690,082	14,322,584
Cars and trucks, used	186,387,419	21,272,087	47,029,152	44,490,709	20,734,560	52,858,957	32,797,857	20,061,120
Used cars	89,481,648	9,117,876	19,124,060	23,823,707	10,764,542	26,650,385	15,475,188	11,175,263
Used trucks	96,905,771	12,154,210	27,905,093	20,667,002	9,970,017	26,208,572	17,322,670	8,885,857
Other vehicles	6,460,305	276,676	2,168,483	1,896,687	759,663	1,359,347	831,505	527,625
New motorcycles	4,575,456	220,950	1,261,861	1,582,248	562,769	948,119	578,309	369,780
Used motorcycles	1,884,850	55,726	906,933	314,439	197,010	410,896	253,196	157,845
Gasoline and motor oil	264,718,029	27,957,204	66,333,166	57,511,142	29,567,919	83,346,697	53,407,823	29,938,921
Other vehicle expenses	279,872,888	23,535,362	63,151,583	58,411,478	31,306,609	103,416,100	65,394,647	38,021,911
Vehicle finance charges	35,392,634	2,866,495	9,020,142	8,524,033	4,141,607	10,839,871	7,027,155	3,812,567
Automobile finance charges	13,893,935	1,200,230	3,421,004	3,176,561	1,552,451	4,543,457	3,018,355	1,525,074
Truck finance charges	19,166,999	1,599,182	4,915,125	4,797,517	2,417,627	5,437,056	3,529,642	1,907,420
Motorcycle and plane finance charges	494,387	14,553	149,443	183,234	46,791	100,064	80,214	19,746
Other vehicle finance charges	1,837,313	52,709	534,571	366,720	124,738	759,293	398,944	360,326
Maintenance and repairs	81,816,275	7,026,747	17,048,044	16,922,641	9,264,789	31,515,644	19,994,635	11,520,870
Coolant, additives, brake and transmission fluids	434,965	67,794	137,301	106,321	41,232	82,113	60,639	21,541
Tires—purchased, replaced, installed	12,280,047	1,090,908	2,588,792	2,502,189	1,534,268	4,563,736	3,080,697	1,483,190
Parts, equipment, and accessories	4,902,274	553,529	1,118,956	1,141,129	669,324	1,419,851	851,931	567,834
Vehicle products and cleaning services	629,868	58,743	151,311	206,107	46,212	170,209	125,747	44,158
Vehicle video equipment	306,615	5,857	4,981	62,083	3,359	230,713	190,216	40,568
Miscellaneous auto repair, servicing	4,890,389	340,387	1,071,321	930,498	431,661	2,087,723	1,300,450	787,907
Body work and painting	3,509,434	326,190	613,651	599,470	481,000	1,489,664	1,037,467	451,994
Clutch, transmission repair	4,388,872	406,939	890,432	1,026,262	609,676	1,455,422	971,508	483,826
Drive shaft and rear-end repair	799,813	36,204	160,029	213,648	83,159	306,842	228,728	78,264
Brake work	7,281,511	466,569	1,603,401	1,518,657	793,483	2,898,877	1,672,372	1,226,498
Repair to steering or front-end	2,345,961	154,576	543,911	533,616	266,618	847,390	583,203	264,231
Repair to engine cooling system	2,622,865	216,513	570,686	654,767	287,118	893,266	628,523	264,949
Motor tune-up	5,648,608	394,871	988,816	995,597	590,450	2,679,134	1,487,050	1,192,033
Lube, oil change, and oil filters	7,947,031	602,333	1,724,512	1,670,723	881,390	3,068,421	1,905,568	1,162,714
Front-end alignment, wheel balance, rotation	1,638,845	132,038	401,629	287,796	199,095	618,338	407,029	211,098
Shock absorber replacement	568,070	62,647	151,311	108,332	27,681	218,413	135,534	83,051
Tire repair and other repair work	5,766,262	474,022	1,135,146	1,072,762	738,005	2,346,029	1,439,176	906,979
Vehicle air conditioning repair	1,418,985	102,400	261,526	385,068	119,295	550,853	384,050	166,820
Exhaust system repair	1,206,256	56,613	261,837	216,412	153,230	518,606	345,964	172,684
Electrical system repair	2,934,234	288,211	544,222	712,829	327,192	1,061,813	623,416	438,351
Motor repair, replacement	8,234,631	933,315	1,731,050	1,677,761	812,130	3,080,389	1,943,228	1,137,224
Auto repair service policy	1,038,688	141,621	112,082	242,050	108,871	434,167	246,175	188,241
Vehicle insurance	105,346,000	10,347,033	26,400,698	22,215,821	11,798,699	34,583,733	22,338,935	12,244,634
Vehicle rental, leases, licenses, other charges	57,317,979	3,295,085	10,682,698	10,749,234	6,101,513	26,476,851	16,033,922	10,443,840
Leased and rented vehicles	34,982,625	1,645,502	6,109,736	6,144,251	3,769,941	17,312,810	10,633,819	6,678,902
Rented vehicles	4,455,424	237,100	579,404	689,704	548,176	2,401,214	1,408,537	992,782
Leased vehicles	30,527,201	1,408,402	5,530,332	5,454,546	3,221,649	14,911,596	9,225,282	5,686,120
Car lease payments	14,631,950	824,171	1,929,374	2,895,552	1,721,896	7,260,822	4,267,102	2,993,665
Truck lease payments	12,974,090	517,503	2,745,707	2,208,864	1,032,535	6,468,950	4,118,163	2,350,797
Vehicle registration, state	10,256,151	930,653	2,399,186	2,247,320	1,159,127	3,519,542	2,241,532	1,277,956
Vehicle registration, local	992,339	103,465	255,299	180,721	133,540	319,142	197,451	121,465
Driver's license	816,451	94,414	214,825	187,256	86,054	234,703	148,939	85,564
Vehicle inspection	1,130,197	114,823	286,744	236,520	113,040	378,649	243,196	135,466

	total consumer units	less than high school graduate	high school graduate	some college	associate's degree	college graduate		
						total	bachelor's degree	master's, professional, doctorate
Parking fees	$4,145,244	$89,977	$416,262	$730,674	$363,096	$2,545,493	$1,355,770	$1,189,639
Parking fees in home city, excluding residence	3,416,736	68,503	324,416	621,589	285,149	2,116,313	1,109,808	1,006,544
Parking fees on trips	729,696	21,474	91,845	108,835	77,831	428,848	245,962	183,095
Tolls	1,785,022	91,929	342,474	351,639	120,916	865,009	491,924	374,088
Tolls on trips	477,749	24,846	87,798	85,962	53,046	226,392	126,385	99,924
Towing charges	607,288	87,848	115,196	163,880	67,176	173,534	101,704	71,802
Global positioning services	190,149	2,130	43,588	36,446	35,673	72,139	39,575	32,550
Automobile service clubs	1,935,952	109,144	411,903	384,566	200,137	830,103	453,626	376,482
Public transportation	**59,971,743**	**3,300,410**	**8,520,442**	**9,940,138**	**6,006,194**	**32,196,149**	**18,545,672**	**13,651,116**
Airline fares	39,764,868	1,646,922	5,312,083	6,310,644	4,313,137	22,182,059	12,518,323	9,663,592
Intercity bus fares	1,346,491	92,994	220,429	251,099	169,560	612,022	346,390	265,548
Intracity mass transit fares	6,071,689	967,566	1,062,603	797,534	444,633	2,798,480	1,765,991	1,032,513
Taxis and local transportation on trips	2,476,688	79,507	291,414	428,552	229,555	1,447,444	852,995	594,401
Taxi fares and limousine service in home town	1,648,352	181,907	230,080	351,387	142,690	735,025	428,944	306,595
Intercity train fares	1,935,952	77,909	281,140	376,522	188,323	1,012,280	569,160	443,018
Ship fares	6,538,742	234,615	1,049,838	1,411,833	518,410	3,324,068	2,017,698	1,306,437
School bus	188,960	18,989	72,542	12,568	–	85,105	46,171	38,893

Note: Numbers may not add to total because some categories are not shown and because of rounding. "–" means sample is too small to make a reliable estimate.
Source: Calculations by New Strategist based on the Bureau of Labor Statistics' 2006 Consumer Expenditure Survey

Table 31. Transportation: Market shares by education, 2006

(percentage of total annual spending on transportation accounted for by education of consumer unit reference person, 2006)

	total consumer units	less than high school graduate	high school graduate	some college	associate's degree	college graduate total	bachelor's degree	master's, professional, doctorate
Share of total consumer units	100.0%	14.9%	26.2%	21.1%	9.7%	28.0%	17.9%	10.1%
Share of total before-tax income	100.0	7.8	19.9	18.8	10.8	42.6	24.5	18.1
Share of total spending	100.0	8.9	21.3	20.1	10.5	39.2	23.6	15.6
TRANSPORTATION	**100.0**	**8.9**	**22.8**	**21.5**	**10.9**	**36.0**	**22.4**	**13.6**
Vehicle purchases	**100.0**	**8.5**	**22.8**	**22.4**	**10.6**	**35.6**	**21.9**	**13.7**
Cars and trucks, new	100.0	6.2	20.4	21.0	10.1	42.4	26.0	16.4
New cars	100.0	6.4	17.8	17.4	10.1	48.4	28.2	20.2
New trucks	100.0	5.9	22.8	24.3	10.1	36.9	24.0	12.9
Cars and trucks, used	100.0	11.4	25.2	23.9	11.1	28.4	17.6	10.8
Used cars	100.0	10.2	21.4	26.6	12.0	29.8	17.3	12.5
Used trucks	100.0	12.5	28.8	21.3	10.3	27.0	17.9	9.2
Other vehicles	100.0	4.3	33.6	29.4	11.8	21.0	12.9	8.2
New motorcycles	100.0	4.8	27.6	34.6	12.3	20.7	12.6	8.1
Used motorcycles	100.0	3.0	48.1	16.7	10.5	21.8	13.4	8.4
Gasoline and motor oil	**100.0**	**10.6**	**25.1**	**21.7**	**11.2**	**31.5**	**20.2**	**11.3**
Other vehicle expenses	**100.0**	**8.4**	**22.6**	**20.9**	**11.2**	**37.0**	**23.4**	**13.6**
Vehicle finance charges	100.0	8.1	25.5	24.1	11.7	30.6	19.9	10.8
Automobile finance charges	100.0	8.6	24.6	22.9	11.2	32.7	21.7	11.0
Truck finance charges	100.0	8.3	25.6	25.0	12.6	28.4	18.4	10.0
Motorcycle and plane finance charges	100.0	2.9	30.2	37.1	9.5	20.2	16.2	4.0
Other vehicle finance charges	100.0	2.9	29.1	20.0	6.8	41.3	21.7	19.6
Maintenance and repairs	100.0	8.6	20.8	20.7	11.3	38.5	24.4	14.1
Coolant, additives, brake, transmission fluids	100.0	15.6	31.6	24.4	9.5	18.9	13.9	5.0
Tires—purchased, replaced, installed	100.0	8.9	21.1	20.4	12.5	37.2	25.1	12.1
Parts, equipment, and accessories	100.0	11.3	22.8	23.3	13.7	29.0	17.4	11.6
Vehicle products and cleaning services	100.0	9.3	24.0	32.7	7.3	27.0	20.0	7.0
Vehicle video equipment	100.0	1.9	1.6	20.2	1.1	75.2	62.0	13.2
Miscellaneous auto repair, servicing	100.0	7.0	21.9	19.0	8.8	42.7	26.6	16.1
Body work and painting	100.0	9.3	17.5	17.1	13.7	42.4	29.6	12.9
Clutch, transmission repair	100.0	9.3	20.3	23.4	13.9	33.2	22.1	11.0
Drive shaft and rear-end repair	100.0	4.5	20.0	26.7	10.4	38.4	28.6	9.8
Brake work	100.0	6.4	22.0	20.9	10.9	39.8	23.0	16.8
Repair to steering or front-end	100.0	6.6	23.2	22.7	11.4	36.1	24.9	11.3
Repair to engine cooling system	100.0	8.3	21.8	25.0	10.9	34.1	24.0	10.1
Motor tune-up	100.0	7.0	17.5	17.6	10.5	47.4	26.3	21.1
Lube, oil change, and oil filters	100.0	7.6	21.7	21.0	11.1	38.6	24.0	14.6
Front-end alignment, wheel balance, rotation	100.0	8.1	24.5	17.6	12.1	37.7	24.8	12.9
Shock absorber replacement	100.0	11.0	26.6	19.1	4.9	38.4	23.9	14.6
Tire repair and other repair work	100.0	8.2	19.7	18.6	12.8	40.7	25.0	15.7
Vehicle air conditioning repair	100.0	7.2	18.4	27.1	8.4	38.8	27.1	11.8
Exhaust system repair	100.0	4.7	21.7	17.9	12.7	43.0	28.7	14.3
Electrical system repair	100.0	9.8	18.5	24.3	11.2	36.2	21.2	14.9
Motor repair, replacement	100.0	11.3	21.0	20.4	9.9	37.4	23.6	13.8
Auto repair service policy	100.0	13.6	10.8	23.3	10.5	41.8	23.7	18.1
Vehicle insurance	100.0	9.8	25.1	21.1	11.2	32.8	21.2	11.6
Vehicle rental, leases, licenses, other charges	100.0	5.7	18.6	18.8	10.6	46.2	28.0	18.2
Leased and rented vehicles	100.0	4.7	17.5	17.6	10.8	49.5	30.4	19.1
Rented vehicles	100.0	5.3	13.0	15.5	12.3	53.9	31.6	22.3
Leased vehicles	100.0	4.6	18.1	17.9	10.6	48.8	30.2	18.6
Car lease payments	100.0	5.6	13.2	19.8	11.8	49.6	29.2	20.5
Truck lease payments	100.0	4.0	21.2	17.0	8.0	49.9	31.7	18.1
Vehicle registration, state	100.0	9.1	23.4	21.9	11.3	34.3	21.9	12.5
Vehicle registration, local	100.0	10.4	25.7	18.2	13.5	32.2	19.9	12.2
Driver's license	100.0	11.6	26.3	22.9	10.5	28.7	18.2	10.5
Vehicle inspection	100.0	10.2	25.4	20.9	10.0	33.5	21.5	12.0

	total consumer units	less than high school graduate	high school graduate	some college	associate's degree	college graduate		
						total	bachelor's degree	master's, professional, doctorate
Parking fees	100.0%	2.2%	10.0%	17.6%	8.8%	61.4%	32.7%	28.7%
Parking fees in home city, excl. residence	100.0	2.0	9.5	18.2	8.3	61.9	32.5	29.5
Parking fees on trips	100.0	2.9	12.6	14.9	10.7	58.8	33.7	25.1
Tolls	100.0	5.2	19.2	19.7	6.8	48.5	27.6	21.0
Tolls on trips	100.0	5.2	18.4	18.0	11.1	47.4	26.5	20.9
Towing charges	100.0	14.5	19.0	27.0	11.1	28.6	16.7	11.8
Global positioning services	100.0	1.1	22.9	19.2	18.8	37.9	20.8	17.1
Automobile service clubs	100.0	5.6	21.3	19.9	10.3	42.9	23.4	19.4
Public transportation	**100.0**	**5.5**	**14.2**	**16.6**	**10.0**	**53.7**	**30.9**	**22.8**
Airline fares	100.0	4.1	13.4	15.9	10.8	55.8	31.5	24.3
Intercity bus fares	100.0	6.9	16.4	18.6	12.6	45.5	25.7	19.7
Intracity mass transit fares	100.0	15.9	17.5	13.1	7.3	46.1	29.1	17.0
Taxis and local transportation on trips	100.0	3.2	11.8	17.3	9.3	58.4	34.4	24.0
Taxi fares and limousine service in home town	100.0	11.0	14.0	21.3	8.7	44.6	26.0	18.6
Intercity train fares	100.0	4.0	14.5	19.4	9.7	52.3	29.4	22.9
Ship fares	100.0	3.6	16.1	21.6	7.9	50.8	30.9	20.0
School bus	100.0	10.0	38.4	6.7	–	45.0	24.4	20.6

Note: Numbers may not add to total because of rounding. "–" means sample is too small to make a reliable estimate.
Source: Calculations by New Strategist based on the Bureau of Labor Statistics' 2006 Consumer Expenditure Survey

Airline Fares

Best customers:
Householders aged 35 to 64
Married couples without children at home
Married couples with school-aged or older children at home
Asians
Households in the West
College graduates

Customer trends:
Average household spending in this category may grow because boomers are in the peak-spending age group—but only if discretionary income rises.

The biggest spenders on airline fares are middle-aged and older adults. Householders aged 35 to 64 spend 14 to 21 percent more than average on this item. Married couples without children at home (most of them empty-nesters) spend 48 percent more than average on airline fares, while those with school-aged or older children at home spend 32 to 36 percent more than average on this item. Asians spend more than twice the average on airline fares, while households in the West—where many Asians live—spend 70 percent more. College graduates spend twice the average on airline fares and account for 56 percent of the market.

Average household spending on airline fares fell 4 percent between 2000 and 2006, after adjusting for inflation. The lackluster economic recovery following the recession of 2001 is one reason for the decline, because it reduced the discretionary income of households. Average household spending on airline fares is likely to grow because boomers are in the peak-spending age group, but only if discretionary income rises.

Table 32. Airline fares			
Total household spending	$39,764,867,800.00		
Average household spends	334.60		
	AVERAGE HOUSEHOLD SPENDING	BEST CUSTOMERS (index)	BIGGEST CUSTOMERS (market share)
AGE OF HOUSEHOLDER			
Average household	$334.60	100	100.0%
Under age 25	143.75	43	3.0
Aged 25 to 34	291.43	87	14.7
Aged 35 to 44	381.28	114	23.0
Aged 45 to 54	405.79	121	25.2
Aged 55 to 64	398.09	119	19.0
Aged 65 to 74	323.16	97	9.6
Aged 75 or older	199.45	60	5.6

	AVERAGE HOUSEHOLD SPENDING	BEST CUSTOMERS (index)	BIGGEST CUSTOMERS (market share)
HOUSEHOLD INCOME			
Average household	**$334.60**	**100**	**100.0%**
Under $20,000	101.46	30	6.7
$20,000 to $39,999	138.55	41	9.6
$40,000 to $49,999	169.88	51	4.9
$50,000 to $69,999	324.64	97	14.4
$70,000 to $79,999	424.63	127	7.4
$80,000 to $99,999	470.34	141	12.1
$100,000 or more	943.78	282	44.9
HOUSEHOLD TYPE			
Average household	**334.60**	**100**	**100.0**
Married couples	458.34	137	68.5
Married couples, no children	494.19	148	31.4
Married couples, with children	431.62	129	31.9
Oldest child under 6	374.60	112	5.4
Oldest child 6 to 17	440.13	132	16.8
Oldest child 18 or older	455.23	136	9.7
Single parent with child under 18	156.08	47	2.8
Single person	222.57	67	19.7
RACE AND HISPANIC ORIGIN			
Average household	**334.60**	**100**	**100.0**
Asian	877.54	262	9.0
Black	137.61	41	4.9
Hispanic	238.53	71	8.2
Non-Hispanic white and other	380.37	114	87.1
REGION			
Average household	**334.60**	**100**	**100.0**
Northeast	335.47	100	19.2
Midwest	279.39	83	19.1
South	223.27	67	23.8
West	569.58	170	37.8
EDUCATION			
Average household	**334.60**	**100**	**100.0**
Less than high school graduate	92.80	28	4.1
High school graduate	170.62	51	13.4
Some college	251.07	75	15.9
Associate's degree	372.40	111	10.8
College graduate	667.25	199	55.8
Bachelor's degree	588.35	176	31.5
Master's, professional, doctoral degree	807.52	241	24.3

Note: Market shares may not sum to 100.0 because of rounding and missing categories by household type. "Asian" and "black" include Hispanics and non-Hispanics who identify themselves as being of the respective race alone. "Hispanic" includes people of any race who identify themselves as Hispanic. "Other" includes people who identify themselves as non-Hispanic and as Alaska Native, American Indian, Asian (who are also included in the Asian row), Native Hawaiian or other Pacific Islander, as well as non-Hispanics reporting more than one race.
Source: Calculations by New Strategist based on the Bureau of Labor Statistics' 2006 Consumer Expenditure Survey

Automobile Service Clubs

Best customers: Householders aged 45 or older
                             Married couples without children at home
                             Married couples with adult children at home

Customer trends: Spending in this category should continue to rise as the population ages.

Older householders are the best customers of automobile service club memberships. Householders aged 45 or older spend 25 to 50 percent more than average on this item and control more than three-quarters of the market. Married couples without children at home (most of them empty-nesters) spend 62 percent more than average. Those with adult children at home spend 53 percent more. Behind the higher spending of older households is their greater interest in security—both on the road and at home.

Average household spending on automobile service club memberships rose 67 percent between 2000 and 2006, after adjusting for inflation. Spending on this item is likely to continue to rise along with the aging of the population.

Table 33. Automobile service clubs

Total household spending $1,935,952,470.00
Average household spends   16.29

	AVERAGE HOUSEHOLD SPENDING	BEST CUSTOMERS (index)	BIGGEST CUSTOMERS (market share)
AGE OF HOUSEHOLDER			
Average household	**$16.29**	**100**	**100.0%**
Under age 25	3.34	21	1.4
Aged 25 to 34	7.57	46	7.8
Aged 35 to 44	11.81	72	14.6
Aged 45 to 54	20.52	126	26.2
Aged 55 to 64	24.49	150	24.0
Aged 65 to 74	23.37	143	14.2
Aged 75 or older	20.30	125	11.8

	AVERAGE HOUSEHOLD SPENDING	BEST CUSTOMERS (index)	BIGGEST CUSTOMERS (market share)
HOUSEHOLD INCOME			
Average household	**$16.29**	**100**	**100.0%**
Under $20,000	6.24	38	8.4
$20,000 to $39,999	12.19	75	17.3
$40,000 to $49,999	16.00	98	9.5
$50,000 to $69,999	17.28	106	15.8
$70,000 to $79,999	17.45	107	6.3
$80,000 to $99,999	21.04	129	11.1
$100,000 or more	32.36	199	31.6
HOUSEHOLD TYPE			
Average household	**16.29**	**100**	**100.0**
Married couples	20.56	126	63.1
Married couples, no children	26.43	162	34.5
Married couples, with children	16.25	100	24.7
Oldest child under 6	9.72	60	2.9
Oldest child 6 to 17	13.94	86	10.9
Oldest child 18 or older	24.87	153	10.9
Single parent with child under 18	5.45	33	2.0
Single person	12.02	74	21.9
RACE AND HISPANIC ORIGIN			
Average household	**16.29**	**100**	**100.0**
Asian	14.37	88	3.0
Black	6.58	40	4.8
Hispanic	8.62	53	6.1
Non-Hispanic white and other	18.95	116	89.1
REGION			
Average household	**16.29**	**100**	**100.0**
Northeast	25.75	158	30.3
Midwest	13.73	84	19.3
South	10.38	64	22.8
West	20.27	124	27.7
EDUCATION			
Average household	**16.29**	**100**	**100.0**
Less than high school graduate	6.15	38	5.6
High school graduate	13.23	81	21.3
Some college	15.30	94	19.9
Associate's degree	17.28	106	10.3
College graduate	24.97	153	42.9
Bachelor's degree	21.32	131	23.4
Master's, professional, doctoral degree	31.46	193	19.4

Note: Market shares may not sum to 100.0 because of rounding and missing categories by household type. "Asian" and "black" include Hispanics and non-Hispanics who identify themselves as being of the respective race alone. "Hispanic" includes people of any race who identify themselves as Hispanic. "Other" includes people who identify themselves as non-Hispanic and as Alaska Native, American Indian, Asian (who are also included in the Asian row), Native Hawaiian or other Pacific Islander, as well as non-Hispanics reporting more than one race.
Source: Calculations by New Strategist based on the Bureau of Labor Statistics' 2006 Consumer Expenditure Survey

Bus Fares, Intercity

Best customers: Householders aged 55 to 74
Married couples without children at home
Asians
Households in the West

Customer trends: Spending in this category may rise, or at least stabilize, if higher gas prices
and airfares encourage more bus travel.

The best customers of intercity bus fares are older travelers. Householders aged 55 to 74 spend 20 to 57 percent more than average on this item and account for 37 percent of the market. Married couples without children at home, most of them empty-nesters, spend over twice the average on this item. Many have children in college who travel back and forth by bus. Asians spend nearly twice the average on intercity bus travel, and households in the West, where many Asians reside, spend 59 percent more than average on this item.

Average household spending on intercity bus fares fell by a substantial 40 percent between 2000 and 2006, after adjusting for inflation. The lackluster recovery following the recession of 2001 is one factor behind the decline, as it reduced the amount spent on travel overall. But spending on bus fares fell more than other travel categories, in part because a growing share of travelers are choosing to get to their destination by car or plane rather than bus. Average household spending on intercity bus fares may rise, or at least stabilize, if higher gas prices and airfares encourage more bus travel.

Table 34. Bus fares, intercity

Total household spending $1,346,491,190.00
Average household spends   11.33

	AVERAGE HOUSEHOLD SPENDING	BEST CUSTOMERS (index)	BIGGEST CUSTOMERS (market share)
AGE OF HOUSEHOLDER			
Average household	**$11.33**	**100**	**100.0%**
Under age 25	7.43	66	4.5
Aged 25 to 34	8.01	71	11.9
Aged 35 to 44	9.42	83	16.8
Aged 45 to 54	11.04	97	20.2
Aged 55 to 64	17.81	157	25.1
Aged 65 to 74	13.60	120	11.9
Aged 75 or older	11.47	101	9.6

	AVERAGE HOUSEHOLD SPENDING	BEST CUSTOMERS (index)	BIGGEST CUSTOMERS (market share)
HOUSEHOLD INCOME			
Average household	**$11.33**	**100**	**100.0%**
Under $20,000	6.38	56	12.4
$20,000 to $39,999	7.77	69	15.9
$40,000 to $49,999	6.11	54	5.2
$50,000 to $69,999	13.08	115	17.2
$70,000 to $79,999	10.18	90	5.3
$80,000 to $99,999	16.50	146	12.5
$100,000 or more	22.47	198	31.6
HOUSEHOLD TYPE			
Average household	**11.33**	**100**	**100.0**
Married couples	14.57	129	64.3
Married couples, no children	23.40	207	44.0
Married couples, with children	7.70	68	16.8
Oldest child under 6	3.58	32	1.5
Oldest child 6 to 17	7.71	68	8.7
Oldest child 18 or older	10.49	93	6.6
Single parent with child under 18	4.13	36	2.2
Single person	8.91	79	23.3
RACE AND HISPANIC ORIGIN			
Average household	**11.33**	**100**	**100.0**
Asian	22.31	197	6.8
Black	5.94	52	6.3
Hispanic	8.05	71	8.2
Non-Hispanic white and other	12.67	112	85.7
REGION			
Average household	**11.33**	**100**	**100.0**
Northeast	12.68	112	21.4
Midwest	10.68	94	21.6
South	6.85	60	21.6
West	18.03	159	35.4
EDUCATION			
Average household	**11.33**	**100**	**100.0**
Less than high school graduate	5.24	46	6.9
High school graduate	7.08	62	16.4
Some college	9.99	88	18.6
Associate's degree	14.64	129	12.6
College graduate	18.41	162	45.5
Bachelor's degree	16.28	144	25.7
Master's, professional, doctoral degree	22.19	196	19.7

Note: Market shares may not sum to 100.0 because of rounding and missing categories by household type. "Asian" and "black" include Hispanics and non-Hispanics who identify themselves as being of the respective race alone. "Hispanic" includes people of any race who identify themselves as Hispanic. "Other" includes people who identify themselves as non-Hispanic and as Alaska Native, American Indian, Asian (who are also included in the Asian row), Native Hawaiian or other Pacific Islander, as well as non-Hispanics reporting more than one race.
Source: Calculations by New Strategist based on the Bureau of Labor Statistics' 2006 Consumer Expenditure Survey

Car Lease Payments

Best customers:	Householders aged 35 to 44 and 55 to 64
	Married couples without children at home
	Married couples with adult children at home
	Households in the Northeast
Customer trends:	Spending in this category will fluctuate depending on vehicle financing incentives.

The best customers of car leasing are middle-aged married couples buying additional cars for teenagers or older children. Householders aged 35 to 44 spend 41 percent more than average on this item, and those aged 55 to 64 spend 52 percent more than average. Married couples without children at home spend 47 percent more than average on car lease payments. Those with adult children at home spend 22 percent more than the average. Households in the Northeast spend 69 percent more than average on car leases.

Average household spending on car lease payments fell 40 percent between 2000 and 2006, after adjusting for inflation, one of the steepest declines in the transportation category. Behind the spending drop was the shift to buying rather than leasing as car dealers offered no-interest loans and other purchasing incentives. Spending on leasing will continue to fluctuate, depending on dealer incentives.

Table 35. Car lease payments

Total household spending $14,631,950,160.00
Average household spends 123.12

	AVERAGE HOUSEHOLD SPENDING	BEST CUSTOMERS (index)	BIGGEST CUSTOMERS (market share)
AGE OF HOUSEHOLDER			
Average household	**$123.12**	**100**	**100.0%**
Under age 25	67.27	55	3.8
Aged 25 to 34	104.47	85	14.3
Aged 35 to 44	174.07	141	28.5
Aged 45 to 54	111.35	90	18.8
Aged 55 to 64	186.71	152	24.2
Aged 65 to 74	79.42	65	6.4
Aged 75 or older	52.81	43	4.1

	AVERAGE HOUSEHOLD SPENDING	BEST CUSTOMERS (index)	BIGGEST CUSTOMERS (market share)
HOUSEHOLD INCOME			
Average household	**$123.12**	**100**	**100.0%**
Under $20,000	39.91	32	7.1
$20,000 to $39,999	44.91	36	8.5
$40,000 to $49,999	112.05	91	8.8
$50,000 to $69,999	120.52	98	14.6
$70,000 to $79,999	126.89	103	6.0
$80,000 to $99,999	168.61	137	11.8
$100,000 or more	334.78	272	43.3
HOUSEHOLD TYPE			
Average household	**123.12**	**100**	**100.0**
Married couples	149.33	121	60.7
Married couples, no children	180.51	147	31.2
Married couples, with children	130.82	106	26.3
Oldest child under 6	119.03	97	4.7
Oldest child 6 to 17	124.32	101	12.9
Oldest child 18 or older	150.54	122	8.7
Single parent with child under 18	78.63	64	3.9
Single person	91.23	74	22.0
RACE AND HISPANIC ORIGIN			
Average household	**123.12**	**100**	**100.0**
Asian	142.34	116	4.0
Black	110.22	90	10.7
Hispanic	112.75	92	10.5
Non-Hispanic white and other	126.51	103	78.7
REGION			
Average household	**123.12**	**100**	**100.0**
Northeast	208.62	169	32.4
Midwest	111.23	90	20.7
South	71.68	58	20.8
West	144.38	117	26.1
EDUCATION			
Average household	**123.12**	**100**	**100.0**
Less than high school graduate	46.44	38	5.6
High school graduate	61.97	50	13.2
Some college	115.20	94	19.8
Associate's degree	148.67	121	11.8
College graduate	218.41	177	49.6
Bachelor's degree	200.55	163	29.2
Master's, professional, doctoral degree	250.16	203	20.5

Note: Market shares may not sum to 100.0 because of rounding and missing categories by household type. "Asian" and "black" include Hispanics and non-Hispanics who identify themselves as being of the respective race alone. "Hispanic" includes people of any race who identify themselves as Hispanic. "Other" includes people who identify themselves as non-Hispanic and as Alaska Native, American Indian, Asian (who are also included in the Asian row), Native Hawaiian or other Pacific Islander, as well as non-Hispanics reporting more than one race.
Source: Calculations by New Strategist based on the Bureau of Labor Statistics' 2006 Consumer Expenditure Survey

Cars, New

Best customers: Householders aged 45 to 54 and 65 to 74
                                        Married couples
                                        Asians

Customer trends: Spending in this category is likely to rise as downsizing boomers replace SUVs and minivans with cars.

The best customers of new cars are older adults. Householders aged 45 to 54 spend 33 percent more than average on new cars, and those aged 65 to 74 spend 49 percent more. Married couples spend 39 percent more than average, with spending peaking at 81 percent above average among couples with adult children at home. Asians, who have the highest incomes, spend almost twice the average on new cars.

Average household spending on new cars fell 20 percent between 2000 and 2006, after adjusting for inflation. Behind the decline in spending on new cars was the growing popularity of sport utility vehicles (considered trucks) during the time period. Rising gasoline prices are likely to turn this trend around, as is the downsizing of transportation needs as boomers become empty-nesters.

Table 36. Cars, new

Total household spending $102,547,247,840.00
Average household spends   862.88

	AVERAGE HOUSEHOLD SPENDING	BEST CUSTOMERS (index)	BIGGEST CUSTOMERS (market share)
AGE OF HOUSEHOLDER			
Average household	**$862.88**	**100**	**100.0%**
Under age 25	384.64	45	3.1
Aged 25 to 34	641.28	74	12.6
Aged 35 to 44	924.06	107	21.6
Aged 45 to 54	1,150.55	133	27.7
Aged 55 to 64	851.85	99	15.7
Aged 65 to 74	1,283.05	149	14.7
Aged 75 or older	422.57	49	4.6

	AVERAGE HOUSEHOLD SPENDING	BEST CUSTOMERS (index)	BIGGEST CUSTOMERS (market share)
HOUSEHOLD INCOME			
Average household	**$862.88**	**100**	**100.0%**
Under $20,000	321.28	37	8.2
$20,000 to $39,999	353.62	41	9.5
$40,000 to $49,999	553.79	64	6.2
$50,000 to $69,999	771.12	89	13.3
$70,000 to $79,999	894.71	104	6.1
$80,000 to $99,999	1,217.41	141	12.2
$100,000 or more	2,419.97	280	44.6
HOUSEHOLD TYPE			
Average household	**862.88**	**100**	**100.0**
Married couples	1,201.16	139	69.6
Married couples, no children	1,139.58	132	28.1
Married couples, with children	1,328.45	154	38.1
Oldest child under 6	1,241.67	144	7.0
Oldest child 6 to 17	1,229.76	143	18.2
Oldest child 18 or older	1,564.70	181	12.9
Single parent with child under 18	152.08	18	1.1
Single person	612.23	71	21.0
RACE AND HISPANIC ORIGIN			
Average household	**862.88**	**100**	**100.0**
Asian	1,656.16	192	6.6
Black	390.78	45	5.4
Hispanic	598.38	69	8.0
Non-Hispanic white and other	975.26	113	86.6
REGION			
Average household	**862.88**	**100**	**100.0**
Northeast	922.15	107	20.5
Midwest	580.64	67	15.4
South	861.39	100	35.7
West	1,104.82	128	28.5
EDUCATION			
Average household	**862.88**	**100**	**100.0**
Less than high school graduate	371.81	43	6.4
High school graduate	585.01	68	17.8
Some college	708.47	82	17.4
Associate's degree	891.91	103	10.1
College graduate	1,491.90	173	48.4
Bachelor's degree	1,358.06	157	28.2
Master's, professional, doctoral degree	1,729.86	200	20.2

Note: Market shares may not sum to 100.0 because of rounding and missing categories by household type. "Asian" and "black" include Hispanics and non-Hispanics who identify themselves as being of the respective race alone. "Hispanic" includes people of any race who identify themselves as Hispanic. "Other" includes people who identify themselves as non-Hispanic and as Alaska Native, American Indian, Asian (who are also included in the Asian row), Native Hawaiian or other Pacific Islander, as well as non-Hispanics reporting more than one race.
Source: Calculations by New Strategist based on the Bureau of Labor Statistics' 2006 Consumer Expenditure Survey

Cars, Used

Best customers: Householders aged 25 to 34
                       Married couples with adult children at home

Customer trends: Spending in this category is likely to rise as the millennial generation fills the young-adult age group.

The best customers of used cars are young adults and married couples with adult children at home. Householders aged 25 to 34 spend 25 percent more than average on used cars. Married couples with adult children at home spend almost twice the average on this item.

Average household spending on used cars fell 36 percent between 2000 and 2006, after adjusting for inflation. Behind the decline was the growing popularity of sport utility vehicles (considered trucks), as well as dealer incentives to buy new rather than used vehicles. Average household spending on used cars may climb along with gas prices, but dealer incentives may steer consumers to buying new rather than used.

Table 37. Cars, used

Total household spending $89,481,648,420.00
Average household spends   752.94

AGE OF HOUSEHOLDER	AVERAGE HOUSEHOLD SPENDING	BEST CUSTOMERS (index)	BIGGEST CUSTOMERS (market share)
Average household	**$752.94**	**100**	**100.0%**
Under age 25	747.58	99	6.8
Aged 25 to 34	941.18	125	21.1
Aged 35 to 44	743.71	99	19.9
Aged 45 to 54	882.38	117	24.4
Aged 55 to 64	623.40	83	13.2
Aged 65 to 74	662.20	88	8.7
Aged 75 or older	469.41	62	5.9

	AVERAGE HOUSEHOLD SPENDING	BEST CUSTOMERS (index)	BIGGEST CUSTOMERS (market share)
HOUSEHOLD INCOME			
Average household	**$752.94**	**100**	**100.0%**
Under $20,000	336.13	45	9.8
$20,000 to $39,999	689.16	92	21.2
$40,000 to $49,999	564.02	75	7.2
$50,000 to $69,999	742.70	99	14.7
$70,000 to $79,999	1,152.84	153	9.0
$80,000 to $99,999	1,006.21	134	11.5
$100,000 or more	1,260.02	167	26.6
HOUSEHOLD TYPE			
Average household	**752.94**	**100**	**100.0**
Married couples	882.60	117	58.6
Married couples, no children	694.32	92	19.6
Married couples, with children	1,015.26	135	33.3
Oldest child under 6	778.48	103	5.0
Oldest child 6 to 17	845.44	112	14.3
Oldest child 18 or older	1,481.41	197	14.0
Single parent with child under 18	832.73	111	6.7
Single person	417.51	55	16.4
RACE AND HISPANIC ORIGIN			
Average household	**752.94**	**100**	**100.0**
Asian	962.61	128	4.4
Black	698.43	93	11.1
Hispanic	628.74	84	9.6
Non-Hispanic white and other	778.99	103	79.3
REGION			
Average household	**752.94**	**100**	**100.0**
Northeast	708.54	94	18.0
Midwest	640.39	85	19.5
South	820.76	109	38.9
West	798.09	106	23.6
EDUCATION			
Average household	**752.94**	**100**	**100.0**
Less than high school graduate	513.77	68	10.2
High school graduate	614.25	82	21.4
Some college	947.83	126	26.6
Associate's degree	929.42	123	12.0
College graduate	801.66	106	29.8
Bachelor's degree	727.32	97	17.3
Master's, professional, doctoral degree	933.84	124	12.5

Note: Market shares may not sum to 100.0 because of rounding and missing categories by household type. "Asian" and "black" include Hispanics and non-Hispanics who identify themselves as being of the respective race alone. "Hispanic" includes people of any race who identify themselves as Hispanic. "Other" includes people who identify themselves as non-Hispanic and as Alaska Native, American Indian, Asian (who are also included in the Asian row), Native Hawaiian or other Pacific Islander, as well as non-Hispanics reporting more than one race.
Source: Calculations by New Strategist based on the Bureau of Labor Statistics' 2006 Consumer Expenditure Survey

Gasoline and Motor Oil (Including on Trips)

Best customers: Householders aged 35 to 54
Married couples with children at home

Customer trends: Spending in this category will rise and fall along with the price of gas.

Gasoline is the biggest transportation expense for the average household, accounting for 26 percent of transportation spending. The biggest spenders on gasoline are middle-aged married couples because they have the largest households and the most vehicles. Householders aged 35 to 54 spend 18 to 21 percent more than average on gasoline and account for 49 percent of the market. Married couples with children at home spend 46 percent more than average on this item. Married couples with adult children at home spend 65 percent more than average on gasoline.

Average household spending on gasoline rose by a substantial 47 percent between 2000 and 2006, after adjusting for inflation. Behind the increase was the rise in gasoline prices. Average household spending on gasoline will fluctuate with gasoline prices.

Table 38. Gasoline and motor oil (including on trips)

Total household spending $264,718,028,780.00
Average household spends 2,227.46

	AVERAGE HOUSEHOLD SPENDING	BEST CUSTOMERS (index)	BIGGEST CUSTOMERS (market share)
AGE OF HOUSEHOLDER			
Average household	**$2,227.46**	**100**	**100.0%**
Under age 25	1,637.15	73	5.1
Aged 25 to 34	2,346.02	105	17.8
Aged 35 to 44	2,635.62	118	23.8
Aged 45 to 54	2,692.71	121	25.1
Aged 55 to 64	2,288.21	103	16.4
Aged 65 to 74	1,765.80	79	7.8
Aged 75 or older	933.80	42	4.0

	AVERAGE HOUSEHOLD SPENDING	BEST CUSTOMERS (index)	BIGGEST CUSTOMERS (market share)
HOUSEHOLD INCOME			
Average household	**$2,227.46**	**100**	**100.0%**
Under $20,000	1,020.62	46	10.1
$20,000 to $39,999	1,733.41	78	18.0
$40,000 to $49,999	2,146.62	96	9.3
$50,000 to $69,999	2,599.07	117	17.4
$70,000 to $79,999	2,909.33	131	7.6
$80,000 to $99,999	3,138.28	141	12.1
$100,000 or more	3,568.09	160	25.5
HOUSEHOLD TYPE			
Average household	**2,227.46**	**100**	**100.0**
Married couples	2,900.65	130	65.1
Married couples, no children	2,419.28	109	23.1
Married couples, with children	3,245.75	146	36.0
Oldest child under 6	2,608.88	117	5.7
Oldest child 6 to 17	3,245.96	146	18.6
Oldest child 18 or older	3,679.66	165	11.7
Single parent with child under 18	1,697.30	76	4.6
Single person	1,187.61	53	15.8
RACE AND HISPANIC ORIGIN			
Average household	**2,227.46**	**100**	**100.0**
Asian	2,191.17	98	3.4
Black	1,740.01	78	9.4
Hispanic	2,318.83	104	12.0
Non-Hispanic white and other	2,289.47	103	78.7
REGION			
Average household	**2,227.46**	**100**	**100.0**
Northeast	1,910.35	86	16.4
Midwest	2,142.22	96	22.0
South	2,355.80	106	37.8
West	2,382.14	107	23.8
EDUCATION			
Average household	**2,227.46**	**100**	**100.0**
Less than high school graduate	1,575.32	71	10.6
High school graduate	2,130.57	96	25.1
Some college	2,288.09	103	21.7
Associate's degree	2,552.92	115	11.2
College graduate	2,507.12	113	31.5
Bachelor's degree	2,510.12	113	20.2
Master's, professional, doctoral degree	2,501.79	112	11.3

Note: Market shares may not sum to 100.0 because of rounding and missing categories by household type. "Asian" and "black" include Hispanics and non-Hispanics who identify themselves as being of the respective race alone. "Hispanic" includes people of any race who identify themselves as Hispanic. "Other" includes people who identify themselves as non-Hispanic and as Alaska Native, American Indian, Asian (who are also included in the Asian row), Native Hawaiian or other Pacific Islander, as well as non-Hispanics reporting more than one race.
Source: Calculations by New Strategist based on the Bureau of Labor Statistics' 2006 Consumer Expenditure Survey

Global Positioning System Services

Best customers: Householders aged 45 to 74
High-income householders
Married couples without children at home

Customer trends: Average household spending on global positioning systems may
increase as prices fall and more families equip their vehicles with these
convenient devices.

The best customers for global positioning system services are affluent, middle-aged and older married couples. Householders aged 45 to 54 spend 44 percent more than average on this item, while those aged 65 to 74 spend over twice the average amount on GPS services. Householders with incomes of $100,000 or more spend three times the average on this item. Married couples without children at home, most of them empty-nesters, spend more than twice the average on GPS services.

Global positioning system services was newly added to the Consumer Expenditure Survey in 2005. Average household spending on global positioning system services may increase as prices fall and more families equip their vehicles with these convenient devices, but spending may be constrained by the addition of these services to cell phones.

Table 39. Global positioning system services

Total household spending $190,148,800.00
Average household spends   1.60

AGE OF HOUSEHOLDER	AVERAGE HOUSEHOLD SPENDING	BEST CUSTOMERS (index)	BIGGEST CUSTOMERS (market share)
Average household	**$1.60**	**100**	**100.0%**
Under age 25	–	–	–
Aged 25 to 34	0.54	34	5.7
Aged 35 to 44	1.30	81	16.4
Aged 45 to 54	2.31	144	30.0
Aged 55 to 64	1.80	113	17.9
Aged 65 to 74	3.29	206	20.4
Aged 75 or older	1.59	99	9.4

	AVERAGE HOUSEHOLD SPENDING	BEST CUSTOMERS (index)	BIGGEST CUSTOMERS (market share)
HOUSEHOLD INCOME			
Average household	**$1.60**	**100**	**100.0%**
Under $20,000	0.21	13	2.8
$20,000 to $39,999	0.74	46	10.7
$40,000 to $49,999	1.54	96	9.3
$50,000 to $69,999	0.87	54	8.1
$70,000 to $79,999	3.01	188	11.0
$80,000 to $99,999	1.98	124	10.7
$100,000 or more	4.86	304	48.3
HOUSEHOLD TYPE			
Average household	**1.60**	**100**	**100.0**
Married couples	2.51	157	78.4
Married couples, no children	3.52	220	46.8
Married couples, with children	1.63	102	25.2
Oldest child under 6	0.87	54	2.6
Oldest child 6 to 17	2.22	139	17.7
Oldest child 18 or older	1.09	68	4.8
Single parent with child under 18	0.64	40	2.4
Single person	0.61	38	11.3
RACE AND HISPANIC ORIGIN			
Average household	**1.60**	**100**	**100.0**
Asian	1.55	97	3.3
Black	0.33	21	2.5
Hispanic	0.37	23	2.7
Non-Hispanic white and other	1.98	124	94.8
REGION			
Average household	**1.60**	**100**	**100.0**
Northeast	1.67	104	20.0
Midwest	2.26	141	32.3
South	1.66	104	37.1
West	0.75	47	10.4
EDUCATION			
Average household	**1.60**	**100**	**100.0**
Less than high school graduate	0.12	8	1.1
High school graduate	1.40	88	22.9
Some college	1.45	91	19.2
Associate's degree	3.08	193	18.8
College graduate	2.17	136	37.9
Bachelor's degree	1.86	116	20.8
Master's, professional, doctoral degree	2.72	170	17.1

Note: Market shares may not sum to 100.0 because of rounding and missing categories by household type. "Asian" and "black" include Hispanics and non-Hispanics who identify themselves as being of the respective race alone. "Hispanic" includes people of any race who identify themselves as Hispanic. "Other" includes people who identify themselves as non-Hispanic and as Alaska Native, American Indian, Asian (who are also included in the Asian row), Native Hawaiian or other Pacific Islander, as well as non-Hispanics reporting more than one race. "–" means sample is too small to make a reliable estimate.
Source: Calculations by New Strategist based on the Bureau of Labor Statistics' 2006 Consumer Expenditure Survey

Local Transportation on Trips (Including Taxis)

Best customers:	**Householders aged 45 to 74**
	Married couples without children at home
	Married couples with adult children at home
	Asians
	Households in the Northeast and West
	College graduates
Customer trends:	**Spending will climb along with travel, but only if discretionary income rises.**

The most avid travelers spend the most on taxi fares, limousine services, and other local transportation on trips. Householders ranging in age from 45 to 74 spend 17 to 51 percent more than average on this item. Married couples without children at home (most of them empty-nesters) spend 74 percent more than average on taxi fares and local transportation on trips, while those with adult children at home surpass average spending by 23 percent. Asians spend more than double the average on local transportation on trips. Households in the Northeast and West spend, respectively, 44 and 46 percent more than average on this item. College graduates spend more than twice the average on these services.

Average household spending on taxi fares, limousine services, and local transportation on trips fell 39 percent between 2000 and 2006, after adjusting for inflation. Behind the decline was the lackluster recovery following the recession of 2001, which reduced the discretionary income of households and overall travel spending. Average household spending on this item should rise along with travel, but only if discretionary income increases.

Table 40. Local transportation on trips (including taxis)

Total household spending $2,476,688,120.00
Average household spends 20.84

	AVERAGE HOUSEHOLD SPENDING	BEST CUSTOMERS (index)	BIGGEST CUSTOMERS (market share)
AGE OF HOUSEHOLDER			
Average household	**$20.84**	**100**	**100.0%**
Under age 25	7.54	36	2.5
Aged 25 to 34	14.14	68	11.5
Aged 35 to 44	19.52	94	18.9
Aged 45 to 54	24.28	117	24.2
Aged 55 to 64	31.41	151	24.0
Aged 65 to 74	25.87	124	12.3
Aged 75 or older	14.61	70	6.6

	AVERAGE HOUSEHOLD SPENDING	BEST CUSTOMERS (index)	BIGGEST CUSTOMERS (market share)
HOUSEHOLD INCOME			
Average household	**$20.84**	**100**	**100.0%**
Under $20,000	9.06	43	9.5
$20,000 to $39,999	11.09	53	12.3
$40,000 to $49,999	10.56	51	4.9
$50,000 to $69,999	17.09	82	12.2
$70,000 to $79,999	19.80	95	5.6
$80,000 to $99,999	28.32	136	11.7
$100,000 or more	57.32	275	43.8
HOUSEHOLD TYPE			
Average household	**20.84**	**100**	**100.0**
Married couples	26.79	129	64.3
Married couples, no children	36.16	174	36.9
Married couples, with children	20.60	99	24.4
Oldest child under 6	9.13	44	2.1
Oldest child 6 to 17	22.19	106	13.6
Oldest child 18 or older	25.59	123	8.7
Single parent with child under 18	5.16	25	1.5
Single person	18.79	90	26.7
RACE AND HISPANIC ORIGIN			
Average household	**20.84**	**100**	**100.0**
Asian	43.11	207	7.1
Black	6.30	30	3.6
Hispanic	11.32	54	6.2
Non-Hispanic white and other	24.52	118	90.1
REGION			
Average household	**20.84**	**100**	**100.0**
Northeast	30.11	144	27.7
Midwest	18.97	91	20.8
South	11.14	53	19.1
West	30.36	146	32.4
EDUCATION			
Average household	**20.84**	**100**	**100.0**
Less than high school graduate	4.48	21	3.2
High school graduate	9.36	45	11.8
Some college	17.05	82	17.3
Associate's degree	19.82	95	9.3
College graduate	43.54	209	58.4
Bachelor's degree	40.09	192	34.4
Master's, professional, doctoral degree	49.67	238	24.0

Note: Market shares may not sum to 100.0 because of rounding and missing categories by household type. "Asian" and "black" include Hispanics and non-Hispanics who identify themselves as being of the respective race alone. "Hispanic" includes people of any race who identify themselves as Hispanic. "Other" includes people who identify themselves as non-Hispanic and as Alaska Native, American Indian, Asian (who are also included in the Asian row), Native Hawaiian or other Pacific Islander, as well as non-Hispanics reporting more than one race.
Source: Calculations by New Strategist based on the Bureau of Labor Statistics' 2006 Consumer Expenditure Survey

Mass Transit Fares, Intracity

Best customers: Householders aged 25 to 54
Married couples with adult children at home
Asians, Hispanics, and blacks
Households in the Northeast

Customer trends: Spending in this category should stabilize as high gas prices encourage workers to use mass transit instead of driving a car on the daily commute.

Workers in the central cities of the Northeast are the best customers of mass transit. Households in the Northeast spend more than three times the average on intracity mass transit fares and account for 58 percent of the market. Householders aged 25 to 54, most in the workforce, spend 16 to 34 percent more than average on intracity mass transit fares. Blacks and Hispanics spend, respectively, 71 and 90 percent more than average on this item because many live in central cities, and Asians spend more than two-and-one-half times the average on mass transit. Married couples with adult children at home spend 43 percent more than average on this item because they have the most workers in the household.

Average household spending on intracity mass transit fares fell 8 percent between 2000 and 2006, after adjusting for inflation. Behind the decline was the continuing shift of jobs from central cities to suburbs, reducing the use of mass transit. Average household spending on this item should stabilize as higher gas prices encourage workers to use mass transit for their daily commute.

Table 41. Mass transit fares, intracity

Total household spending $6,071,688,870.00
Average household spends   51.09

	AVERAGE HOUSEHOLD SPENDING	BEST CUSTOMERS (index)	BIGGEST CUSTOMERS (market share)
AGE OF HOUSEHOLDER			
Average household	**$51.09**	**100**	**100.0%**
Under age 25	42.69	84	5.7
Aged 25 to 34	62.36	122	20.6
Aged 35 to 44	68.41	134	27.0
Aged 45 to 54	59.16	116	24.1
Aged 55 to 64	49.42	97	15.4
Aged 65 to 74	21.61	42	4.2
Aged 75 or older	16.09	31	3.0

	AVERAGE HOUSEHOLD SPENDING	BEST CUSTOMERS (index)	BIGGEST CUSTOMERS (market share)
HOUSEHOLD INCOME			
Average household	**$51.09**	**100**	**100.0%**
Under $20,000	43.68	85	18.8
$20,000 to $39,999	43.32	85	19.6
$40,000 to $49,999	41.12	80	7.8
$50,000 to $69,999	45.63	89	13.3
$70,000 to $79,999	41.43	81	4.7
$80,000 to $99,999	33.04	65	5.6
$100,000 or more	97.04	190	30.2
HOUSEHOLD TYPE			
Average household	**51.09**	**100**	**100.0**
Married couples	46.39	91	45.4
Married couples, no children	32.99	65	13.7
Married couples, with children	53.53	105	25.9
Oldest child under 6	38.74	76	3.7
Oldest child 6 to 17	48.37	95	12.1
Oldest child 18 or older	72.87	143	10.1
Single parent with child under 18	52.49	103	6.2
Single person	47.43	93	27.5
RACE AND HISPANIC ORIGIN			
Average household	**51.09**	**100**	**100.0**
Asian	132.91	260	9.0
Black	87.56	171	20.6
Hispanic	96.84	190	21.8
Non-Hispanic white and other	38.52	75	57.8
REGION			
Average household	**51.09**	**100**	**100.0**
Northeast	154.65	303	58.0
Midwest	25.64	50	11.5
South	16.33	32	11.4
West	43.93	86	19.1
EDUCATION			
Average household	**51.09**	**100**	**100.0**
Less than high school graduate	54.52	107	15.9
High school graduate	34.13	67	17.5
Some college	31.73	62	13.1
Associate's degree	38.39	75	7.3
College graduate	84.18	165	46.1
Bachelor's degree	83.00	162	29.1
Master's, professional, doctoral degree	86.28	169	17.0

Note: Market shares may not sum to 100.0 because of rounding and missing categories by household type. "Asian" and "black" include Hispanics and non-Hispanics who identify themselves as being of the respective race alone. "Hispanic" includes people of any race who identify themselves as Hispanic. "Other" includes people who identify themselves as non-Hispanic and as Alaska Native, American Indian, Asian (who are also included in the Asian row), Native Hawaiian or other Pacific Islander, as well as non-Hispanics reporting more than one race.
Source: Calculations by New Strategist based on the Bureau of Labor Statistics' 2006 Consumer Expenditure Survey

Motorcycles, New and Used

Best customers: Householders aged 25 to 64
Married couples with school-aged or older children at home
Households in the West

Customer trends: Average household spending on motorcycles may rise along with gasoline prices.

The best customers of motorcycles are middle-aged adults buying fuel-efficient two-wheelers for daily commuting and weekend cruising. Householders aged 25 to 64 spend 30 to 57 percent more than the average on motorcycles and account for 86 percent of the market. Married couples with school-aged or older children at home spend 73 to 104 percent more than average on this item. Households in the West, including sunny southern California, spend almost twice the average on motorcycles.

Average household spending on motorcycles rose 30 percent from 2000 to 2006, after adjusting for inflation. Behind the increase was aging boomers grasping at youth, as well as rising fuel prices. Average household spending on motorcycles should continue to rise along with gasoline prices.

Table 42. Motorcycles, new and used

Total household spending $6,460,305,480.00
Average household spends 54.36

	AVERAGE HOUSEHOLD SPENDING	BEST CUSTOMERS (index)	BIGGEST CUSTOMERS (market share)
AGE OF HOUSEHOLDER			
Average household	**$54.36**	**100**	**100.0%**
Under age 25	46.88	86	5.9
Aged 25 to 34	70.62	130	21.9
Aged 35 to 44	84.61	156	31.4
Aged 45 to 54	85.17	157	32.6
Aged 55 to 64	27.99	51	8.2
Aged 65 to 74	–	–	–
Aged 75 or older	–	–	–

	AVERAGE HOUSEHOLD SPENDING	BEST CUSTOMERS (index)	BIGGEST CUSTOMERS (market share)
HOUSEHOLD INCOME			
Average household	**$54.36**	**100**	**100.0%**
Under $20,000	10.72	20	4.3
$20,000 to $39,999	13.37	25	5.7
$40,000 to $49,999	50.93	94	9.0
$50,000 to $69,999	55.57	102	15.2
$70,000 to $79,999	25.48	47	2.7
$80,000 to $99,999	155.69	286	24.7
$100,000 or more	137.05	252	40.1
HOUSEHOLD TYPE			
Average household	**54.36**	**100**	**100.0**
Married couples	78.86	145	72.5
Married couples, no children	66.97	123	26.2
Married couples, with children	83.42	153	37.9
Oldest child under 6	15.77	29	1.4
Oldest child 6 to 17	93.93	173	22.1
Oldest child 18 or older	110.70	204	14.5
Single parent with child under 18	11.63	21	1.3
Single person	6.37	12	3.5
RACE AND HISPANIC ORIGIN			
Average household	**54.36**	**100**	**100.0**
Asian	–	–	–
Black	36.05	66	8.0
Hispanic	49.69	91	10.5
Non-Hispanic white and other	57.85	106	81.5
REGION			
Average household	**54.36**	**100**	**100.0**
Northeast	38.09	70	13.4
Midwest	43.59	80	18.4
South	37.76	69	24.8
West	106.17	195	43.4
EDUCATION			
Average household	**54.36**	**100**	**100.0**
Less than high school graduate	15.59	29	4.3
High school graduate	69.65	128	33.6
Some college	75.46	139	29.4
Associate's degree	65.59	121	11.8
College graduate	40.89	75	21.0
Bachelor's degree	39.08	72	12.9
Master's, professional, doctoral degree	44.09	81	8.2

Note: Market shares may not sum to 100.0 because of rounding and missing categories by household type. "Asian" and "black" include Hispanics and non-Hispanics who identify themselves as being of the respective race alone. "Hispanic" includes people of any race who identify themselves as Hispanic. "Other" includes people who identify themselves as non-Hispanic and as Alaska Native, American Indian, Asian (who are also included in the Asian row), Native Hawaiian or other Pacific Islander, as well as non-Hispanics reporting more than one race. "–" means sample is too small to make a reliable estimate.
Source: Calculations by New Strategist based on the Bureau of Labor Statistics' 2006 Consumer Expenditure Survey

Oil Change, Lube, and Oil Filters

Best customers: Householders aged 35 to 64
Married couples

Customer trends: Spending in this category may decline as boomers become empty-nesters and reduce the number of vehicles they own.

Middle-aged married couples are the biggest spenders on oil changes, lubes, and oil filters. Householders ranging in age from 35 to 64 spend 10 to 19 percent more than average on this item. Married couples, particularly those with children, own more cars than average, which boosts spending on this item. Overall, married couples spend 25 percent more than average on oil changes. Couples with adult children at home (many with three cars) spend 39 percent more than average on this item.

Average household spending on oil changes, lubes, and oil filters fell 3 percent between 2000 and 2006, after adjusting for inflation. Behind the decline is increasing competition from discount oil change shops and big-box retailers. Average household spending on this item may continue to decline as boomers become empty-nesters and reduce the number of vehicles they own.

Table 43. Oil change, lube, and oil filters

Total household spending $7,947,031,410.00
Average household spends 66.87

	AVERAGE HOUSEHOLD SPENDING	BEST CUSTOMERS (index)	BIGGEST CUSTOMERS (market share)
AGE OF HOUSEHOLDER			
Average household	**$66.87**	**100**	**100.0%**
Under age 25	39.71	59	4.1
Aged 25 to 34	61.59	92	15.6
Aged 35 to 44	73.59	110	22.2
Aged 45 to 54	79.60	119	24.7
Aged 55 to 64	77.74	116	18.5
Aged 65 to 74	64.58	97	9.6
Aged 75 or older	37.89	57	5.4

	AVERAGE HOUSEHOLD SPENDING	BEST CUSTOMERS (index)	BIGGEST CUSTOMERS (market share)
HOUSEHOLD INCOME			
Average household	**$66.87**	**100**	**100.0%**
Under $20,000	31.36	47	10.3
$20,000 to $39,999	49.54	74	17.2
$40,000 to $49,999	64.12	96	9.2
$50,000 to $69,999	75.68	113	16.8
$70,000 to $79,999	88.61	133	7.8
$80,000 to $99,999	96.31	144	12.4
$100,000 or more	110.58	165	26.3
HOUSEHOLD TYPE			
Average household	**66.87**	**100**	**100.0**
Married couples	83.66	125	62.6
Married couples, no children	81.03	121	25.8
Married couples, with children	87.38	131	32.3
Oldest child under 6	77.18	115	5.6
Oldest child 6 to 17	88.30	132	16.9
Oldest child 18 or older	92.71	139	9.9
Single parent with child under 18	51.60	77	4.7
Single person	45.64	68	20.2
RACE AND HISPANIC ORIGIN			
Average household	**66.87**	**100**	**100.0**
Asian	65.40	98	3.4
Black	45.68	68	8.2
Hispanic	54.53	82	9.4
Non-Hispanic white and other	71.98	108	82.5
REGION			
Average household	**66.87**	**100**	**100.0**
Northeast	56.41	84	16.2
Midwest	72.67	109	24.9
South	66.21	99	35.4
West	70.99	106	23.6
EDUCATION			
Average household	**66.87**	**100**	**100.0**
Less than high school graduate	33.94	51	7.6
High school graduate	55.39	83	21.7
Some college	66.47	99	21.0
Associate's degree	76.10	114	11.1
College graduate	92.30	138	38.6
Bachelor's degree	89.56	134	24.0
Master's, professional, doctoral degree	97.16	145	14.6

Note: Market shares may not sum to 100.0 because of rounding and missing categories by household type. "Asian" and "black" include Hispanics and non-Hispanics who identify themselves as being of the respective race alone. "Hispanic" includes people of any race who identify themselves as Hispanic. "Other" includes people who identify themselves as non-Hispanic and as Alaska Native, American Indian, Asian (who are also included in the Asian row), Native Hawaiian or other Pacific Islander, as well as non-Hispanics reporting more than one race.
Source: Calculations by New Strategist based on the Bureau of Labor Statistics' 2006 Consumer Expenditure Survey

Parking Fees (Excluding Residence)

Best customers: Householders aged 25 to 64
High-income households
Married couples
Households in the Northeast
College graduates

Customer trends: Spending in this category should continue to rise as localities recoup infrastructure costs by raising parking fees.

The biggest spenders on parking fees (excluding residential parking) are affluent, educated, middle-aged married couples out and about with their children and grandchildren—many of them shopping, visiting museums, going to concerts, and participating in other events. Married couples with preschoolers spend 70 percent more than average on this item. Couples with older children at home spend 13 to 17 percent more. Households with incomes of $100,000 or more spend more than three times the average on parking fees. College graduates (who dominate the affluent) spend more than twice the average and account for 61 percent of the market. Households in the Northeast spend 57 percent more than average on parking fees.

Average household spending on parking fees rose 62 percent between 2000 and 2006, after adjusting for inflation. Spending on parking fees should continue to rise as localities recover infrastructure costs by raising parking fees.

Table 44. Parking fees (excluding residence)

Total household spending $8,291,676,110.00
Average household spends   69.77

	AVERAGE HOUSEHOLD SPENDING	BEST CUSTOMERS (index)	BIGGEST CUSTOMERS (market share)
AGE OF HOUSEHOLDER			
Average household	**$69.77**	**100**	**100.0%**
Under age 25	71.80	103	7.1
Aged 25 to 34	76.40	110	18.5
Aged 35 to 44	80.90	116	23.4
Aged 45 to 54	77.16	111	23.0
Aged 55 to 64	84.78	122	19.4
Aged 65 to 74	42.00	60	6.0
Aged 75 or older	20.16	29	2.7

	AVERAGE HOUSEHOLD SPENDING	BEST CUSTOMERS (index)	BIGGEST CUSTOMERS (market share)
HOUSEHOLD INCOME			
Average household	**$69.77**	**100**	**100.0%**
Under $20,000	27.83	40	8.8
$20,000 to $39,999	29.29	42	9.7
$40,000 to $49,999	43.98	63	6.1
$50,000 to $69,999	59.99	86	12.8
$70,000 to $79,999	56.94	82	4.8
$80,000 to $99,999	74.68	107	9.2
$100,000 or more	213.26	306	48.6
HOUSEHOLD TYPE			
Average household	**69.77**	**100**	**100.0**
Married couples	81.18	116	58.2
Married couples, no children	79.55	114	24.3
Married couples, with children	87.72	126	31.1
Oldest child under 6	118.74	170	8.3
Oldest child 6 to 17	79.14	113	14.5
Oldest child 18 or older	81.93	117	8.4
Single parent with child under 18	43.93	63	3.8
Single person	59.95	86	25.5
RACE AND HISPANIC ORIGIN			
Average household	**69.77**	**100**	**100.0**
Asian	100.32	144	5.0
Black	30.31	43	5.2
Hispanic	39.88	57	6.6
Non-Hispanic white and other	80.38	115	88.3
REGION			
Average household	**69.77**	**100**	**100.0**
Northeast	109.76	157	30.1
Midwest	77.74	111	25.5
South	36.64	53	18.8
West	80.34	115	25.6
EDUCATION			
Average household	**69.77**	**100**	**100.0**
Less than high school graduate	10.14	15	2.2
High school graduate	26.74	38	10.0
Some college	58.13	83	17.6
Associate's degree	62.69	90	8.8
College graduate	153.13	219	61.4
Bachelor's degree	127.44	183	32.7
Master's, professional, doctoral degree	198.82	285	28.7

Note: Market shares may not sum to 100.0 because of rounding and missing categories by household type. "Asian" and "black" include Hispanics and non-Hispanics who identify themselves as being of the respective race alone. "Hispanic" includes people of any race who identify themselves as Hispanic. "Other" includes people who identify themselves as non-Hispanic and as Alaska Native, American Indian, Asian (who are also included in the Asian row), Native Hawaiian or other Pacific Islander, as well as non-Hispanics reporting more than one race.
Source: Calculations by New Strategist based on the Bureau of Labor Statistics' 2006 Consumer Expenditure Survey

Ship Fares

Best customers:	Householders aged 45 or older
	Married couples without children at home
	Married couples with adult children at home
Customer trends:	Spending in this category will continue to grow as boomers fill the peak-spending lifestage.

The biggest spenders on ship fares are older Americans. Householders aged 45 or older spend more than average on this item, with spending peaking at 68 percent above average among those aged 75 or older. Married couples without children at home (most of them empty-nesters) spend 78 percent more than average on cruises and account for 38 percent of household spending on this item. Married couples with adult children at home spend 63 percent more than average on ship fares.

Average household spending on ship fares rose 28 percent between 2000 and 2006, after adjusting for inflation. Average household spending on ship fares should grow substantially in the years ahead as boomers fill the peak-spending lifestage.

Table 45. Ship fares

Total household spending $6,538,741,860.00
Average household spends   55.02

	AVERAGE HOUSEHOLD SPENDING	BEST CUSTOMERS (index)	BIGGEST CUSTOMERS (market share)
AGE OF HOUSEHOLDER			
Average household	**$55.02**	**100**	**100.0%**
Under age 25	3.36	6	0.4
Aged 25 to 34	43.11	78	13.2
Aged 35 to 44	47.93	87	17.6
Aged 45 to 54	68.51	125	25.9
Aged 55 to 64	56.29	102	16.3
Aged 65 to 74	59.62	108	10.7
Aged 75 or older	92.35	168	15.9

	AVERAGE HOUSEHOLD SPENDING	BEST CUSTOMERS (index)	BIGGEST CUSTOMERS (market share)
HOUSEHOLD INCOME			
Average household	**$55.02**	**100**	**100.0%**
Under $20,000	13.74	25	5.5
$20,000 to $39,999	12.35	22	5.2
$40,000 to $49,999	23.28	42	4.1
$50,000 to $69,999	79.18	144	21.4
$70,000 to $79,999	33.81	61	3.6
$80,000 to $99,999	102.77	187	16.1
$100,000 or more	152.61	277	44.1
HOUSEHOLD TYPE			
Average household	**55.02**	**100**	**100.0**
Married couples	74.69	136	67.9
Married couples, no children	97.77	178	37.8
Married couples, with children	59.12	107	26.6
Oldest child under 6	16.76	30	1.5
Oldest child 6 to 17	58.32	106	13.5
Oldest child 18 or older	89.43	163	11.6
Single parent with child under 18	26.46	48	2.9
Single person	33.55	61	18.1
RACE AND HISPANIC ORIGIN			
Average household	**55.02**	**100**	**100.0**
Asian	70.57	128	4.4
Black	28.24	51	6.2
Hispanic	28.08	51	5.9
Non-Hispanic white and other	63.32	115	88.2
REGION			
Average household	**55.02**	**100**	**100.0**
Northeast	46.12	84	16.1
Midwest	44.48	81	18.5
South	39.29	71	25.5
West	98.81	180	39.9
EDUCATION			
Average household	**55.02**	**100**	**100.0**
Less than high school graduate	13.22	24	3.6
High school graduate	33.72	61	16.1
Some college	56.17	102	21.6
Associate's degree	44.76	81	7.9
College graduate	99.99	182	50.8
Bachelor's degree	94.83	172	30.9
Master's, professional, doctoral degree	109.17	198	20.0

Note: Market shares may not sum to 100.0 because of rounding and missing categories by household type. "Asian" and "black" include Hispanics and non-Hispanics who identify themselves as being of the respective race alone. "Hispanic" includes people of any race who identify themselves as Hispanic. "Other" includes people who identify themselves as non-Hispanic and as Alaska Native, American Indian, Asian (who are also included in the Asian row), Native Hawaiian or other Pacific Islander, as well as non-Hispanics reporting more than one race.
Source: Calculations by New Strategist based on the Bureau of Labor Statistics' 2006 Consumer Expenditure Survey

Taxi Fares and Limousine Service in Home Town

Best customers:	Householders aged 45 to 54
	Married couples with adult children at home
	People living alone
	Households in the Northeast
Customer trends:	Spending in this category may fall if mass transit improves.

Households in the highly urbanized Northeast are the best customers of taxi and limousine services. They spend well over twice the average on this item and control 44 percent of the market. Much of this spending probably occurs in New York City, where many households do not own cars. Householders aged 45 to 54 spend 68 percent more than average on this item. Married couples with adult children at home spend 76 percent more than average on taxis, and householders who live alone spend 26 percent more than average.

Average household spending on taxi fares and limousine services rose 29 percent between 2000 and 2006, after adjusting for inflation. One factor that may account for this increase is the growing use of taxis rather than mass transit for the commute to work.

Table 46. Taxi fares and limousine service in home town

Total household spending $1,648,352,410.00
Average household spends   13.87

	AVERAGE HOUSEHOLD SPENDING	BEST CUSTOMERS (index)	BIGGEST CUSTOMERS (market share)
AGE OF HOUSEHOLDER			
Average household	**$13.87**	**100**	**100.0%**
Under age 25	9.79	71	4.9
Aged 25 to 34	16.33	118	19.9
Aged 35 to 44	10.90	79	15.8
Aged 45 to 54	23.30	168	34.9
Aged 55 to 64	8.60	62	9.9
Aged 65 to 74	11.58	83	8.3
Aged 75 or older	9.72	70	6.6

	AVERAGE HOUSEHOLD SPENDING	BEST CUSTOMERS (index)	BIGGEST CUSTOMERS (market share)
HOUSEHOLD INCOME			
Average household	**$13.87**	**100**	**100.0%**
Under $20,000	7.88	57	12.5
$20,000 to $39,999	10.40	75	17.4
$40,000 to $49,999	14.18	102	9.8
$50,000 to $69,999	8.88	64	9.5
$70,000 to $79,999	18.65	134	7.9
$80,000 to $99,999	12.69	91	7.9
$100,000 or more	29.09	210	33.4
HOUSEHOLD TYPE			
Average household	**13.87**	**100**	**100.0**
Married couples	11.54	83	41.6
Married couples, no children	9.32	67	14.3
Married couples, with children	12.44	90	22.2
Oldest child under 6	4.78	34	1.7
Oldest child 6 to 17	9.03	65	8.3
Oldest child 18 or older	24.44	176	12.5
Single parent with child under 18	10.47	75	4.6
Single person	17.43	126	37.2
RACE AND HISPANIC ORIGIN			
Average household	**13.87**	**100**	**100.0**
Asian	14.17	102	3.5
Black	10.21	74	8.8
Hispanic	18.24	132	15.1
Non-Hispanic white and other	13.76	99	76.0
REGION			
Average household	**13.87**	**100**	**100.0**
Northeast	32.02	231	44.2
Midwest	10.47	75	17.3
South	5.87	42	15.1
West	15.01	108	24.1
EDUCATION			
Average household	**13.87**	**100**	**100.0**
Less than high school graduate	10.25	74	11.0
High school graduate	7.39	53	14.0
Some college	13.98	101	21.3
Associate's degree	12.32	89	8.7
College graduate	22.11	159	44.6
Bachelor's degree	20.16	145	26.0
Master's, professional, doctoral degree	25.62	185	18.6

Note: Market shares may not sum to 100.0 because of rounding and missing categories by household type. "Asian" and "black" include Hispanics and non-Hispanics who identify themselves as being of the respective race alone. "Hispanic" includes people of any race who identify themselves as Hispanic. "Other" includes people who identify themselves as non-Hispanic and as Alaska Native, American Indian, Asian (who are also included in the Asian row), Native Hawaiian or other Pacific Islander, as well as non-Hispanics reporting more than one race.
Source: Calculations by New Strategist based on the Bureau of Labor Statistics' 2006 Consumer Expenditure Survey

Tires (Purchased, Replaced, Installed)

Best customers: Householders aged 35 to 54
                             Married couples with school-aged or older children at home

Customer trends: Spending in this category will decline as competition drives prices down and as
                             boomers reduce the number of vehicles they own.

The best customers of tires are households with the most cars—those headed by middle-aged married couples, particularly households with teenage or adult children at home. Householders aged 35 to 54, many with teens and young adults at home, spend 18 to 28 percent more than the average household on tires and account for over half the market. Married couples with school-aged or older children at home spend 44 to 73 percent more than average on tires.

Average household spending on tires remained essentially flat between 2000 and 2006, after adjusting for inflation. Behind the minimal 1 percent gain in spending was increased competition from discounters, which lowered prices. Average household spending will fall in the years ahead as boomers reduce the number of vehicles they own.

Table 47. Tires (purchased, replaced, installed)

| Total household spending | $12,280,047,190.00 |
| Average household spends | 103.33 |

	AVERAGE HOUSEHOLD SPENDING	BEST CUSTOMERS (index)	BIGGEST CUSTOMERS (market share)
AGE OF HOUSEHOLDER			
Average household	**$103.33**	**100**	**100.0%**
Under age 25	67.49	65	4.5
Aged 25 to 34	99.33	96	16.2
Aged 35 to 44	121.48	118	23.7
Aged 45 to 54	132.73	128	26.7
Aged 55 to 64	107.13	104	16.5
Aged 65 to 74	87.94	85	8.4
Aged 75 or older	42.97	42	3.9

	AVERAGE HOUSEHOLD SPENDING	BEST CUSTOMERS (index)	BIGGEST CUSTOMERS (market share)
HOUSEHOLD INCOME			
Average household	**$103.33**	**100**	**100.0%**
Under $20,000	40.24	39	8.5
$20,000 to $39,999	64.36	62	14.4
$40,000 to $49,999	89.52	87	8.3
$50,000 to $69,999	124.20	120	17.9
$70,000 to $79,999	133.87	130	7.6
$80,000 to $99,999	161.75	157	13.5
$100,000 or more	193.01	187	29.7
HOUSEHOLD TYPE			
Average household	**103.33**	**100**	**100.0**
Married couples	137.03	133	66.3
Married couples, no children	122.41	118	25.2
Married couples, with children	154.03	149	36.9
Oldest child under 6	98.26	95	4.6
Oldest child 6 to 17	178.39	173	22.0
Oldest child 18 or older	148.34	144	10.2
Single parent with child under 18	78.01	75	4.6
Single person	54.48	53	15.6
RACE AND HISPANIC ORIGIN			
Average household	**103.33**	**100**	**100.0**
Asian	71.73	69	2.4
Black	71.30	69	8.3
Hispanic	86.03	83	9.6
Non-Hispanic white and other	111.06	107	82.3
REGION			
Average household	**103.33**	**100**	**100.0**
Northeast	88.33	85	16.4
Midwest	93.75	91	20.8
South	105.35	102	36.4
West	122.86	119	26.4
EDUCATION			
Average household	**103.33**	**100**	**100.0**
Less than high school graduate	61.47	59	8.9
High school graduate	83.15	80	21.1
Some college	99.55	96	20.4
Associate's degree	132.47	128	12.5
College graduate	137.28	133	37.2
Bachelor's degree	144.79	140	25.1
Master's, professional, doctoral degree	123.94	120	12.1

Note: Market shares may not sum to 100.0 because of rounding and missing categories by household type. "Asian" and "black" include Hispanics and non-Hispanics who identify themselves as being of the respective race alone. "Hispanic" includes people of any race who identify themselves as Hispanic. "Other" includes people who identify themselves as non-Hispanic and as Alaska Native, American Indian, Asian (who are also included in the Asian row), Native Hawaiian or other Pacific Islander, as well as non-Hispanics reporting more than one race.
Source: Calculations by New Strategist based on the Bureau of Labor Statistics' 2006 Consumer Expenditure Survey

Towing Charges

Best customers: Householders aged 25 to 54
                          Married couples with adult children at home
                          Single parents
                          Hispanics

Customer trends: Spending in this category should fall as boomers age and reduce the number of vehicles they own.

The biggest spenders on towing charges are householders who do not spend on automobile service clubs (which usually cover towing charges). They are also the heads of the largest households and most likely to own multiple and used vehicles, with frequent breakdowns. Householders aged 25 to 54 spend 15 to 36 percent more than the average on towing charges. Married couples with adult children at home spend 72 percent more than average on towing charges, while single parents spend 63 percent more. Hispanics, who tend to have the largest families, spend 47 percent more than average on towing charges.

Average household spending on towing charges fell 7 percent between 2000 and 2006, after adjusting for inflation, reflecting the increasing reliability of vehicles and tires. Average household spending on this item may decline as boomers age and reduce the number of vehicles they own.

Table 48. Towing charges

Total household spending $607,287,730.00
Average household spends   5.11

	AVERAGE HOUSEHOLD SPENDING	BEST CUSTOMERS (index)	BIGGEST CUSTOMERS (market share)
AGE OF HOUSEHOLDER			
Average household	**$5.11**	**100**	**100.0%**
Under age 25	5.24	103	7.0
Aged 25 to 34	5.88	115	19.4
Aged 35 to 44	6.19	121	24.4
Aged 45 to 54	6.97	136	28.3
Aged 55 to 64	4.17	82	13.0
Aged 65 to 74	2.59	51	5.0
Aged 75 or older	1.49	29	2.8

	AVERAGE HOUSEHOLD SPENDING	BEST CUSTOMERS (index)	BIGGEST CUSTOMERS (market share)
HOUSEHOLD INCOME			
Average household	**$5.11**	**100**	**100.0%**
Under $20,000	3.48	68	14.9
$20,000 to $39,999	4.58	90	20.8
$40,000 to $49,999	6.03	118	11.4
$50,000 to $69,999	4.61	90	13.4
$70,000 to $79,999	8.85	173	10.1
$80,000 to $99,999	4.47	87	7.5
$100,000 or more	7.01	137	21.8
HOUSEHOLD TYPE			
Average household	**5.11**	**100**	**100.0**
Married couples	5.56	109	54.4
Married couples, no children	2.92	57	12.2
Married couples, with children	6.42	126	31.1
Oldest child under 6	4.44	87	4.2
Oldest child 6 to 17	5.86	115	14.6
Oldest child 18 or older	8.77	172	12.2
Single parent with child under 18	8.33	163	9.9
Single person	3.15	62	18.3
RACE AND HISPANIC ORIGIN			
Average household	**5.11**	**100**	**100.0**
Asian	3.18	62	2.1
Black	5.63	110	13.2
Hispanic	7.51	147	16.9
Non-Hispanic white and other	4.66	91	69.9
REGION			
Average household	**5.11**	**100**	**100.0**
Northeast	4.72	92	17.7
Midwest	5.69	111	25.5
South	3.97	78	27.8
West	6.69	131	29.1
EDUCATION			
Average household	**5.11**	**100**	**100.0**
Less than high school graduate	4.95	97	14.5
High school graduate	3.70	72	19.0
Some college	6.52	128	27.0
Associate's degree	5.80	114	11.1
College graduate	5.22	102	28.6
Bachelor's degree	4.78	94	16.7
Master's, professional, doctoral degree	6.00	117	11.8

Note: Market shares may not sum to 100.0 because of rounding and missing categories by household type. "Asian" and "black" include Hispanics and non-Hispanics who identify themselves as being of the respective race alone. "Hispanic" includes people of any race who identify themselves as Hispanic. "Other" includes people who identify themselves as non-Hispanic and as Alaska Native, American Indian, Asian (who are also included in the Asian row), Native Hawaiian or other Pacific Islander, as well as non-Hispanics reporting more than one race.
Source: Calculations by New Strategist based on the Bureau of Labor Statistics' 2006 Consumer Expenditure Survey

Train Fares, Intercity

Best customers: Householders aged 35 to 64
                   Married couples without children at home
                   Married couples with adult children at home
                   Households in the West

Customer trends: Average household spending may continue to decline unless train service
                   improves.

Middle-aged and older Americans are the best customers of intercity train fares. Householders aged 35 to 64 spend 15 to 35 percent more than average on intercity train tickets. Married couples without children at home (most of them empty-nesters) spend 49 percent more than average on intercity train fares, while those with adult children at home spend 59 percent more than average. Households in the West spend 60 percent more than average on intercity train fares.

Average household spending on intercity train fares fell 34 percent between 2000 and 2006, after adjusting for inflation. Behind the decline is the increasingly limited train service available in the United States. Unless train service improves, average household spending on this item is likely to continue to decline.

Table 49. Train fares, intercity

Total household spending $1,935,952,470.00
Average household spends   16.29

	AVERAGE HOUSEHOLD SPENDING	BEST CUSTOMERS (index)	BIGGEST CUSTOMERS (market share)
AGE OF HOUSEHOLDER			
Average household	**$16.29**	**100**	**100.0%**
Under age 25	5.77	35	2.4
Aged 25 to 34	12.18	75	12.6
Aged 35 to 44	18.75	115	23.2
Aged 45 to 54	20.62	127	26.3
Aged 55 to 64	21.94	135	21.5
Aged 65 to 74	13.04	80	7.9
Aged 75 or older	10.39	64	6.0

	AVERAGE HOUSEHOLD SPENDING	BEST CUSTOMERS (index)	BIGGEST CUSTOMERS (market share)
HOUSEHOLD INCOME			
Average household	**$16.29**	**100**	**100.0%**
Under $20,000	5.78	35	7.8
$20,000 to $39,999	10.13	62	14.4
$40,000 to $49,999	9.59	59	5.7
$50,000 to $69,999	10.59	65	9.7
$70,000 to $79,999	17.53	108	6.3
$80,000 to $99,999	19.38	119	10.3
$100,000 or more	47.02	289	45.9
HOUSEHOLD TYPE			
Average household	**16.29**	**100**	**100.0**
Married couples	20.26	124	62.2
Married couples, no children	24.27	149	31.7
Married couples, with children	17.81	109	27.0
Oldest child under 6	9.95	61	3.0
Oldest child 6 to 17	16.32	100	12.8
Oldest child 18 or older	25.82	159	11.3
Single parent with child under 18	6.09	37	2.3
Single person	13.91	85	25.3
RACE AND HISPANIC ORIGIN			
Average household	**16.29**	**100**	**100.0**
Asian	27.20	167	5.8
Black	9.35	57	6.9
Hispanic	8.56	53	6.0
Non-Hispanic white and other	18.52	114	87.1
REGION			
Average household	**16.29**	**100**	**100.0**
Northeast	16.92	104	19.9
Midwest	15.48	95	21.8
South	10.40	64	22.8
West	26.06	160	35.6
EDUCATION			
Average household	**16.29**	**100**	**100.0**
Less than high school graduate	4.39	27	4.0
High school graduate	9.03	55	14.5
Some college	14.98	92	19.4
Associate's degree	16.26	100	9.7
College graduate	30.45	187	52.3
Bachelor's degree	26.75	164	29.4
Master's, professional, doctoral degree	37.02	227	22.9

Note: Market shares may not sum to 100.0 because of rounding and missing categories by household type. "Asian" and "black" include Hispanics and non-Hispanics who identify themselves as being of the respective race alone. "Hispanic" includes people of any race who identify themselves as Hispanic. "Other" includes people who identify themselves as non-Hispanic and as Alaska Native, American Indian, Asian (who are also included in the Asian row), Native Hawaiian or other Pacific Islander, as well as non-Hispanics reporting more than one race.
Source: Calculations by New Strategist based on the Bureau of Labor Statistics' 2006 Consumer Expenditure Survey

Truck Lease Payments

Best customers: Householders aged 35 to 44

Married couples with children under age 18

Customer trends: Spending in this category will fluctuate depending on vehicle financing incentives.

The best customers of truck leasing are married couples with children, leasing a pickup, minivan, or sport utility vehicle (all are considered trucks). Householders aged 35 to 44 spend 71 percent more than average on truck lease payments. Married couples with children under age 18 at home spend well over twice the average on truck lease payments.

Average household spending on truck lease payments fell a substantial 37 percent between 2000 and 2006, after adjusting for inflation. Behind the spending decline was the shift to buying rather than leasing as automotive dealers offered no-interest loans and other purchasing incentives. Spending on leasing will continue to fluctuate, depending on dealer incentives.

Table 50. Truck lease payments

Total household spending $12,974,090,310.00
Average household spends 109.17

	AVERAGE HOUSEHOLD SPENDING	BEST CUSTOMERS (index)	BIGGEST CUSTOMERS (market share)
AGE OF HOUSEHOLDER			
Average household	**$109.17**	**100**	**100.0%**
Under age 25	50.14	46	3.2
Aged 25 to 34	118.65	109	18.4
Aged 35 to 44	186.41	171	34.4
Aged 45 to 54	108.16	99	20.6
Aged 55 to 64	128.76	118	18.8
Aged 65 to 74	40.16	37	3.6
Aged 75 or older	11.95	11	1.0

	AVERAGE HOUSEHOLD SPENDING	BEST CUSTOMERS (index)	BIGGEST CUSTOMERS (market share)
HOUSEHOLD INCOME			
Average household	**$109.17**	**100**	**100.0%**
Under $20,000	24.25	22	4.9
$20,000 to $39,999	46.55	43	9.9
$40,000 to $49,999	57.09	52	5.0
$50,000 to $69,999	151.05	138	20.6
$70,000 to $79,999	145.11	133	7.8
$80,000 to $99,999	173.25	159	13.7
$100,000 or more	261.83	240	38.2
HOUSEHOLD TYPE			
Average household	**109.17**	**100**	**100.0**
Married couples	180.93	166	82.9
Married couples, no children	139.67	128	27.2
Married couples, with children	220.52	202	49.9
Oldest child under 6	307.51	282	13.7
Oldest child 6 to 17	242.78	222	28.4
Oldest child 18 or older	121.26	111	7.9
Single parent with child under 18	67.88	62	3.8
Single person	29.20	27	7.9
RACE AND HISPANIC ORIGIN			
Average household	**109.17**	**100**	**100.0**
Asian	162.56	149	5.1
Black	81.48	75	9.0
Hispanic	91.17	84	9.6
Non-Hispanic white and other	116.28	107	81.6
REGION			
Average household	**109.17**	**100**	**100.0**
Northeast	142.72	131	25.0
Midwest	165.25	151	34.7
South	71.70	66	23.5
West	82.73	76	16.8
EDUCATION			
Average household	**109.17**	**100**	**100.0**
Less than high school graduate	29.16	27	4.0
High school graduate	88.19	81	21.2
Some college	87.88	80	17.0
Associate's degree	89.15	82	8.0
College graduate	194.59	178	49.9
Bachelor's degree	193.55	177	31.7
Master's, professional, doctoral degree	196.44	180	18.1

Note: Market shares may not sum to 100.0 because of rounding and missing categories by household type. "Asian" and "black" include Hispanics and non-Hispanics who identify themselves as being of the respective race alone. "Hispanic" includes people of any race who identify themselves as Hispanic. "Other" includes people who identify themselves as non-Hispanic and as Alaska Native, American Indian, Asian (who are also included in the Asian row), Native Hawaiian or other Pacific Islander, as well as non-Hispanics reporting more than one race.
Source: Calculations by New Strategist based on the Bureau of Labor Statistics' 2006 Consumer Expenditure Survey

Trucks, New

Best customers: Householders aged 25 to 34

                                       Married couples

Customer trends: Spending in this category may decline because of surging gas prices and aging boomers.

The best customers of new trucks (a category that includes minivans, sport utility vehicles, and pickups) are young married couples, many with children. Householders aged 25 to 34 spend 41 percent more than average on new trucks. Married couples with children at home spend 76 percent more than average on this item, while couples without children at home spend 34 percent more.

Average household spending on new trucks climbed 16 percent between 2000 and 2006, after adjusting for inflation. Behind the increase was the popularity of sport utility vehicles for families with children. Spending on new trucks may decline in the years ahead because of surging gas prices. Also, as boomers become empty-nesters, they are likely to replace their family-sized trucks with smaller, more fuel-efficient cars.

Table 51. Trucks, new

Total household spending $111,145,538,890.00
Average household spends   935.23

	AVERAGE HOUSEHOLD SPENDING	BEST CUSTOMERS (index)	BIGGEST CUSTOMERS (market share)
AGE OF HOUSEHOLDER			
Average household	**$935.23**	**100**	**100.0%**
Under age 25	558.55	60	4.1
Aged 25 to 34	1,318.52	141	23.8
Aged 35 to 44	1,075.38	115	23.2
Aged 45 to 54	936.53	100	20.8
Aged 55 to 64	1,014.90	109	17.3
Aged 65 to 74	927.43	99	9.8
Aged 75 or older	97.06	10	1.0

	AVERAGE HOUSEHOLD SPENDING	BEST CUSTOMERS (index)	BIGGEST CUSTOMERS (market share)
HOUSEHOLD INCOME			
Average household	**$935.23**	**100**	**100.0%**
Under $20,000	116.45	12	2.7
$20,000 to $39,999	483.99	52	12.0
$40,000 to $49,999	373.54	40	3.8
$50,000 to $69,999	989.50	106	15.7
$70,000 to $79,999	1,371.04	147	8.6
$80,000 to $99,999	1,576.10	169	14.5
$100,000 or more	2,541.21	272	43.2
HOUSEHOLD TYPE			
Average household	**935.23**	**100**	**100.0**
Married couples	1,463.39	156	78.2
Married couples, no children	1,252.80	134	28.5
Married couples, with children	1,649.18	176	43.6
Oldest child under 6	1,822.97	195	9.5
Oldest child 6 to 17	1,848.48	198	25.2
Oldest child 18 or older	1,173.07	125	8.9
Single parent with child under 18	400.71	43	2.6
Single person	213.60	23	6.8
RACE AND HISPANIC ORIGIN			
Average household	**935.23**	**100**	**100.0**
Asian	1,015.86	109	3.7
Black	655.09	70	8.4
Hispanic	1,062.66	114	13.1
Non-Hispanic white and other	958.61	102	78.5
REGION			
Average household	**935.23**	**100**	**100.0**
Northeast	695.20	74	14.2
Midwest	736.22	79	18.0
South	1,027.82	110	39.3
West	1,198.12	128	28.5
EDUCATION			
Average household	**935.23**	**100**	**100.0**
Less than high school graduate	369.65	40	5.9
High school graduate	813.99	87	22.8
Some college	1,072.82	115	24.3
Associate's degree	972.60	104	10.1
College graduate	1,233.68	132	36.9
Bachelor's degree	1,254.41	134	24.0
Master's, professional, doctoral degree	1,196.84	128	12.9

Note: Market shares may not sum to 100.0 because of rounding and missing categories by household type. "Asian" and "black" include Hispanics and non-Hispanics who identify themselves as being of the respective race alone. "Hispanic" includes people of any race who identify themselves as Hispanic. "Other" includes people who identify themselves as non-Hispanic and as Alaska Native, American Indian, Asian (who are also included in the Asian row), Native Hawaiian or other Pacific Islander, as well as non-Hispanics reporting more than one race.
Source: Calculations by New Strategist based on the Bureau of Labor Statistics' 2006 Consumer Expenditure Survey

Trucks, Used

Best customers:	**Householders aged 35 to 44**
	Married couples with children at home
	Hispanics
	Households in the West
Customer trends:	**Spending in this category may fall as gas prices encourage consumers to buy cars.**

The best customers of used trucks (a category that includes minivans, sport utility vehicles, and pickups) are married couples with children, a group that spends 81 percent more than average on used trucks. Householders aged 35 to 44, most with children, spend 51 percent more than average on used trucks and control 30 percent of the market. Married couples with children at home spend 81 percent more than average on this item. Hispanics spend 30 percent more than average on used trucks. Households in the West, where many Hispanics live, spend 25 percent more than average on used trucks.

Average household spending on used trucks fell 8 percent between 2000 and 2006, after adjusting for inflation. Behind the decline were the generous incentives car dealers offered on new trucks. Average household spending on used trucks may decline in the years ahead as rising gas prices encourage consumers to buy cars.

Table 52. Trucks, used

Total household spending	$96,905,770,630.00
Average household spends	815.41

	AVERAGE HOUSEHOLD SPENDING	BEST CUSTOMERS (index)	BIGGEST CUSTOMERS (market share)
AGE OF HOUSEHOLDER			
Average household	**$815.41**	**100**	**100.0%**
Under age 25	658.20	81	5.5
Aged 25 to 34	940.03	115	19.5
Aged 35 to 44	1,229.00	151	30.4
Aged 45 to 54	928.75	114	23.7
Aged 55 to 64	647.14	79	12.7
Aged 65 to 74	400.37	49	4.9
Aged 75 or older	295.06	36	3.4

	AVERAGE HOUSEHOLD SPENDING	BEST CUSTOMERS (index)	BIGGEST CUSTOMERS (market share)
HOUSEHOLD INCOME			
Average household	**$815.41**	**100**	**100.0%**
Under $20,000	217.03	27	5.8
$20,000 to $39,999	768.20	94	21.8
$40,000 to $49,999	687.18	84	8.1
$50,000 to $69,999	1,037.79	127	18.9
$70,000 to $79,999	877.95	108	6.3
$80,000 to $99,999	1,199.65	147	12.7
$100,000 or more	1,347.75	165	26.3
HOUSEHOLD TYPE			
Average household	**815.41**	**100**	**100.0**
Married couples	1,118.72	137	68.6
Married couples, no children	649.50	80	17.0
Married couples, with children	1,476.34	181	44.8
Oldest child under 6	1,352.23	166	8.0
Oldest child 6 to 17	1,568.97	192	24.6
Oldest child 18 or older	1,394.76	171	12.2
Single parent with child under 18	519.86	64	3.9
Single person	308.58	38	11.2
RACE AND HISPANIC ORIGIN			
Average household	**815.41**	**100**	**100.0**
Asian	188.33	23	0.8
Black	581.36	71	8.6
Hispanic	1,060.83	130	15.0
Non-Hispanic white and other	819.47	100	77.0
REGION			
Average household	**815.41**	**100**	**100.0**
Northeast	530.26	65	12.5
Midwest	728.83	89	20.5
South	894.78	110	39.2
West	1,022.62	125	27.9
EDUCATION			
Average household	**815.41**	**100**	**100.0**
Less than high school graduate	684.86	84	12.5
High school graduate	896.29	110	28.8
Some college	822.24	101	21.3
Associate's degree	860.82	106	10.3
College graduate	788.37	97	27.0
Bachelor's degree	814.15	100	17.9
Master's, professional, doctoral degree	742.53	91	9.2

Note: Market shares may not sum to 100.0 because of rounding and missing categories by household type. "Asian" and "black" include Hispanics and non-Hispanics who identify themselves as being of the respective race alone. "Hispanic" includes people of any race who identify themselves as Hispanic. "Other" includes people who identify themselves as non-Hispanic and as Alaska Native, American Indian, Asian (who are also included in the Asian row), Native Hawaiian or other Pacific Islander, as well as non-Hispanics reporting more than one race.
Source: Calculations by New Strategist based on the Bureau of Labor Statistics' 2006 Consumer Expenditure Survey

Vehicle Finance Charges

Best customers: **Householders aged 25 to 44**
     Married couples with children at home

Customer trends: **Spending in this category will rise along with interest rates.**

The biggest spenders on vehicle finance charges are households with little savings and lots of vehicles—primarily young adults and couples with kids. Householders aged 25 to 44 spend 26 to 35 percent more than average on vehicle finance charges and account for 48 percent of household spending on this item. Married couples with children at home spend 67 percent more than average on vehicle finance charges.

Average household spending on vehicle finance charges fell 23 percent between 2000 and 2006, after adjusting for inflation. Behind the decline were low-interest and no-interest loans on vehicles during the time period. Average household spending on this item will increase along with interest rates.

Table 53. Vehicle finance charges

Total household spending $35,392,633,830.00
Average household spends   297.81

	AVERAGE HOUSEHOLD SPENDING	BEST CUSTOMERS (index)	BIGGEST CUSTOMERS (market share)
AGE OF HOUSEHOLDER			
Average household	**$297.81**	**100**	**100.0%**
Under age 25	198.78	67	4.6
Aged 25 to 34	401.36	135	22.8
Aged 35 to 44	374.18	126	25.3
Aged 45 to 54	334.18	112	23.3
Aged 55 to 64	299.26	100	16.0
Aged 65 to 74	189.81	64	6.3
Aged 75 or older	52.82	18	1.7

	AVERAGE HOUSEHOLD SPENDING	BEST CUSTOMERS (index)	BIGGEST CUSTOMERS (market share)
HOUSEHOLD INCOME			
Average household	**$297.81**	**100**	**100.0%**
Under $20,000	65.56	22	4.8
$20,000 to $39,999	186.44	63	14.5
$40,000 to $49,999	298.12	100	9.6
$50,000 to $69,999	374.24	126	18.7
$70,000 to $79,999	471.95	158	9.3
$80,000 to $99,999	496.95	167	14.4
$100,000 or more	536.60	180	28.7
HOUSEHOLD TYPE			
Average household	**297.81**	**100**	**100.0**
Married couples	418.78	141	70.3
Married couples, no children	323.31	109	23.1
Married couples, with children	496.97	167	41.3
Oldest child under 6	518.91	174	8.4
Oldest child 6 to 17	494.49	166	21.2
Oldest child 18 or older	486.44	163	11.6
Single parent with child under 18	192.60	65	3.9
Single person	116.64	39	11.6
RACE AND HISPANIC ORIGIN			
Average household	**297.81**	**100**	**100.0**
Asian	219.86	74	2.5
Black	245.75	83	9.9
Hispanic	326.48	110	12.6
Non-Hispanic white and other	301.56	101	77.6
REGION			
Average household	**297.81**	**100**	**100.0**
Northeast	236.68	79	15.2
Midwest	249.98	84	19.2
South	337.94	113	40.5
West	335.21	113	25.0
EDUCATION			
Average household	**297.81**	**100**	**100.0**
Less than high school graduate	161.52	54	8.1
High school graduate	289.72	97	25.5
Some college	339.13	114	24.1
Associate's degree	357.59	120	11.7
College graduate	326.07	109	30.6
Bachelor's degree	330.27	111	19.9
Master's, professional, doctoral degree	318.59	107	10.8

Note: Market shares may not sum to 100.0 because of rounding and missing categories by household type. "Asian" and "black" include Hispanics and non-Hispanics who identify themselves as being of the respective race alone. "Hispanic" includes people of any race who identify themselves as Hispanic. "Other" includes people who identify themselves as non-Hispanic and as Alaska Native, American Indian, Asian (who are also included in the Asian row), Native Hawaiian or other Pacific Islander, as well as non-Hispanics reporting more than one race.
Source: Calculations by New Strategist based on the Bureau of Labor Statistics' 2006 Consumer Expenditure Survey

Vehicle Insurance

Best customers: Householders aged 45 to 54
                                            Married couples with school-aged or older children at home

Customer trends: Spending in this category should fall as boomers become empty-nesters and
                                            no longer have teen drivers at home.

The biggest spenders on vehicle insurance are households with multiple cars and drivers—particularly teens and young adults. Householders aged 45 to 54 (the age group most likely to have teen or young-adult children in the home) spend 25 percent more than average on vehicle insurance. Married couples with school-aged or adult children at home spend 28 to 81 percent more than average on this item.

Average household spending on vehicle insurance declined 3 percent between 2000 and 2006, after adjusting for inflation. Behind the decline is competition in the auto insurance industry, as well as the aging of boomers out of the peak-spending lifestage. Average household spending on this item may continue to fall in the years ahead as boomers become empty-nesters and no longer need to insure teen and young-adult drivers.

Table 54. Vehicle insurance

Total household spending $105,346,000,490.00
Average household spends   886.43

	AVERAGE HOUSEHOLD SPENDING	BEST CUSTOMERS (index)	BIGGEST CUSTOMERS (market share)
AGE OF HOUSEHOLDER			
Average household	**$886.43**	**100**	**100.0%**
Under age 25	548.03	62	4.2
Aged 25 to 34	822.19	93	15.7
Aged 35 to 44	976.08	110	22.2
Aged 45 to 54	1,105.17	125	25.9
Aged 55 to 64	941.06	106	16.9
Aged 65 to 74	805.89	91	9.0
Aged 75 or older	567.68	64	6.1

	AVERAGE HOUSEHOLD SPENDING	BEST CUSTOMERS (index)	BIGGEST CUSTOMERS (market share)
HOUSEHOLD INCOME			
Average household	**$886.43**	**100**	**100.0%**
Under $20,000	374.10	42	9.3
$20,000 to $39,999	694.68	78	18.2
$40,000 to $49,999	911.00	103	9.9
$50,000 to $69,999	1,042.81	118	17.5
$70,000 to $79,999	1,159.07	131	7.7
$80,000 to $99,999	1,175.85	133	11.4
$100,000 or more	1,453.89	164	26.1
HOUSEHOLD TYPE			
Average household	**886.43**	**100**	**100.0**
Married couples	1,131.80	128	63.8
Married couples, no children	993.80	112	23.9
Married couples, with children	1,234.92	139	34.4
Oldest child under 6	947.36	107	5.2
Oldest child 6 to 17	1,137.36	128	16.4
Oldest child 18 or older	1,606.06	181	12.9
Single parent with child under 18	665.61	75	4.6
Single person	507.90	57	17.0
RACE AND HISPANIC ORIGIN			
Average household	**886.43**	**100**	**100.0**
Asian	1,037.37	117	4.0
Black	709.87	80	9.6
Hispanic	814.24	92	10.6
Non-Hispanic white and other	925.06	104	80.0
REGION			
Average household	**886.43**	**100**	**100.0**
Northeast	859.79	97	18.6
Midwest	823.68	93	21.3
South	874.24	99	35.2
West	993.60	112	24.9
EDUCATION			
Average household	**886.43**	**100**	**100.0**
Less than high school graduate	583.03	66	9.8
High school graduate	847.97	96	25.1
Some college	883.86	100	21.1
Associate's degree	1,018.71	115	11.2
College graduate	1,040.30	117	32.8
Bachelor's degree	1,049.91	118	21.2
Master's, professional, doctoral degree	1,023.20	115	11.6

Note: Market shares may not sum to 100.0 because of rounding and missing categories by household type. "Asian" and "black" include Hispanics and non-Hispanics who identify themselves as being of the respective race alone. "Hispanic" includes people of any race who identify themselves as Hispanic. "Other" includes people who identify themselves as non-Hispanic and as Alaska Native, American Indian, Asian (who are also included in the Asian row), Native Hawaiian or other Pacific Islander, as well as non-Hispanics reporting more than one race.
Source: Calculations by New Strategist based on the Bureau of Labor Statistics' 2006 Consumer Expenditure Survey

Vehicle Maintenance and Repair (Including Oil Changes and Tires)

Best customers: Householders aged 45 to 54

Married couples with school-aged or older children at home

Customer trends: Spending in this category may decline if vehicle quality and warranties continue to improve.

The biggest spenders on vehicle maintenance and repair are households with the most vehicles—middle-aged married couples with teenagers and young adults at home. Householders aged 45 to 54, many living with teens and young adults, spend 26 percent more than average on vehicle maintenance and repair. Married couples with school-aged or older children at home spend 45 to 60 percent more than average on this item.

Average household spending on vehicle maintenance and repair fell 6 percent between 2000 and 2006, after adjusting for inflation. Behind the decline in spending was the increased ownership of new vehicles as dealers offered low-interest loans and other incentives. With more households owning new vehicles covered by warranties, spending on vehicle repair fell. Average household spending on this item may fall further in the years ahead if vehicle quality and warranties continue to improve.

Table 55. Vehicle maintenance and repair (including oil changes and tires)

Total household spending $81,816,274,920.00
Average household spends   688.44

	AVERAGE HOUSEHOLD SPENDING	BEST CUSTOMERS (index)	BIGGEST CUSTOMERS (market share)
AGE OF HOUSEHOLDER			
Average household	**$688.44**	**100**	**100.0%**
Under age 25	400.25	58	4.0
Aged 25 to 34	623.56	91	15.3
Aged 35 to 44	743.81	108	21.8
Aged 45 to 54	866.14	126	26.1
Aged 55 to 64	799.05	116	18.5
Aged 65 to 74	639.76	93	9.2
Aged 75 or older	370.62	54	5.1

	AVERAGE HOUSEHOLD SPENDING	BEST CUSTOMERS (index)	BIGGEST CUSTOMERS (market share)
HOUSEHOLD INCOME			
Average household	**$688.44**	**100**	**100.0%**
Under $20,000	300.63	44	9.6
$20,000 to $39,999	485.61	71	16.3
$40,000 to $49,999	614.99	89	8.6
$50,000 to $69,999	788.64	115	17.0
$70,000 to $79,999	861.29	125	7.3
$80,000 to $99,999	897.09	130	11.2
$100,000 or more	1,287.06	187	29.8
HOUSEHOLD TYPE			
Average household	**688.44**	**100**	**100.0**
Married couples	882.02	128	64.1
Married couples, no children	789.86	115	24.4
Married couples, with children	957.79	139	34.4
Oldest child under 6	645.87	94	4.5
Oldest child 6 to 17	995.06	145	18.4
Oldest child 18 or older	1,102.10	160	11.4
Single parent with child under 18	467.44	68	4.1
Single person	418.96	61	18.0
RACE AND HISPANIC ORIGIN			
Average household	**688.44**	**100**	**100.0**
Asian	677.61	98	3.4
Black	456.41	66	8.0
Hispanic	609.71	89	10.2
Non-Hispanic white and other	736.28	107	81.9
REGION			
Average household	**688.44**	**100**	**100.0**
Northeast	651.45	95	18.1
Midwest	625.35	91	20.8
South	650.33	94	33.7
West	847.06	123	27.4
EDUCATION			
Average household	**688.44**	**100**	**100.0**
Less than high school graduate	395.94	58	8.6
High school graduate	547.57	80	20.8
Some college	673.27	98	20.7
Associate's degree	799.93	116	11.3
College graduate	948.01	138	38.5
Bachelor's degree	939.73	137	24.4
Master's, professional, doctoral degree	962.72	140	14.1

Note: Market shares may not sum to 100.0 because of rounding and missing categories by household type. "Asian" and "black" include Hispanics and non-Hispanics who identify themselves as being of the respective race alone. "Hispanic" includes people of any race who identify themselves as Hispanic. "Other" includes people who identify themselves as non-Hispanic and as Alaska Native, American Indian, Asian (who are also included in the Asian row), Native Hawaiian or other Pacific Islander, as well as non-Hispanics reporting more than one race.
Source: Calculations by New Strategist based on the Bureau of Labor Statistics' 2006 Consumer Expenditure Survey

Vehicle Rentals (Including Rentals on Trips)

Best customers: Householders aged 35 to 74
                       Married couples without children at home
                       Married couples with school-aged or older children at home

Customer trends: Spending in this category will rise if discretionary income increases.

The biggest spenders on rented vehicles are travelers, since more than two-thirds of spending on rented vehicles occurs on trips. Middle-aged and older married couples are the biggest travelers, which accounts for their above-average spending on rented vehicles. Householders ranging in age from 35 to 74 spend 11 to 39 percent more than average on rented vehicles. Married couples without children at home (most of them empty-nesters) spend 41 percent more than average on this item. Those with school-aged or older children at home spend 37 to 40 percent more.

Average household spending on rented vehicles fell 29 percent between 2000 and 2006, after adjusting for inflation. Behind the decline was the lackluster recovery following the recession of 2001, reducing discretionary income and limiting travel. Spending on this item will rise if discretionary income increases.

Table 56. Vehicle rentals (including rentals on trips)

Total household spending $4,455,424,070.00
Average household spends   37.49

	AVERAGE HOUSEHOLD SPENDING	BEST CUSTOMERS (index)	BIGGEST CUSTOMERS (market share)
AGE OF HOUSEHOLDER			
Average household	**$37.49**	**100**	**100.0%**
Under age 25	18.47	49	3.4
Aged 25 to 34	29.07	78	13.1
Aged 35 to 44	41.75	111	22.4
Aged 45 to 54	52.25	139	29.0
Aged 55 to 64	42.32	113	18.0
Aged 65 to 74	42.80	114	11.3
Aged 75 or older	11.19	30	2.8

	AVERAGE HOUSEHOLD SPENDING	BEST CUSTOMERS (index)	BIGGEST CUSTOMERS (market share)
HOUSEHOLD INCOME			
Average household	**$37.49**	**100**	**100.0%**
Under $20,000	9.01	24	5.3
$20,000 to $39,999	20.84	56	12.9
$40,000 to $49,999	24.51	65	6.3
$50,000 to $69,999	33.76	90	13.4
$70,000 to $79,999	41.19	110	6.4
$80,000 to $99,999	51.11	136	11.7
$100,000 or more	103.60	276	44.0
HOUSEHOLD TYPE			
Average household	**37.49**	**100**	**100.0**
Married couples	49.96	133	66.6
Married couples, no children	52.93	141	30.1
Married couples, with children	49.06	131	32.4
Oldest child under 6	36.71	98	4.7
Oldest child 6 to 17	52.41	140	17.8
Oldest child 18 or older	51.46	137	9.8
Single parent with child under 18	27.86	74	4.5
Single person	24.12	64	19.1
RACE AND HISPANIC ORIGIN			
Average household	**37.49**	**100**	**100.0**
Asian	51.79	138	4.8
Black	27.19	73	8.7
Hispanic	20.61	55	6.3
Non-Hispanic white and other	41.60	111	85.0
REGION			
Average household	**37.49**	**100**	**100.0**
Northeast	44.76	119	22.9
Midwest	30.87	82	18.9
South	24.45	65	23.3
West	59.00	157	35.0
EDUCATION			
Average household	**37.49**	**100**	**100.0**
Less than high school graduate	13.36	36	5.3
High school graduate	18.61	50	13.0
Some college	27.44	73	15.5
Associate's degree	47.33	126	12.3
College graduate	72.23	193	53.9
Bachelor's degree	66.20	177	31.6
Master's, professional, doctoral degree	82.96	221	22.3

Note: Market shares may not sum to 100.0 because of rounding and missing categories by household type. "Asian" and "black" include Hispanics and non-Hispanics who identify themselves as being of the respective race alone. "Hispanic" includes people of any race who identify themselves as Hispanic. "Other" includes people who identify themselves as non-Hispanic and as Alaska Native, American Indian, Asian (who are also included in the Asian row), Native Hawaiian or other Pacific Islander, as well as non-Hispanics reporting more than one race.
Source: Calculations by New Strategist based on the Bureau of Labor Statistics' 2006 Consumer Expenditure Survey

Appendix: Spending by product and service, Ranked by amount spent, 2006

(average annual spending of consumer units on products and services, ranked by amount spent, 2006)

1.	Deductions for Social Security	$3,810.60
2.	Mortgage interest (or rent, $2,436.89)	3,460.96
3.	Vehicle purchases (net outlay)	3,420.83
4.	Groceries (also shown by individual category)	3,416.86
5.	Restaurants (also shown by meal category)	2,317.68
6.	Gasoline and motor oil	2,227.46
7.	Federal income taxes	1,711.22
8.	Property taxes	1,648.73
9.	Health insurance	1,464.98
10.	Electricity	1,265.88
11.	Dinner at restaurants	1,072.70
12.	Vehicle insurance	886.43
13.	Lunch at restaurants	768.62
14.	Cash contributions to church, religious organizations	752.84
15.	Vehicle maintenance and repairs	688.44
16.	Women's clothes	628.59
17.	Deductions for private pensions	607.42
18.	Maintenance and repair services, owner	559.60
19.	Residential phone service	541.95
20.	Cable TV and community antenna	539.04
21.	College tuition	523.87
22.	Cellular phone service	523.78
23.	State and local income taxes	519.09
24.	Natural gas	508.74
25.	Nonpayroll deposit to retirement plans	447.76
26.	Cash gifts to members of other households	408.70
27.	Prescription drugs	392.97
28.	Men's clothes	352.58
29.	Homeowner's insurance	342.52
30.	Airline fares	334.60
31.	Life and other personal insurance	322.14
32.	Lodging on trips	320.64
33.	Cigarettes	302.20
34.	Vehicle finance charges	297.81
35.	Water and sewerage maintenance	286.49
36.	Personal care services	274.04
37.	Day care centers, nurseries, and preschools	265.09
38.	Leased vehicles	256.87
39.	Restaurant meals on trips	242.93
40.	Dental services	238.96
41.	Beef	236.25
42.	Breakfast at restaurants	233.43
43.	Child support expenditures	215.79
44.	Finance charges other than mortgage and vehicle	202.66
45.	Other taxes	202.01
46.	Fresh fruits	195.44

47.	Fresh vegetables	$193.26
48.	Cash contributions to charities and other organizations	192.20
49.	Owned vacation homes	184.63
50.	Computer information services	176.44
51.	Snacks at restaurants	174.63
52.	Physician's services	167.90
53.	Motorized recreational vehicles	163.78
54.	Movie, theater, opera, ballet admissions	160.62
55.	Legal fees	158.97
56.	Pork	157.24
57.	Elementary and high school tuition	156.46
58.	Cosmetics, perfume, bath preparations	152.51
59.	Laundry and cleaning supplies	151.22
60.	Expenses for other properties	146.50
61.	Women's footwear	143.64
62.	Computers and computer hardware for nonbusiness use	142.59
63.	Poultry	140.52
64.	Decorative items for the home	137.88
65.	Carbonated drinks	134.55
66.	Pet food	133.01
67.	Miscellaneous household products	132.92
68.	Prepared foods except frozen, salads, and desserts	132.68
69.	Television sets	130.39
70.	Jewelry	125.39
71.	Fresh milk	124.47
72.	Beer and ale at home	123.84
73.	Social, recreation, civic club membership	123.48
74.	Girls' (aged 2 to 15) clothes	122.44
75.	Fish and seafood	121.67
76.	Sofas	116.05
77.	Housekeeping services	114.30
78.	Cash contributions to educational institutions	112.31
79.	Cheese	110.75
80.	Gardening, lawn care service	109.13
81.	Fees for participant sports	108.83
82.	Trash and garbage collection	108.51
83.	Wine at home	102.77
84.	Fees for recreational lessons	101.57
85.	Cleansing and toilet tissue, paper towels, and napkins	99.86
86.	Men's footwear	98.81
87.	Lawn and garden supplies	97.05
88.	Maintenance and repair materials, owner	96.42
89.	Children's (under age 2) clothes	95.73
90.	Potato chips and other snacks	95.22
91.	Vehicle registration, state and local	94.65
92.	Support for college students	94.35
93.	Hospital room and services	93.81
94.	Vet services	93.77
95.	Interest paid, home equity loan or line of credit	93.50
96.	Boys' (aged 2 to 15) clothes	90.94
97.	Toys, games, arts and crafts, and tricycles	86.32
98.	Stationery, stationery supplies, giftwraps	85.97
99.	Bedroom furniture except mattresses and springs	84.98
100.	Beer and ale at bars, restaurants	84.81

101.	Ready-to-eat and cooked cereals	$84.73
102.	Fuel oil	82.65
103.	Nonprescription drugs	80.58
104.	Babysitting and child care	80.57
105.	Candy and chewing gum	79.13
106.	Deductions for government retirement	76.98
107.	Lunch meats (cold cuts)	75.62
108.	Bedroom linens	75.44
109.	Lotteries and gambling losses	70.99
110.	Postage	69.38
111.	Frozen meals	69.04
112.	Rent as pay	68.96
113.	Catered affairs	68.61
114.	School lunches	67.82
115.	Frozen prepared foods, except meals	67.54
116.	Mattresses and springs	65.27
117.	Other alcoholic beverages at bars, restaurants	64.90
118.	Wall units, cabinets, and other occasional furniture	63.27
119.	Refrigerators, freezers	62.80
120.	Accounting fees	62.35
121.	Housing while attending school	62.01
122.	Professional laundry and dry cleaning	61.95
123.	Ice cream products	61.62
124.	School books, supplies, equipment for college	60.27
125.	Maintenance and repair materials, renter	59.51
126.	Athletic gear, game tables, and exercise equipment	58.11
127.	Funeral expenses	57.47
128.	Recreational expenses on trips	56.50
129.	Hair care products	56.05
130.	Canned and bottled fruit juice	55.29
131.	Bottled water	55.23
132.	Pet purchase, supplies, medicine	55.21
133.	Admission to sporting events	55.12
134.	Ship fares	55.02
135.	School expenses and supplies (except tuition, books)	54.71
136.	Bread, other than white	54.23
137.	Eyeglasses and contact lenses	53.99
138.	Books	53.55
139.	Intracity mass transit fares	51.09
140.	Ground rent	51.08
141.	Coffee	49.89
142.	Lawn and garden equipment	49.68
143.	Bottled gas	49.25
144.	Service by professionals other than physician	49.14
145.	Newspaper and magazine subscriptions	48.66
146.	Property management, owner	48.46
147.	Nonalcoholic beverages (except carbonated, coffee, fruit-flavored drinks, tea, and water) and ice	48.44
148.	Sauces and gravies	48.25
149.	Unmotored recreational vehicles	46.86
150.	Kitchen, dining room furniture	46.44
151.	Indoor plants, fresh flowers	46.17
152.	Alimony	46.16
153.	Living room chairs	45.48
154.	Occupational expenses	44.53

155.	Cookies	$44.38
156.	Alcoholic beverages purchased on trips	43.36
157.	Lab tests, X-rays	43.23
158.	Care for elderly, invalids, handicapped, etc.	43.17
159.	Groceries on trips	42.89
160.	Canned and packaged soups	42.18
161.	Biscuits and rolls	41.84
162.	Wine at bars, restaurants	41.62
163.	Moving, storage, freight express	41.57
164.	Video cassettes, tapes, and discs	41.20
165.	Miscellaneous personal services	41.17
166.	Nonprescription vitamins	40.12
167.	Coin-operated apparel laundry and dry cleaning	38.85
168.	Eyecare services	38.81
169.	Food or board at school	38.39
170.	Washing machines	37.99
171.	Rented vehicles	37.49
172.	Eggs	36.67
173.	Boys' footwear	36.04
174.	Deodorants, feminine hygiene, miscellaneous personal care products	35.08
175.	Cakes and cupcakes	35.02
176.	Parking fees	34.88
177.	Video game hardware and software	34.10
178.	Compact discs, records, and audio tapes	34.03
179.	Pet services	34.01
180.	Telephones and accessories	34.01
181.	Cooking stoves, ovens	33.71
182.	Baby food	33.65
183.	Photographic equipment and supplies (except film)	32.56
184.	Nuts	32.48
185.	Canned vegetables	32.31
186.	Prepared salads	32.31
187.	Topicals and dressings	32.09
188.	Crackers	31.83
189.	White bread	31.77
190.	Rental of video cassettes, tapes, discs, films	31.44
191.	Electric floor-cleaning equipment	31.34
192.	Frozen vegetables	30.54
193.	Hunting and fishing equipment	28.68
194.	Outdoor equipment	28.66
195.	Fats and oils	28.36
196.	Oral hygiene products	28.19
197.	Clothes dryers	28.10
198.	Meals as pay	27.17
199.	Other alcoholic beverages at home	26.92
200.	Bathroom linens	26.77
201.	Window coverings	26.67
202.	Tea	26.31
203.	Salad dressings	26.13
204.	Wall-to-wall carpeting	25.68
205.	Frozen and refrigerated bakery products	25.60
206.	Girls' footwear	25.42
207.	Salt, spices, other seasonings	25.34
208.	Schools tuition (except college, elementary, high school)	24.58

209.	Curtains and draperies	$24.45
210.	Power tools	24.41
211.	Tableware, nonelectric kitchenware	24.33
212.	Gifts of stocks, bonds, and mutual funds to members of other households	24.30
213.	Pasta, cornmeal, and other cereal products	24.23
214.	Jams, preserves, other sweets	23.04
215.	Baking needs	22.96
216.	Tobacco products except cigarettes	22.51
217.	Photographer fees	22.44
218.	Sound equipment	22.34
219.	Cash contributions to political organizations	22.19
220.	Floor coverings, nonpermanent	21.82
221.	Computer software and accessories for nonbusiness use	21.70
222.	Taxi fares and limousine services	21.58
223.	Phone cards	21.16
224.	Checking accounts, other bank service charges	21.15
225.	Watches	21.06
226.	Sweetrolls, coffee cakes, doughnuts	20.81
227.	Nonelectric cookware	20.61
228.	Frankfurters	20.19
229.	Home security system service fee	19.93
230.	Cemetery lots, vaults, maintenance fees	19.38
231.	Small electric kitchen appliances	19.08
232.	Tolls	19.04
233.	Dishwashers (built-in), garbage disposals, range hoods	19.01
234.	Termite and pest control	18.44
235.	Canned fruits	18.42
236.	Butter	18.32
237.	Living room tables	18.30
238.	Appliance repair, including at service center	17.98
239.	Photo processing	17.88
240.	Noncarbonated fruit-flavored drinks	17.75
241.	Closet and storage items	17.70
242.	Rice	17.51
243.	Fresh fruit juice	17.43
244.	Personal digital audio players	17.41
245.	Care in convalescent or nursing home	17.20
246.	Hearing aids	16.94
247.	Lamps and lighting fixtures	16.88
248.	Shaving needs	16.84
249.	School books, supplies, equipment for elementary, high school	16.68
250.	Sugar	16.54
251.	Infants' equipment	16.42
252.	Automobile service clubs	16.29
253.	Intercity train fares	16.29
254.	VCRs and video disc players	16.12
255.	Glassware	15.76
256.	Cream	15.71
257.	Musical instruments and accessories	15.67
258.	Outdoor furniture	15.67
259.	Laundry and cleaning equipment	15.32
260.	Maintenance and repair services, renter	14.88
261.	Newspapers and magazines, nonsubscription	14.55
262.	Pies, tarts, turnovers	13.93

263.	Local transportation on out-of-town trips	$13.13
264.	Vegetable juice	13.11
265.	Material for making clothes	13.07
266.	Bicycles	13.05
267.	China and other dinnerware	12.98
268.	Nondairy cream and imitation milk	12.80
269.	Olives, pickles, relishes	12.78
270.	Electric personal care appliances	12.74
271.	Sewing materials for slipcovers and curtains, other sewing materials for the home	12.05
272.	Prepared desserts	12.02
273.	Dried vegetables	11.79
274.	Intercity bus fares	11.33
275.	Prepared flour mixes	11.28
276.	Peanut butter	11.25
277.	Security services, owner	10.72
278.	Camping equipment	10.40
279.	Microwave ovens	9.71
280.	Tenant's insurance	9.52
281.	Vehicle inspection	9.51
282.	Lamb, organ meats, and others	9.08
283.	Office furniture for home use	9.07
284.	Dried fruit	8.96
285.	Whiskey at home	8.83
286.	Kitchen and dining room linens	8.64
287.	Repair and rental of lawn and garden equipment, hand or power tools, other household equipment	8.31
288.	Luggage	7.83
289.	Infants' furniture	7.77
290.	Shopping club membership fees	7.57
291.	Hand tools	7.51
292.	Hair accessories	7.30
293.	Margarine	7.30
294.	Reupholstering, furniture repair	7.11
295.	Supportive and convalescent medical equipment	7.10
296.	Drivers' license	6.87
297.	Rental of recreational vehicles	6.54
298.	Repair of computer systems for nonbusiness use	6.45
299.	Film	6.39
300.	Sewing machines	6.31
301.	Docking and landing fees	6.29
302.	Coal, wood, and other fuels	6.11
303.	Parking at owned home	6.08
304.	Radios	5.95
305.	Fireworks	5.94
306.	Alteration, repair, and tailoring of apparel and accessories	5.93
307.	Artificial sweeteners	5.80
308.	Portable heating and cooling equipment	5.76
309.	Stamp and coin collecting	5.62
310.	Tape recorders and players	5.62
311.	Winter sports equipment	5.62
312.	Repair of TV, radio, and sound equipment	5.53
313.	Water sports equipment	5.51
314.	Window air conditioners	5.45

315.	Sewing patterns and notions	$5.43
316.	Towing charges	5.11
317.	Frozen fruit juice	5.05
318.	Flour	4.95
319.	Medical equipment for general use	4.94
320.	Slipcovers, decorative pillows	4.90
321.	Deductions for railroad retirement	4.77
322.	Playground equipment	4.55
323.	Bread and cracker products	4.35
324.	Watch and jewelry repair	4.24
325.	Flatware	4.16
326.	Personal digital assistants	4.12
327.	Frozen fruits	4.07
328.	Water softening service	4.04
329.	Safe deposit box rental	3.73
330.	Clocks	3.70
331.	Rental and repair of miscellaneous sports equipment	3.64
332.	Streaming and downloading audio	3.62
333.	School books, supplies, equipment for day care, nursery, other	3.53
334.	Delivery services	3.16
335.	Coin-operated household laundry and dry cleaning (nonclothing)	3.00
336.	Rental of furniture	2.96
337.	Business equipment for home use	2.50
338.	Septic tank cleaning	2.40
339.	Silver serving pieces	2.30
340.	Rental of medical equipment	2.19
341.	Smoking accessories	2.12
342.	Wigs and hairpieces	2.01
343.	Clothing rental	1.96
344.	Plastic dinnerware	1.95
345.	Pinball, electronic video games	1.90
346.	Credit card memberships	1.89
347.	Internet services away from home	1.64
348.	Appliance rental	1.63
349.	Global positioning services	1.60
350.	School bus	1.59
351.	Smoke alarms	1.42
352.	Shoe repair and other shoe service	1.37
353.	Repair and rental of photographic equipment	1.30
354.	Repair and rental of musical instruments	1.16
355.	Household nonclothing laundry and dry cleaning, sent out, not coin-operated	1.09
356.	Streaming and downloading video	1.03
357.	Satellite dishes	0.92
358.	Portable dishwasher	0.91
359.	Dating services	0.72
360.	Telephone answering devices	0.69
361.	Clothing storage	0.44
362.	Rental of television sets	0.44

Source: Calculations by New Strategist based on the 2006 Consumer Expenditure Survey

Glossary

age The age of the reference person.

alcoholic beverages Includes beer and ale, wine, whiskey, gin, vodka, rum, and other alcoholic beverages.

annual spending The annual amount spent per household. The Bureau of Labor Statistics calculates the annual average for all households in a segment, not just for those that purchased an item. The averages are calculated by integrating the results of the diary (weekly) and interview (quarterly) portions of the Consumer Expenditure Survey. For items purchased by most households—such as bread—average annual spending figures are a fairly accurate account of actual spending. For products and services purchased by few households during a year's time—such as cars—the average annual amount spent is much less than what purchasers spend.

apparel, accessories, and related services Includes the following:
• *men's and boys' apparel* Includes coats, jackets, sweaters, vests, sport coats, tailored jackets, slacks, shorts and short sets, sportswear, shirts, underwear, nightwear, hosiery, uniforms, and other accessories.
• *women's and girls' apparel* Includes coats, jackets, furs, sport coats, tailored jackets, sweaters, vests, blouses, shirts, dresses, dungarees, culottes, slacks, shorts, sportswear, underwear, nightwear, uniforms, hosiery, and other accessories.
• *infants' apparel* Includes coats, jackets, snowsuits, underwear, diapers, dresses, crawlers, sleeping garments, hosiery, footwear, and other accessories for children.
• *footwear* Includes articles such as shoes, slippers, boots, and other similar items. It excludes footwear for babies and footwear used for sports such as bowling or golf shoes.
• *other apparel products and services* Includes material for making clothes, shoe repair, alterations and sewing patterns and notions, clothing rental, clothing storage, dry cleaning, sent-out laundry, watches, jewelry, and repairs to watches and jewelry.

baby boom Americans born between 1946 and 1964.

cash contributions Includes cash contributed to persons or organizations outside the consumer unit including court-ordered alimony, child support payments, and support for college students, and contributions to religious, educational, charitable, or political organizations.

consumer unit (1) All members of a household who are related by blood, marriage, adoption, or other legal arrangements; (2) a person living alone or sharing a household with others or living as a roomer in a private home or lodging house or in permanent living quarters in a hotel or motel, but who is financially independent; or (3) two or more persons living together who pool their income to make joint expenditure decisions. Financial independence is determined by the three major expense categories: housing, food, and other living expenses. To be considered financially independent, at least two of the three major expense categories have to be provided by the respondent. For convenience, called household in the text of this report.

consumer unit, composition of The classification of interview households by type according to (1) relationship of other household members to the reference person; (2) age of the children of the reference person; and (3) combination of relationship to the reference person and age of the children. Stepchildren and adopted children are included with the reference person's own children.

earner A consumer unit member aged 14 or older who worked at least one week during the twelve months prior to the interview date.

education Includes tuition, fees, books, supplies, and equipment for public and private nursery schools, elementary and high schools, colleges and universities, and other schools.

entertainment Includes the following:
• *fees and admissions* Includes fees for participant sports; admissions to sporting events, movies, concerts, plays; health, swimming, tennis, and country club memberships, and other social recreational and fraternal organizations; recreational lessons or instructions; and recreational expenses on trips.
• *audio and visual equipment and services* Includes television sets; radios; cable TV; tape recorders and players; video cassettes, tapes, and discs; video cassette recorders and video disc players; video game hardware and software; personal digital audio players; streaming and downloading audio and video; sound components; CDs, records, and tapes; musical instruments; and rental and repair of TV and sound equipment.
• *pets, toys, hobbies, and playground equipment* Includes pet food, pet services, veterinary expenses, toys, games, hobbies, and playground equipment.
• *other entertainment equipment and services* Includes indoor exercise equipment, athletic shoes, bicycles, trailers, campers, camping equipment, rental of cameras and trailers, hunting and fishing equipment, sports equipment, winter sports equipment, water sports equipment, boats, boat motors and boat trailers, rental of boats, landing and docking fees, rental and repair of sports equipment, photographic equipment, film, photo processing, photographer fees, repair and rental of photo equipment, fireworks, pinball and electronic video games.

expenditure The transaction cost including excise and sales taxes of goods and services acquired during the survey period. The full cost of each purchase is recorded even though full payment may not have been made at the date of purchase. Expenditure estimates include gifts. Excluded from expenditures are purchases or portions of purchases directly assignable to business purposes and periodic credit or installment payments on goods and services already acquired.

federal income tax Includes federal income tax withheld in the survey year to pay for income earned in survey year plus additional tax paid in survey year to cover any underpayment or underwithholding of tax in the year prior to the survey.

financial products and services Includes accounting fees, legal fees, union dues, professional dues and fees, other occupational expenses, funerals, cemetery lots, dating services, shopping club memberships, and unclassified fees and personal services.

food Includes the following:
• *food at home* Refers to the total expenditures for food at grocery stores or other food stores during the interview period. It is calculated by multiplying the number of visits to a grocery or other food store by the average amount spent per visit. It excludes the purchase of nonfood items.
• *food away from home* Includes all meals (breakfast, lunch, brunch, and dinner) at restaurants, carry-outs, and vending machines, including tips, plus meals as pay, special catered affairs such as weddings, bar mitzvahs, and confirmations, and meals away from home on trips.

generation X Americans born between 1965 and 1976; also known as the baby-bust generation.

gifts for people in other households Includes gift expenditures for people living in other consumer units. The amount spent on gifts is also included in individual product and service categories.

health care Includes the following:
• *health insurance* Includes health maintenance plans (HMOs), Blue Cross / Blue Shield, commercial health insurance, Medicare, Medicare supplemental insurance, long-term care insurance, and other health insurance.
• *medical services* Includes hospital room and services, physicians' services, services of a practitioner other than a physician, eye and dental care, lab tests, X-rays, nursing, therapy services, care in convalescent or nursing home, and other medical care.
• *drugs* Includes prescription and nonprescription drugs, internal and respiratory over-the-counter drugs.
• *medical supplies* Includes eyeglasses and contact lenses, topicals and dressings, antiseptics, bandages, cotton, first aid kits, contraceptives; medical equipment for general use such as syringes, ice bags, thermometers, vaporizers, heating pads; supportive or convalescent medical equipment such as hearing aids, braces, canes, crutches, and walkers.

Hispanic origin The self-identified Hispanic origin of the consumer unit reference person. All consumer units are included in one of two Hispanic origin groups based on the reference person's Hispanic origin: Hispanic or non-Hispanic. Hispanics may be of any race.

household According to the Census Bureau, all the people who occupy a household. A group of unrelated people who share a housing unit as roommates or unmarried partners is also counted as a household. Households do not include group quarters such as college dormitories, prisons, or nursing homes. A household may contain more than one consumer unit. The terms "household" and "consumer unit" are used interchangeably in this report.

household furnishings and equipment Includes the following:
• *household textiles* Includes bathroom, kitchen, dining room, and other linens, curtains and drapes, slipcovers and decorative pillows, and sewing materials.
• *furniture* Includes living room, dining room, kitchen, bedroom, nursery, porch, lawn, and other outdoor furniture.
• *carpet, rugs, and other floor coverings* Includes installation and replacement of wall-to-wall carpets, room-size rugs, and other soft floor coverings.

• *major appliances* Includes refrigerators, freezers, dishwashers, stoves, ovens, garbage disposals, vacuum cleaners, microwave ovens, air-conditioners, sewing machines, washing machines, clothes dryers, and floor-cleaning equipment.
• *small appliances and miscellaneous housewares* Includes small electrical kitchen appliances, portable heating and cooling equipment, china and other dinnerware, flatware, glassware, silver and other serving pieces, nonelectric cookware, and plastic dinnerware. Excludes personal care appliances.
• *miscellaneous household equipment* Includes computer hardware and software, luggage, lamps and other lighting fixtures, window coverings, clocks, lawn mowers and gardening equipment, hand and power tools, telephone answering devices, personal digital assistants, Internet services away from home, office equipment for home use, fresh flowers and house plants, rental of furniture, closet and storage items, household decorative items, infants' equipment, outdoor equipment, smoke alarms, other household appliances, and small miscellaneous furnishing.

household services Includes the following:
• *personal services* Includes baby sitting, day care, and care of elderly and handicapped persons.
• *other household services* Includes computer information services; housekeeping services; gardening and lawn care services; coin-operated laundry and dry-cleaning of household textiles; termite and pest control products; moving, storage, and freight expenses; repair of household appliances and other household equipment; reupholstering and furniture repair; rental and repair of lawn and gardening tools; and rental of other household equipment.

housekeeping supplies Includes soaps, detergents, other laundry cleaning products, cleansing and toilet tissue, paper towels, napkins, and miscellaneous household products; lawn and garden supplies, postage, stationery, stationery supplies, and gift wrap.

housing tenure "Owner" includes households living in their own homes, cooperatives, condominiums, or townhouses. "Renter" includes households paying rent as well as families living rent free in lieu of wages.

income before taxes The total money earnings and selected money receipts accruing to a consumer unit during the 12 months prior to the interview date. Income includes the following components:
• *wages and salaries* Includes total money earnings for all members of the consumer unit aged 14 or older from all jobs, including civilian wages and salaries, Armed Forces pay and allowances, piece-rate payments, commissions, tips, National Guard or Reserve pay (received for training periods), and cash bonuses before deductions for taxes, pensions, union dues, etc.
• *self-employment income* Includes net business and farm income, which consists of net income (gross receipts minus operating expenses) from a profession or unincorporated business or from the operation of a farm by an owner, tenant, or sharecropper. If the business or farm is a partnership, only an appropriate share of net income is recorded. Losses are also recorded.

• *Social Security, private and government retirement* Includes payments by the federal government made under retirement, survivor, and disability insurance programs to retired persons, dependents of deceased insured workers, or to disabled workers; and private pensions or retirement benefits received by retired persons or their survivors, either directly or through an insurance company.

• *interest, dividends, rental income, and other property income* Includes interest income on savings or bonds; payments made by a corporation to its stockholders, periodic receipts from estates or trust funds; net income or loss from the rental of property, real estate, or farms, and net income or loss from roomers or boarders.

• *unemployment and workers' compensation and veterans' benefits* Includes income from unemployment compensation and workers' compensation, and veterans' payments including educational benefits, but excluding military retirement.

• *public assistance, supplemental security income, and food stamps* Includes public assistance or welfare, including money received from job training grants; supplemental security income paid by federal, state, and local welfare agencies to low-income persons who are aged 65 or older, blind, or disabled; and the value of food stamps obtained.

• *regular contributions for support* Includes alimony and child support as well as any regular contributions from persons outside the consumer unit.

• *other income* Includes money income from care of foster children, cash scholarships, fellowships, or stipends not based on working; and meals and rent as pay.

indexed spending Indexed spending figures compare the spending of particular demographic segments with that of the average household. To compute an index, the amount spent on an item by a demographic segment is divided by the amount spent on the item by the average household. That figure is then multiplied by 100. An index of 100 is the average for all households. An index of 132 means average spending by households in a segment is 32 percent above average (100 plus 32). An index of 75 means average spending by households in a segment is 25 percent below average (100 minus 25). Indexed spending figures identify the consumer units that spend the most on a product or service.

life and other personal insurance Includes premiums from whole life and term insurance; endowments; income and other life insurance; mortgage guarantee insurance; mortgage life insurance; premiums for personal life liability, accident and disability; and other non–health insurance other than homes and vehicles.

market share The market share is the percentage of total household spending on an item that is accounted for by a demographic segment. Market shares are calculated by dividing a demographic segment's total spending on an item by the total spending of all households on the item. Total spending on an item for all households is calculated by multiplying average spending by the total number of households. Total spending on an item for each demographic segment is calculated by multiplying the segment's average spending by the number of households in the segment. Market shares reveal the demographic segments that account for the largest share of spending on a product or service.

millennial generation Americans born between 1977 and 1994.

occupation The occupation in which the reference person received the most earnings during the survey period. The occupational categories follow those of the Census of Population. Categories shown in the tables include the following:

• *self-employed* Includes all occupational categories; the reference person is self-employed in own business, professional practice, or farm.

• *wage and salary earners, managers and professionals* Includes executives, administrators, managers, and professional specialties such as architects, engineers, natural and social scientists, lawyers, teachers, writers, health diagnosis and treatment workers, entertainers, and athletes.

• *wage and salary earners, technical, sales, and clerical workers* Includes technicians and related support workers; sales representatives, sales workers, cashiers, and sales-related occupations; and administrative support, including clerical.

• *retired* People who did not work either full- or part-time during the survey period.

owner *See* housing tenure.

pensions and Social Security Includes all Social Security contributions paid by employees; employees' contributions to railroad retirement, government retirement and private pensions programs; retirement programs for self-employed.

personal care Includes products for the hair, oral hygiene products, shaving needs, cosmetics, bath products, suntan lotions, hand creams, electric personal care appliances, incontinence products, other personal care products, personal care services such as hair care services (haircuts, bleaching, tinting, coloring, conditioning treatments, permanents, press, and curls), styling and other services for wigs and hairpieces, body massages or slenderizing treatments, facials, manicures, pedicures, shaves, electrolysis.

quarterly spending Quarterly spending data are collected in the interview portion of the Consumer Expenditure Survey. The quarterly spending tables show the percentage of households that purchased an item during an average quarter, and the amount spent during the quarter on the item by purchasers. Not all items are included in the interview portion of the Consumer Expenditure Survey.

reading Includes subscriptions for newspapers, magazines, and books through book clubs; purchase of single-copy newspapers and magazines, books, and encyclopedias and other reference books.

reference person The first member mentioned by the respondent when asked to "Start with the name of the person or one of the persons who owns or rents the home." It is with respect to this person that the relationship of other consumer unit members is determined. Also called the householder or head of household.

region Consumer units are classified according to their address at the time of their participation in the survey. The four major census regions of the United States are the following state groupings:
• *Northeast* Connecticut, Maine, Massachusetts, New Hampshire, New Jersey, New York, Pennsylvania, Rhode Island, and Vermont.
• *Midwest* Illinois, Indiana, Iowa, Kansas, Michigan, Minnesota, Mississippi, Nebraska, North Dakota, Ohio, South Dakota, and Wisconsin.
• *South* Alabama, Arkansas, Delaware, District of Columbia, Florida, Georgia, Kentucky, Louisiana, Maryland, Mississippi, North Carolina, Oklahoma, South Carolina, Tennessee, Texas, Virginia, and West Virginia.
• *West* Alaska, Arizona, California, Colorado, Hawaii, Idaho, Minnesota, Nevada, New Mexico, Oregon, Utah, Washington, and Wyoming.

renter *See* housing tenure.

shelter Includes the following:
• *owned dwellings* Includes interest on mortgages, property taxes and insurance, refinancing and prepayment charges, ground rent, expenses for property management and security, homeowner's insurance, fire insurance and extended coverage, landscaping expenses for repairs and maintenance contracted out (including periodic maintenance and service contracts), and expenses of materials for owner-performed repairs and maintenance for dwellings used or maintained by the consumer unit, but not dwellings maintained for business or rent.
• *rented dwellings* Includes rent paid for dwellings, rent received as pay, parking fees, maintenance, and other expenses.
• *other lodging* Includes all expenses for vacation homes, school, college, hotels, motels, cottages, trailer camps, and other lodging while out of town.
• *utilities, fuels, and public services* Includes natural gas, electricity, fuel oil, coal, bottled gas, wood, other fuels; residential telephone service, cell phone service, phone cards; water, garbage, trash collection; sewerage maintenance, septic tank cleaning; and other public services.

size of consumer unit The number of people whose usual place of residence at the time of the interview is in the consumer unit.

state and local income taxes Includes state and local income taxes withheld in the survey year to pay for income earned in survey year plus additional taxes paid in the survey year to cover any underpayment or underwithholding of taxes in the year prior to the survey.

tobacco and smoking supplies Includes cigarettes, cigars, snuff, loose smoking tobacco, chewing tobacco, and smoking accessories such as cigarette or cigar holders, pipes, flints, lighters, pipe cleaners, and other smoking products and accessories.

transportation Includes the following:
• *vehicle purchases (net outlay)* Includes the net outlay (purchase price minus trade-in value) on new and used domestic and imported cars and trucks and other vehicles, including motorcycles and private planes.

• *gasoline and motor oil* Includes gasoline, diesel fuel, and motor oil.
• *other vehicle expenses* Includes vehicle finance charges, maintenance and repairs, vehicle insurance, and vehicle rental licenses and other charges.
• *vehicle finance charges* Includes the dollar amount of interest paid for a loan contracted for the purchase of vehicles described above.
• *maintenance and repairs* Includes tires, batteries, tubes, lubrication, filters, coolant, additives, brake and transmission fluids, oil change, brake adjustment and repair, front-end alignment, wheel balancing, steering repair, shock absorber replacement, clutch and transmission repair, electrical system repair, repair to cooling system, drive train repair, drive shaft and rear-end repair, tire repair, vehicle video equipment, other maintenance and services, and auto repair policies.
• *vehicle insurance* Includes the premium paid for insuring cars, trucks, and other vehicles.
• *vehicle rental, licenses, and other charges* Includes leased and rented cars, trucks, motorcycles, and aircraft, inspection fees, state and local registration, drivers' license fees, parking fees, towing charges, tolls on trips, and global positioning services.
• *public transportation* Includes fares for mass transit, buses, trains, airlines, taxis, private school buses, and fares paid on trips for trains, boats, taxis, buses, and trains.

weekly spending Weekly spending data are collected in the diary portion of the Consumer Expenditure Survey. The data show the percentage of households that purchased an item during the average week, and the amount spent per week on the item by purchasers. Not all items are included in the diary portion of the Consumer Expenditure Survey.